YEATS &
AMERICAN
POETRY

YEATS &
AMERICAN
POETRY

THE TRADITION
OF THE SELF

TERENCE DIGGORY

PRINCETON UNIVERSITY PRESS

8/1983
am. Lit.

Copyright © 1983 by Princeton University Press
Published by Princeton University Press, 41 William Street,
Princeton, New Jersey
In the United Kingdom: Princeton University Press
Guildford, Surrey

Library of Congress Cataloging in Publication Data will be
found on the last printed page of this book

This book has been composed in Linotron Sabon

Publication of this book has been aided by a grant from
The Andrew W. Mellon Foundation

Clothbound editions of Princeton University Press books
are printed on acid-free paper, and binding materials are
chosen for strength and durability. Paperbacks,
while satisfactory for personal collections,
are not usually suitable for library rebinding

Printed in the United States of America by Princeton
University Press, Princeton, New Jersey

TO MY MOTHER

CONTENTS

	ACKNOWLEDGMENTS	ix
	PERMISSIONS	xi
	NOTE ON CITATIONS AND ABBREVIATIONS	xv

I.   INTRODUCTION: "THE TRADITION OF MYSELF"   3

II. AN AMERICAN TRADITION: EMERSON, POE,
     THOREAU, AND WHITMAN   11

III. A LIVE TRADITION: EZRA POUND   31

IV. NATURAL SPEECH: THE NINETEEN-TENS   59
     Midwestern Rhetoric: *Poetry* Magazine
        and Vachel Lindsay   59
     New England Reticence: Robert Frost   66
     American Rhythm: William Carlos Williams   76

V.   ARTIFICIAL LIVES: THE NINETEEN-TWENTIES   87
     The Racial Self: Wallace Stevens   88
     The Traditional Self: T. S. Eliot   101
     The Inhuman Self: Robinson Jeffers   118

VI   PUBLIC SPEECH: THE NINETEEN-THIRTIES   134
     Versions of Pastoral: Tate, Ransom, and Warren 135
     Vision of Survival: Horace Gregory   156
     Language of Belief: Archibald MacLeish   166

VII. PRIVATE LIVES: THE NINETEEN-FORTIES   181
     A Father's Authority: Theodore Roethke   182
     A Father's Fatality: John Berryman   197
     A Father's Nonentity: Robert Lowell   212

VIII. CONCLUSION: THE END OF TRADITION   225

     NOTES   229

     INDEX   249

ACKNOWLEDGMENTS

THIS BOOK BEGAN in conversations with Richard Ellmann, and a first draft was completed under his generous and patient supervision. To him also I owe the debt incurred by all who have read his essential works on Yeats. My notes record my obligations to other scholars, but to at least three of them, Harold Bloom, Robert Langbaum, and George T. Wright, my debt is greater, because more pervasive, than notes can convey. Their work has proven equally valuable both for their reassuring agreements and for their challenging disagreements with each other's views and with my own.

Christopher Butler and Jon Stallworthy served as readers for the version of this study that was submitted as a doctoral thesis in Oxford University. I have greatly benefited from their comments, as I have from the advice and assistance of the following: A. Alvarez, Cleanth Brooks, Paul E. Cohen, Malcolm Cowley, William T. Dameron of the Kenyon College Library, Richard Eberhart, Lawrence Ferlinghetti, Robert Fitzgerald, John Fuller, Dame Helen Gardner, Horace Gregory, Daryl Hine, William Ingoldsby of the Henry E. Huntington Library, Laura (Riding) Jackson, Kenneth A. Lohf of the Columbia University Library, Denise Levertov, Robert Lowell, Archibald MacLeish, Gavin Millar, Liam Miller, Samuel French Morse, William M. Murphy, Norman Holmes Pearson, Karl Shapiro, Holly Stevens, Karin Strand, Allen Tate, Peter Taylor, John Unterecker, Louis Untermeyer, Robert Penn Warren, William Wasserstrom, James S. Watson, Jr., John Hall Wheelock, Richard Wilbur, Senator Michael Yeats.

Richard Finneran, David Perkins, and Carol Smith devoted to the final draft an illuminating attention matched only by the kind concern shown for its author by Marjorie Sherwood and Gretchen Oberfranc of Princeton University Press. At Skidmore College, Carol Steiger, Zeke Finkelstein, and Tammy Tatsey assisted in the preparation and typing of the manuscript, which was funded in part by a Skidmore College Faculty Research Grant. Elizabeth Farrey painstakingly prepared the index. The Skidmore College librarians went out of their way to obtain out-of-the-way material.

An incalculable debt must be acknowledged to Anne Parker Diggory, who became my wife while this project was under way and, more remarkably, remained my wife through its completion.

TERENCE DIGGORY
Skidmore College
Saratoga Springs, New York
1982

PERMISSIONS

of Robinson Jeffers (1959): by permission of Random House, Inc. *Flagons and Apples* (1970): by permission of Cayucos Books. *Be Angry at the Sun* (1941): by permission of Jeffers Literary Properties.

Vachel Lindsay, unpublished letters to Harriet Monroe: by permission of the University of Chicago Library and the Estate of Vachel Lindsay.

Robert Lowell, *Day by Day* copyright © 1975, 1976, 1977 by Robert Lowell; *The Dolphin* copyright © 1973 by Robert Lowell; *History* copyright © 1967, 1968, 1969, 1970, 1973 by Robert Lowell; *For the Union Dead* copyright © 1956, 1960, 1961, 1962, 1963, 1964 by Robert Lowell; *Life Studies* copyright © 1956, 1959 by Robert Lowell; *Near the Ocean* copyright © 1963, 1965, 1966, 1967 by Robert Lowell; *Notebook* copyright © 1967, 1968, 1969, 1970 by Robert Lowell. By permission of Farrar, Straus and Giroux, Inc., and Faber and Faber Ltd.

Archibald MacLeish, *Collected Poems 1917-1952* copyright 1952 by Archibald MacLeish; *The Happy Marriage and Other Poems* copyright 1924 by Archibald MacLeish, copyright renewed 1952 by Archibald MacLeish; *New and Collected Poems 1917-1976* copyright © 1976 by Archibald MacLeish; *Panic* copyright 1935, copyright renewed © 1963 by Archibald MacLeish. By permission of Houghton Mifflin Company.

Ezra Pound, *The Cantos of Ezra Pound* copyright 1934, 1948, © 1962 by Ezra Pound; *Personae* copyright 1926 by Ezra Pound; *Collected Early Poems of Ezra Pound* copyright © 1976 by the Trustees of the Ezra Pound Literary Property Trust. Reprinted by permission of New Directions Publishing Corporation. *Collected Early Poems*; *Collected Shorter Poems*; *The Cantos*: by permission of Faber and Faber Ltd.

John Crowe Ransom, *Selected Poems*, Third Ed., Revised and Enlarged (1969): by permission of Random House, Inc.

Theodore Roethke, lines from "The Summons" in *Selected Letters of Theodore Roethke*, ed. Ralph J. Mills: by permission of the University of Washington Press, *Poetry* Magazine, and Beatrice Lushington. Lines from "The Dying

NOTE ON CITATIONS AND ABBREVIATIONS

UNLESS otherwise indicated, dates in parentheses in the text represent the year of first publication, as nearly as this can be determined. Poems by Yeats are cited as they appear in *The Variorum Edition of the Poems of W. B. Yeats*, ed. Peter Allt and Russell K. Alspach (1957; rpt. New York: Macmillan, 1973). Where the version that would have been available at the relevant period differs from the version now commonly printed, this fact has been noted. Frequently cited texts are identified by the abbreviations in the following list.

John Berryman
    FP   *The Freedom of the Poet*. New York: Farrar, Straus and Giroux, 1976.
    HMB   *Homage to Mistress Bradstreet and Other Poems*. New York: Noonday Press/Farrar, Straus and Giroux, 1970.
    LF   *Love and Fame*. New York: Farrar, Straus and Giroux, 1970.
    Songs cited by number.
           The Dream Songs. New York: Farrar, Straus and Giroux, 1969.

T. S. Eliot
    CPP   *The Complete Poems and Plays, 1909-1950*. 1952; rpt. New York: Harcourt, Brace and World, 1971.
    PP   *On Poetry and Poets*. 1957; rpt. New York: Noonday Press/Farrar, Straus and Giroux, 1961.

SE   *Selected Essays.* New York: Harcourt, Brace and World, 1964.

Ralph Waldo Emerson

     Works   *Works of Ralph Waldo Emerson.* London: Routledge, 1895.

FR   *Fugitives' Reunion: Conversations at Vanderbilt, May 3-5, 1956.* Ed. Rob Roy Purdy. Nashville: Vanderbilt University Press, 1959.

Robert Frost

     FL   *Selected Letters of Robert Frost.* Ed. Lawrance Thompson. New York: Holt, Rinehart and Winston, 1964.

     PRF   *The Poetry of Robert Frost.* Ed. Edward Connery Lathem. New York: Holt, Rinehart and Winston, 1969.

Horace Gregory

     CS   *Chorus for Survival.* New York: Covici, Friede, 1935.

     HJS   *The House on Jefferson Street: A Cycle of Memories.* New York: Holt, Rinehart and Winston, 1971.

Robinson Jeffers

     BAS   *Be Angry at the Sun.* New York: Random House, 1941.

     DJ   *Dear Judas and Other Poems.* New York: Horace Liveright, 1929.

     FA   *Flagons and Apples.* Los Angeles: Grafton Publishing Company, 1912.

     HOP   *Hungerfield and Other Poems.* New York: Random House, 1954.

     SPRJ   *The Selected Poetry of Robinson Jeffers.* 1938; rpt. New York: Random House, 1959.

Vachel Lindsay

     LCP   *Collected Poems.* 1925; rpt. New York: Macmillan, 1959.

Robert Lowell

     DD   *Day by Day.* New York: Farrar, Straus and Giroux, 1977.

LS   *Life Studies.* In *Life Studies and For the Union Dead.* Combined ed. New York: Noonday Press/Farrar, Straus and Giroux, 1969.

NO   *Near the Ocean.* New York: Farrar, Straus and Giroux, 1967.

UD   *For the Union Dead.* In *Life Studies and For the Union Dead.* Combined ed. New York: Noonday Press/Farrar, Straus and Giroux, 1969.

Archibald MacLeish

Music   *This Music Crept by Me Upon the Waters.* Cambridge, Mass.: Harvard University Press, 1953.

NCP   *New and Collected Poems, 1917-1976.* Boston: Houghton Mifflin, 1976.

Edgar Allan Poe

Works   *The Works of Edgar Allan Poe.* Vol. V. Philadelphia: J. B. Lippincott, 1908.

Ezra Pound

Cantos   *The Cantos of Ezra Pound.* New York: New Directions, 1972.

CEP   *Collected Early Poems of Ezra Pound.* Ed. Michael John King. New York: New Directions, 1976.

GB   *Gaudier-Brzeska: A Memoir.* 1970; rpt. New York: New Directions, 1974.

LE   *Literary Essays of Ezra Pound.* Ed. T. S. Eliot. 1954; rpt. New York: New Directions, 1968.

Personae   *Personae: The Collected Shorter Poems.* 1949; rpt. New York: New Directions, 1971.

PL   *The Letters of Ezra Pound, 1907-1941.* Ed. D. D. Paige. New York: Harcourt, Brace, 1950.

SP   *Selected Prose 1909-1965.* Ed. William Cookson. New York: New Directions, 1973.

SR   *The Spirit of Romance.* 1952; rpt. New York: New Directions, 1968.

John Crowe Ransom

PAG   *Poems About God.* New York: Holt, 1919.

Theodore Roethke
   PC   *On the Poet and His Craft: Selected Prose of
            Theodore Roethke.* Ed. Ralph J. Mills, Jr.
            Seattle: University of Washington Press, 1965.
   RCP   *The Collected Poems of Theodore Roethke.*
            Garden City, N.Y.: Anchor Press/Doubleday,
            1975.
   RL   *Selected Letters of Theodore Roethke.* Ed.
            Ralph J. Mills, Jr. Seattle: University of
            Washington Press, 1968.
   SF   *Straw for the Fire: From the Notebooks of
            Theodore Roethke 1943-1963.* Ed. David
            Wagoner. Garden City, N.Y.: Doubleday,
            1972.
SRev   *Southern Review,* 7 (Winter 1941). Yeats me-
            morial issue.

Wallace Stevens
   OP   *Opus Posthumous.* Ed. Samuel French Morse.
            New York: Knopf, 1957.
   PEM   *The Palm at the End of the Mind.* Ed. Holly
            Stevens. New York: Vintage Books/Random
            House, 1972.
   SCP   *The Collected Poems of Wallace Stevens.* New
            York: Knopf, 1954.
   SL   *Letters of Wallace Stevens.* Ed. Holly Stevens.
            New York: Knopf, 1966.

Allen Tate
   EFD   *Essays of Four Decades.* Chicago: Swallow
            Press, 1968.
   TCP   *Collected Poems 1919-1976.* New York: Far-
            rar, Straus and Giroux, 1977.

Robert Penn Warren
   WSP   *Selected Poems 1923-1975.* New York: Ran-
            dom House, 1976.

Walt Whitman
   LG   *Leaves of Grass.* Ed. Harold W. Blodgett and
            Sculley Bradley. 1965; rpt. New York: Nor-
            ton, 1968.

William Carlos Williams

Paterson	*Paterson.* New York: New Directions, 1963.
WL	*The Selected Letters of William Carlos Williams.* Ed. John C. Thirwall. New York: McDowell, Obolensky, 1957.

W. B. Yeats

Au	*Autobiographies.* 1955; rpt. London: Macmillan, 1973.
EI	*Essays and Introductions.* London: Macmillan, 1961.
Ex	*Explorations.* London: Macmillan, 1962.
L	*The Letters of W. B. Yeats.* Ed. Allan Wade. New York: Macmillan, 1955.
Memoirs	*Memoirs.* Ed. Denis Donoghue. New York: Macmillan, 1973.
OBMV	"Introduction." *The Oxford Book of Modern Verse 1892-1935.* 1936; rpt. Oxford: Oxford University Press, 1972.
UP I	*Uncollected Prose by W. B. Yeats.* Vol. I: *First Reviews and Articles, 1886-1896.* Ed. John P. Frayne. New York: Columbia University Press, 1970.
UP II	*Uncollected Prose by W. B. Yeats.* Vol. II: *Reviews, Articles and Other Miscellaneous Prose, 1897-1939.* Ed. John P. Frayne and Colton Johnson. New York: Columbia University Press, 1976.
Vision A	*A Critical Edition of Yeats's "A Vision" (1925).* Ed. George Mills Harper and Walter Kelly Hood. London: Macmillan, 1978.
Vision B	*A Vision.* London: Macmillan, 1962.
VPl	*The Variorum Edition of the Plays of W. B. Yeats.* Ed. Russell K. Alspach. 1966; rpt. New York: Macmillan, 1969.
VPo	*The Variorum Edition of the Poems of W. B. Yeats.* Ed. Peter Allt and Russell K. Alspach. 1957; rpt. New York: Macmillan, 1973.

YEATS &
AMERICAN
POETRY

INTRODUCTION:
"THE TRADITION OF MYSELF"

NOT LONG AGO, any study concerned with the concept of tradition in twentieth-century poetry would inevitably have revolved around T. S. Eliot. His most famous essay, "Tradition and the Individual Talent," is still the standard classroom introduction to the modernist preoccupation with tradition. Recent scholarship and poetry have helped to redefine that preoccupation, however. Contrary to the view that in other essays Eliot implicitly adopts toward himself, as a restorer of a tradition that had lain dormant for more than two hundred years, numerous scholars have argued that Eliot's work is in fact a continuation of the romantic tradition that has flourished since the late eighteenth century. Meanwhile, the "postmodernist" poets of the last two decades have shifted the question entirely, from "Which is the relevant tradition?" to "Is there a relevant tradition?" Robert Lowell's attitude to "Those Before Us" (1964) is that "We have stopped watching them. They have stopped watching" (UD 17).

Whichever perspective we adopt, that of the scholars or that of the poets, the modernist in whom the problem of tradition now finds its focus is not Eliot but William Butler Yeats. Measuring himself against Eliot, Yeats could assert, in his edition of the *Oxford Book of Modern Verse* (1936), that "I too have tried to be modern" (*OBMV* xxxvi). Yet he saw no contradiction in his claim, in "Coole Park and Ballylee, 1931" (1932), to be also one of "the last romantics." Identifying himself as an Irishman, Yeats tried at first to revive the ancient Irish tradition, but he soon realized that his real task was to create a tradition where none seemed to exist.

Yeats's commitment to creating a tradition for Ireland in particular helps to explain why his relevance to the question of tradition in a broader sense has not been fully perceived. To do so requires a recognition of the complex resemblance between Yeats's situation in Ireland and the situation of poets in America, for since World War I the American absence of tradition has increasingly come to be acknowledged as the situation of modern art generally. Long before World War I, Yeats acknowledged that poems analogous to Whitman's "Song of Myself" were being written in response to the failure of tradition in Europe, but he specifically excluded Ireland from the analogy. In 1906 an Irish newspaper reported Yeats's belief that "although, so far as cultivated Europe was concerned, the days of symbols and myths had gone, something had been gained as well as lost. Individuality stood out in stronger relief, and painters as well as poets had all learned to sing the song of themselves—the song of their own souls, more gladly, more confidently than ever before" (*UP* II, 344-45). Though he later emphasized their bitterness rather than their gaiety, the poets whom Yeats has in mind here are those of the eighteen-nineties, men like Lionel Johnson and Ernest Dowson, "who more and more must make all out of the privacy of their thought" (1922; *Au* 314). In 1906 Yeats still thought he might be spared the bitterness of his friends because he was from Ireland, where "this great tradition that they called a nation" (*UP* II, 345) might rescue the artist from his privacy.

Nationhood, rather than selfhood, was the issue in which Yeats first perceived the relevance to his own situation of Whitman and the other nineteenth-century American writers whom the Irishman admired. The Americans had succeeded in declaring aesthetic independence from England. Yeats wanted the Irish to follow the American lead—officially because English rationalism denied the authority of tradition; unofficially, perhaps, because English poetry embodied a tradition that threatened to overwhelm a young poet who had a strong attraction to romanticism. Once the Americans had determined not to make use of English tradition, they found themselves without any tradition, because America had no past of its own. Yeats hoped that the past embodied in Ireland's ancient legends and persisting folk beliefs would supply the tradition that gives poetry its essential resonance, but his attempt to found a national theater during the first decade of this century led him to abandon that hope. The sort of tradition he envisioned required the consent of a community, but the Irish community exhibited only dissension. In effect, then, Yeats found himself without a tradition as much as the Americans, and Whitman's "Song of Myself" became immediately relevant to him as well as to his English friends. American poets like Emerson and Whitman had discovered in the self an alternative to tradition that was at the same time a new source of tradition. This is the tradition Yeats had in mind when he resolved in his journal for 1909: "To oppose the new ill-breeding of Ireland, . . . I can only set up a secondary or interior personality created out of the tradition of myself."[1]

The view that personality is *created* distinguishes the tradition of the self from its origin in the romantic theory of artistic self-expression. Both doctrines lead logically to poems in which the speaker is identified through autobiographical detail with the poet himself, as in Wordsworth's "Tintern Abbey" or Yeats's "The Tower." These two poems symbolize an important difference, however. Whereas Wordsworth views himself in terms of past stages of his life—the child sensualist and adolescent pantheist—Yeats views himself in terms of past creations—the fictional Hanrahan and even the restored tower itself. For Wordsworth, the self was given or, at most, discovered; for Yeats, the self was created. In the process of being created, the self becomes distanced or externalized. It is literally *ex-pressed*, but not as in romantic expression, because Yeats's externalized self differs from the internal self where it originated.[2] Once externalized, the self is viewed not as the poet's content but rather as a form to be entered into; it is the mask or antiself that must be pursued throughout life.

Though it has roots in Blake's *The Four Zoas* and Shelley's *Alastor*, Yeats's postulation of a dual or even multiple self marks another signal divergence from romantic self-expression, since that theory demands an identity between what is expressed and what is contained in the poet's true self. The romantic desires harmony between subjective and objective experience, a harmony that Yeats could preserve only by expanding the definition of the self to include what appeared to him as quite disparate modes of experience. Subjectively, Yeats felt himself to be the creator of the world, but, objectively, he felt himself the helpless victim of the world's intransigence. By granting a measure of truth to both selves, Yeats could adopt a heroic stance in his poetry without diminishing the obstacles he faced.[3] Further, Yeats was able to retain a sense of inspiration as coming from outside—a sense demanded by the feeling of helplessness before the world—and yet to know also that his inspiration came from himself, since there was also a self that was outside. To enjoy the sanction of external authority and yet to recognize that authority as the self is the definitive experience of the tradition of the self.

Experience does not demand the distinction between inside and outside, subject and object, that intellect attempts to impose upon it. At least, this is the assumption of poets in the tradition of the self who, following their romantic predecessors, regard experience as a sense of wholeness that includes intellect but that is destroyed when that faculty functions exclusively. Robert Langbaum has stressed the continuity of modern poetry and romanticism by showing how "the poetry of experience" is designed to create experience for the reader.[4] However, a discontinuity emerges between romanticism and modernism, particularly Yeats's brand of modernism, if the same poetry is considered from the perspective of the writer. Because a poet in the tradition of the self creates a self when he writes, the act of writing extends his experience as well as that of the reader, whereas the romantic poet, in expressing a self that already exists, merely records preexisting experience. Thus, another intellective distinction, that between art and life, is obliterated when we arrive at the tradition of the self, and such modifications of theory are bound to affect the reader's experience of the poetry that results. For instance, the reader must adjust to an enlargement of the romantic's claim for the poet's heroic role, since in the tradition of the self the poet is not merely a seer but a man of action whose deeds are his poems.

This conviction of the power of language is one of the points of agreement between the tradition of the self as developed by Yeats and the second principal source of that tradition: the American poetry that regards the poet as another Adam who names the world anew.[5] Contrasting scientists and artists in a 1908 lecture, Yeats described artists as "Adams of a different Eden" who "must name and number the passions and motives of men" (*UP* II, 369-70). But English romanticism checked Yeats's American Adamic impulse, freeing him to conceive a poetry distinct from either of its sources. The tradition of the self grows less distinctively American as Yeats shapes it to accommodate the communal concerns that he shared with the English romantics.[6] The American Adam, as the first man, stands apart from society. Yeats felt that he had gone beyond the Adamic Whitman by asserting the public responsibility of the artist. At the same time, the public that interested Yeats was different from that to which the English romantics responded. Like the self, Yeats's public world was created by the artist, not given to him.

In the beginning, then, the self for Yeats stands alone, and if poetry is to be produced from that situation, the self is the poet's only available subject. Since that generating postulate of the tradition of the self derives immediately from American poetry, the next chapter of this study will be devoted to a fuller examination of Yeats's ties to nineteenth-century American writers. In the twentieth century many American writers came in touch with the tradition through Yeats. What they found, however, was not necessarily the core of the tradition but one of four corollaries derived from the generating postulate. The man most responsible for transmitting Yeats's influence to America, Ezra Pound, eventually embraced the tradition in its entirety, as I show in Chapter III, but for other poets, one of the corollaries usually remained of primary importance. If the poem's subject was to be an actual man, the poet himself, then the speech of the poem must convincingly convey that actuality (Chapter IV). But even though he spoke a natural speech, the self that entered the poem was in fact artificial, a created being, as Yeats would argue against the English romantics (Chapter V). Moreover, Yeats maintained against his American forebears that the dimensions of the self in the poem were not merely individual but also communal (Chapter VI). So that the self did not lose its individuality, however, it was located amid the special circumstances of the poet's private existence (Chapter VII). Understandably, given the conflicting demands embodied in this set of principles, few poets could embrace the entire system, but, taken as a whole, the system reflects the notion of the duality of the self that was fundamental to Yeats's thought.

To talk of postulates and corollaries is, of course, to employ a logical schematization available only to hindsight. A poet attracted to what I have called a corollary would have seen it rather as an aspect of Yeats's poetry that had value in itself or, more important, that might instill similar value in his own poetry. Because Yeats's poetry cohered as a system, however, a poet who explored one element of the system was likely at least to confront other elements, provided he devoted sufficient time and attention to his exploration. As an acknowledgment of the importance of time in this study, I have used an organization that is chronological as well as logical. Chapters IV through VII each represent a decade during which one of the corollaries of the tradition of the self received special attention. Though these chapters embrace the entire career of each relevant American poet, the decade divisions serve to define stages of Yeats's career as it was shaped by the poets who read him. In Yeats's case, the issues raised by his readers cluster around volumes that seem to announce decades: *The Green Helmet* volume in 1910, *Four Plays for Dancers* in 1921, and *The Tower* in 1928. Yeats's death in 1939 marks off another decade.

This book concludes with three poets who published their first volumes during the nineteen-forties, the sort of poets whom M. L. Rosenthal describes as "carrying on where Yeats left off when he proposed that the time had come to make the literal Self poetry's central redeeming symbol."[7] Rosenthal is speaking of confessional poetry, which indeed represents the culmination of the tradition of the self. To appreciate the scope of that tradition, we need to recognize that "confessional" poems have been written not only within the school so designated but also by poets as diverse as William Carlos Williams, Robinson Jeffers, and Archibald MacLeish. Although most of these poems were written from the forties through the sixties, the phenomenon is too widespread to be considered merely the leading fashion of a period. These poets shared a common experience, World War II and its aftermath, and a common tradition, derived from Yeats.[8] Within the confessional school more strictly defined, especially in the work of Robert Lowell, there are signs that the tradition has come to an end.

What signs allow us to trace a tradition? The question is especially problematic when applied to the tradition of the self, because far more important than any of the characteristics I have designated as corollaries of the tradition is the central lesson: a poet is to be himself in his poems. Yet to say that a poem betrays the influence of Yeats especially at those moments when the author presents himself most persuasively sounds either like nonsense or like an extremely subtle paradox. Harold Bloom traces that paradox to its origin in American poetry when he attributes to Emerson "the only poetic influence that counsels against itself, and against the idea of influence."[9] Though Emerson certainly opened the way to the tradition of the self, that fact provides further proof of the difficulty of tracing such a tradition. For as far as Yeats was concerned, Whitman, not Emerson, was the central figure in American poetry. Yeats's opinion would not matter to Bloom, because he is interested in the Emersonian tradition as a pure idea. Yeats's opinion matters greatly to me, however, because I wish to study the tradition of the self as a movement in literary history.

For that reason, the following chapters will trace the tradition of the self not solely through a succession of poems that fully embody the tradition, but also through the careers of poets who, continually struggling either to invest themselves in or to divest themselves of the tradition, meet only rarely with complete success. The opinion of Yeats and other poets, as expressed in their prose and implied in their poetry, will be attended to closely, because in a historical study it is just as important to know what poets thought they were doing as it is to analyze what they were actually writing. In a historical study of tradition, it is especially important to know whom poets were reading and what they thought of their reading, and to this end prose statements, biographical data, and even the much maligned verbal and structural echoes prove useful, so long as we bear in mind the advice of Wellek and Warren that echoes "establish, at the most, the mere fact of relationship."[10] That is an important fact, from which we can proceed to fill in the larger patterns of influence that transmit the functional values of tradition. Thus, when a poet's letters discuss Yeats, when specific lines in certain poems echo Yeats, and when those poems reveal a concern for one of the corollaries of the tradition of the self—such superficial signs, if they agree with each other, indicate that Yeats may have penetrated deeper into the poems, to the level at which the poet creates his identity.

If Yeats plays no other part in such a poet's self-creation, he at least offers support to the self by providing access to tradition. To those for whom tradition is preserved through formal technique, Yeats shows how the trimeter line or the eight-line stanza can be made freshly contemporary. To those for whom tradition is a pattern of belief, Yeats shows how the modern world can be set parallel to myth. But to all the poets studied here, Yeats presents a possibility that can be vividly inspiring or fatally intimidating: the possibility that, when inheritance fails to provide tradition, tradition can be generated from the self.

AN AMERICAN TRADITION:
EMERSON, POE, THOREAU,
AND WHITMAN

AFTER YEATS RETURNED from his first visit to America during
the winter of 1903-1904, he recorded his impression of the
American poetic scene in which he was just beginning to play
a part. In an article entitled "America and the Arts," he agreed
with many contemporary critics, as well as with later literary
historians, that turn-of-the-century America was not produc-
ing great art. Yet in the greatness of the nation's past, he saw
hope for its future (*UP* II, 338-42). He found contemporary
American poetry disappointing because it "had followed the
modern way of [James Russell] Lowell, who mistook the imag-
inative reason for poetry, not that ancient way Whitman,
Thoreau and Poe had lit upon." Even without reflecting on
the work of the poets Yeats mentions, it is possible to see his
point in the adjectives he uses to characterize the two types.
Lowell is "modern"; Whitman, Thoreau, and Poe are "an-
cient," or, in other words, traditional. Though it may seem
strange to find in Yeats's traditional category work that is
famous for defying traditions, it is not surprising to find Yeats
respecting tradition. To discover what he meant by tradition
in this context is to discover what he valued most highly in
nineteenth-century American literature, which is in turn what
made Yeats valuable to American poets in the twentieth cen-
tury.

Yeats's list of the writers of the "ancient way" ranks in
descending order the American writers whom he most ad-
mired. Just off the list, but at the foundation of the writing
of his time, lies Ralph Waldo Emerson, who appears in a

slightly expanded list elsewhere in "America and the Arts": "there is Poe and Thoreau and Whitman, and there is Emerson, who seems to me of a lesser order because he loved the formless infinite too well to delight in form." Emerson seemed more concerned with the Oversoul than with the individual souls that give it expression, whereas that expression was emphasized in the tradition to which Yeats was attracted. Nevertheless, Yeats's allusions to Emerson prove that the American offered a useful entry into tradition, although his counsel against certain sources of tradition was equally important. In opposition to the worn-out literary formulas of a book he reviewed in 1893, Yeats slightly misquoted lines from Emerson's "Saadi"—"To thine orchard's edge belong / All the brass and plume of song"—which, he claimed, "should be writ over the mantelpiece of every poet" (*UP* I, 289). As Yeats recognized, Emerson's lines prescribe a poetry that is not solipsistic but local, like the American art that grew out of Emerson or the Irish art that Yeats was trying to encourage. Yeats associated Emerson's lines specifically with William Allingham's poems centered on the Irish village of Ballyshannon. In such work the poet was still offered a tradition of a sort; his art need not be pure invention. But it was up to him to claim tradition. Continuing Emerson's metaphor, Yeats insisted that each artist must stake out his own orchard (*UP* I, 291).

For both Yeats and Emerson, moral or religious teaching necessarily lay beyond the poet's pale. This prohibition is part of the Muse's instruction to Saadi, and it is what Emerson had in mind—at least as Yeats read him—when he called Shakespeare "master of the revels to mankind" (*Works* 193), a role with which Yeats thought Spenser should have been content (1906; *EI* 368). Spenser's gift, the argument runs, was for celebrating "beautiful and sensuous life," from which his didactic allegories only distract the reader. In the essay on "Shakespeare; or, The Poet," where Yeats found Emerson's phrase, he would also have found that the experience celebrated by the true poet has a traditional dimension. Emerson recalls the brilliant results that Shakespeare could achieve by adapting an old play: "The rude warm blood of the living

England circulated in the play, as in street-ballads, and gave body which he wanted to his airy and majestic fancy. The poet needs a ground in popular tradition on which he may work, and which, again, may restrain his art within the due temperance" (*Works* 188). Through the theater, Yeats hoped to come in touch with popular tradition and thereby give body to his dangerously ethereal verse. He became disillusioned when he discovered that the "people" themselves seemed to have lost touch with tradition, but Emerson had helped to put him in touch with an alternative source.

Emerson did not intend his designation of Shakespeare as "master of the revels" to be entirely complimentary. He was indicating a limitation in Shakespeare's work, the poet's willingness to rest content with the spectacle of appearances instead of pressing on to the underlying reality. The world still waits, concluded Emerson, for a man who will combine the best points of Shakespeare and Swedenborg. Emerson's interest in Swedenborg and Jacob Boehme, his willingness to listen to claims of animal magnetism and self-healing, allied him to the tradition of the occult that attracted Yeats throughout his life. If tradition no longer survived among the people, it had been preserved among the magical coteries. Both sources must have been valued all the more by Emerson and Yeats because they were separate from the literary tradition against which the two men rebelled.

One proof of that separation is the consistently high esteem accorded Emerson among British Theosophists during the nineteenth century, despite fluctuations in his literary reputation. The Theosophists were especially eager to point out the similarities between Emerson's philosophy and the religions of the East. In 1887 Yeats's school friend Charles Johnston contributed an article on "Emerson and Occultism" to Madame Blavatsky's magazine *Lucifer*, to which Yeats himself contributed in 1889.[1] Johnston drew on a number of passages from Emerson's works to argue that the transcendentalist was in essential agreement with, among other doctrines, a belief in reincarnation, in karma, and in mahatmahood.

If the aura of tradition bestowed value on Emerson in Yeats's eyes, Emerson helped to make tradition more valuable by making it more readily understood. In his critical assessment of his fellow Dublin hermeticist, George Russell (AE), Yeats wondered what Russell "would have been had he not met in early life the poetry of Emerson and Walt Whitman . . . and those translations of the Upanishads, which it is so much harder to study by the sinking flame of Indian tradition than by the serviceable lamp of Emerson and Walt Whitman" (*Au* 246). Once Emerson's principle of self-reliance was fully grasped, the Indian's talk of seedless Samadhi became much clearer. Once Emerson's thought was understood as "a reverie about the adventures of the soul, or of the personality" (*Ex* 141), Yeats could explain Bhagwan Shri Hamsa's "meditation upon a divine personality, a personality at once historical and yet his own spiritual Self" (*EI* 452). In discovering the self, one discovered the past. Even in America, where there was no history, men such as Emerson who looked into themselves discovered a source of tradition.

"Personality" became a key term for Yeats during the first decade of the twentieth century, as he struggled to instill that quality into his verse. At this time, the American writer with whom Yeats most strongly associated personality was Edgar Allan Poe, despite Poe's differences with Emerson, the founder of the tradition that gave the term its meaning. Yeats was not responding to the historical Poe, however. In the light of Emerson, the French Symbolists, and the English Decadents, Yeats discovered personality in the legend of Poe as the tortured, dissolute dreamer who turned in on himself in retreat from a hostile world. "Characters and personality alike, as is perhaps true in the instance of Poe," wrote Yeats in 1904, "may draw half their life not from the solid earth but from some dreamy drug" (*Ex* 144). Part of the mystery of personality was that its origin might be "dreamy," yet it had the power to bring a poem, or a nation, into focus. In 1905 Yeats claimed that, before Synge, Irish literature had lacked a true personality. The nearest candidate, James Clarence Mangan, "was not a personality as Edgar Poe was" (*L* 447). Still, the extreme type of personality represented by Poe was not entirely an advantage. An entry in Yeats's diary for 1909 states, "The work of some writers, of Edgar Allan Poe for instance, suggests to the imagination a fever of the personality which keeps admiration from being ever complete" (*Memoirs* 166).

The Poe legend seemed to offer an extreme example of a man who created a tradition out of himself. Poe's own writings, though, offered little evidence that this had been his intention, and it was perhaps for this reason that Yeats felt uncomfortable with them. His statement to a Poe centenary commemoration group that their author was "the greatest of American poets" must be read in light of the fact that Yeats did not approach Poe's competitors as poets but as thinkers.[2] As a poet, Poe made up for Emerson's formlessness through devotion to technique, but this, too, like his "fever of the personality," seemed to Yeats to be misapplied. Instead of using his command of technique to express his own genuinely felt emotion, Poe had sought to arouse emotion in his readers. "The Raven" was "insincere and vulgar," Yeats declared in a letter of 1899, and "The Pit and the Pendulum" was "an appeal to the nerves by tawdry physical affrightments" (*L* 325). This attention to effect can be understood in terms of Poe's claims for "The Raven" in "The Philosophy of Composition" (*Works* 180-94), but it conflicts with the legendary image, which Yeats evidently preferred, of the writer whose uncontrollable anguish separated him from a genteel public.

Despite his implicit rejection of "The Philosophy of Composition," Yeats's letter of 1899 professes a qualified admiration for Poe's critical essays. Qualification and admiration are isolated in two statements from the previous year in which Yeats refers to Poe's "The Poetic Principle." In "The Autumn of the Body" (*EI* 194), Yeats explicitly denies Poe's belief that long poems could no longer be written (*Works* 101), though he does not connect Poe's name with the doctrine. In "John Eglinton and Spiritual Art" (*UP* II, 131), Yeats characterizes the art he favors by adapting a phrase of Poe's to read "the beauty that is beyond the grave" (cf. *Works* 108). For Yeats, such beauty consists of "great passions" rather than the ideas

that concern didactic writers. Poe repeatedly attacked didac-
ticism on much the same basis. Though both men modified
their views in later life, Poe (e.g., *Works* 95) and Yeats began
by identifying the passions as the source of poetry and re-
jecting the concerns of the intellect as irrelevant to an art that
was created for its own sake. Poe's understanding of the pas-
sions allowed Yeats to place him, in "America and the Arts,"
among the writers of the "ancient way" who rejected the
"imaginative reason" of James Russell Lowell. The way of
passion was ancient because the fundamental passions repeat
themselves endlessly and derive force from the cumulative
weight of past embodiments. The strength and weakness of
reason is that its past is no more distant than a premise; here
self-sufficiency appeared to Yeats as a shallowness.

Strength of passion is what made Poe a "personality" for
Yeats, but that passion was divorced from "the solid earth,"
rendering it less than completely admirable. In contrast, Yeats
praised the "relation to concrete reality" that he found in the
American transcendentalists (*Ex* 303). It is doubtful that Yeats
was thinking of Emerson in this connection, for that writer
was attracted to the "formless infinite," whereas concrete real-
ity, Yeats implied, is measurably finite. The measuring tran-
scendentalist was preeminently the writer-surveyor Henry David
Thoreau. Thoreau's balance of the more metaphysical pas-
sages of *Walden* with the most precise measurements may
have inspired Yeats to specify the "nine bean-rows" in his
dream of "The Lake Isle of Innisfree" (1890). Yeats acknowl-
edged that "Innisfree" was written particularly with Thoreau
in mind. As a boy Yeats had heard *Walden* read by his father,
who held that "Thoreau writes like an immortal."[3] As in his
acquaintance with Emerson, however, Yeats learned more from
Thoreau's philosophy than from his style. "Innisfree" is based
on an ideal not of writing but "of living in imitation of Thor-
eau" (*Au* 153).

Walden would have encouraged Yeats's desire to disencum-
ber himself of the English past. "I look upon England to-day,"
Thoreau wrote, "as an old gentleman who is travelling with
a great deal of baggage, trumpery which has accumulated from

long housekeeping, which he has not the courage to burn; great trunk, little trunk, bandbox and bundle. Throw away the first three at least."⁴ Although they differ in degree of practicality, Thoreau's experiment of living at Walden Pond and Yeats's dream of abandoning London and living on Innisfree are both expressions of a desire for simplification, but in both cases the motive of escape is easily overemphasized. Thoreau sought not to renounce humanity but to examine himself as the one representative of humanity whom he could know best. Similarly, Yeats was escaping to, as well as from, something. "Innisfree," in its quiet way, is another example of Yeats's urge to get at the fundamental passions. He hears lake water "in the deep heart's core," and there is where he will seek it.

Yeats's assessment of Thoreau's advance over Emerson and Poe can be estimated through reference to Yeats's description of his own development in *Discoveries* (1907): "I had set out on life with the thought of putting my very self into poetry, and had understood this as a representation of my own visions and an attempt to cut away the non-essential, but as I imagined the visions outside myself my imagination became full of decorative landscape and of still life" (*EI* 271). On this path, Yeats arrived at an "impersonal beauty" like that achieved through Poe's aestheticism but with which Yeats soon became dissatisfied. "Presently I found," Yeats continued in *Discoveries*, "that I entered into myself and pictured myself and not some essence when I was not seeking beauty at all, but merely to lighten the mind of some burden of love or bitterness thrown upon it by the events of life." On this path, Yeats found he could carry "the personality as a whole." The difference lies in a greater engagement with circumstance. That engagement was found both at Walden and at Innisfree, as I have suggested, but those worlds remain comparatively narrow. Far more of the "events of life" are embraced by the American writer who was most important to Yeats, Walt Whitman. His aim in *Leaves of Grass* was to record "my own physical, emotional, moral, intellectual, and aesthetic Personality, in the midst of, and tallying, the momentous spirit and facts of

its immediate days, and of current America—and to exploit
that Personality, identified with place and date, in a far more
candid and comprehensive sense than any hitherto poem or
book" (*LG* 563).

In Whitman, Yeats discovered the culmination of the tra-
dition of the self in nineteenth-century America. Yeats's ear-
liest references to Whitman already make use of that key term,
"personality," which Whitman uses in the passage just quoted.
Writing in 1892 of Edwin Ellis's *Fate in Arcadia*, Yeats ob-
served that, "Exquisite as the verse constantly is, it is almost
impossible to criticise it as verse alone, 'for he who touches
this book touches a man,' as Whitman puts it" (*UP* I, 234;
see *LG* 505). "Every verse seems the deeper," Yeats continued,
"because of the all-pervading personality of the writer." In
the following year Yeats called Charles Weekes's *Reflections
and Refractions* "a rugged, obscure personal book" like that
which had forced Whitman to become his own bookseller (*UP*
I, 303). Yeats's special notion of personality, which he shared
with Whitman to a large extent, must be kept in mind. It was
a writer's self, but it was by no means the self with which he
was born. He had imagined it and sought to create it in his
work. Even though Whitman, in the statement quoted above,
identifies his personality with place and date, he speaks not
merely of recording his personality but of exploiting it. He
did so, for instance, in projecting the image of the "Good
Gray Poet," but an even more important role was antiliterary:
his claim to reach out to his reader directly and not through
a book.

Whitman reinforced the attempt to make his presence di-
rectly felt by placing his self amid the "events of life," so that
those events were taken to be part of the life of the man, Walt
Whitman. The extent to which he developed this basically
confessional method distinguishes him from his American
contemporaries. Yeats could have learned that method from
English poets, however, principally Wordsworth and Ten-
nyson. What distinguished Whitman from these writers, and
made him so important to Yeats, was his notion that the self
he placed among circumstances was his own creation, not a

product of the circumstances, which in themselves were often fictional. This is the principle that Yeats used to contrast Whitman and Wordsworth in his journal for 1909: "One constantly notices in very active natures a tendency to pose, or a preoccupation with the effect they are producing if the pose has become a second self. One notices this in Plutarch's heroes, and every now and then in some modern who has tried to live by classical ideas, in Oscar Wilde, for instance, and less obviously in men like Walt Whitman. Wordsworth is so often flat and heavy partly because his moral sense has no theatrical element, it is an obedience, a discipline which he has not created" (*Memoirs* 151). A version of this passage in a lecture delivered in 1910 replaces Wilde and Whitman with Shelley and Byron, perhaps because more traditional examples would be more comprehensible to Yeats's audience.[5] Another difference between the two sets of examples, however, is that Shelley and Byron still drew a line between art and life that Wilde, by seeing his life as art, and Whitman, by seeing his art as life, attempted to abolish. For the two later writers, self and pose become indistinguishable.

Yeats's use of the term "pose" is left over from the deliberately provocative vocabulary of the Decadents and risks obscuring his meaning. Wordsworth would be playing a role no less than Wilde or Whitman, in Yeats's view. The difference would be that, unlike Wordsworth, Wilde and Whitman realized they were playing a role because they created it, whereas Wordsworth received his from social convention. The issue at stake is the integrity of the self, which is violated by a coercive relationship with other selves in either of two directions. It is the same whether a man receives a role from others, as Yeats accused Wordsworth of doing, or whether he tries to impose a role on others. In art, the latter project can result in Poe's sensationalism, which attempts to arouse the reader's emotion rather than express the writer's, or it can lead to the fault of didacticism that both Poe (*Works* 94) and Yeats (*UP* I, 334) condemned in Wordsworth. Tennyson also seemed a writer whose acceptance of external discipline betrayed his art. Yeats quoted Paul Verlaine's assessment of the author of

In Memoriam: "too noble, too *anglais*, and, when he should have been broken-hearted, had many reminiscences" (*EI* 270). By trying to transform his reaction to grief into an example for others, this view would have it, Tennyson removed himself from his own emotion. The only way for the poet to defend himself against the distraction of the audience is to limit the audience to himself. A man like Wilde, in contrast to Poe, is concerned with his effect on others only as a way of watching his own reflection. Whitman formulated the principle in "A Song of the Rolling Earth," as Yeats remembered when he quoted from that poem in 1901: "The oration is to the orator, the acting is to the actor and actress, not to the audience: / And no man understands any greatness or goodness, but his own or the indication of his own" (*EI* 207; cf. *LG* 223). It was necessary to write both of the self and for the self, if the self was to be its own tradition.

Late in his life, Yeats was willing to admit an admiration for Wordsworth and Tennyson that probably expresses the truth of his relationship to them more accurately than any of his early pronouncements. At the time of those pronouncements, however, it was inevitable that a poet of Yeats's generation and background should claim to dismiss Wordsworth and Tennyson and direct serious attention to Whitman. During the latter part of the nineteenth century, critics had paid so much attention to Wordsworth the moralist that by 1879 Matthew Arnold had to protest that more attention should be paid to the poet. For adherents of aestheticism, the claims of moralist and poet could not be reconciled. Yeats spoke of Dante Gabriel Rossetti reacting violently against what Yeats called "the pedantic composure of Wordsworth" and "the passionless sentiment of Tennyson." Yeats's father, who regarded himself as a follower of Rossetti, declared an abhorrence of Wordsworth and a love of Whitman. The latter preference owes less to Dante Gabriel Rossetti than to his brother, William Michael, who was instrumental in gaining Whitman's first recognition in England. In 1868 Willliam Michael Rossetti pointed to a similarity between Whitman and Swedenborg in the preface to his selection from Whitman's poems.

In the same year, Swinburne concluded his study of Blake by invoking comparison with Whitman. Dr. John Todhunter, a neighbor of the Yeats family in Bedford Park, London, published in 1880 a study of Shelley in which he compared Shelley and Whitman as great poets of democracy. The American poet was being placed in a context that W. B. Yeats was bound to find congenial.[6]

The circle in which Yeats moved as a young man admired Whitman for his iconoclasm, his transcendentalism, his liberalism, his humanity, and his prophetic pose, but they had little praise for his poetry. Oscar Wilde, who visited Whitman in 1882, concluded seven years later that "the chief value of his work is in its prophecy not in its performance. . . . If Poetry has passed him by, Philosophy will take note of him."[7] In 1887 Ernest Rhys brought Yeats to a meeting of the Society of the New Life, which "seeks to carry out some of the ideas of Thoreau and Whitman," Yeats reported (L 39-40). These were of course ideas not of poetic but of social reform. The closest Yeats came to acknowledging Whitman as a poet was his observation that Todhunter's "wild, irregular verses" were "something between Walt Whitman and the Scotch Ossian" (UP I, 216). For the most part, it was as "the greatest teacher of these decades" that Whitman won Yeats's respect (L 32).

Such praise for a teacher may seem strange in the light of Yeats's condemnation of Wordsworth's didacticism. In fact, Yeats eventually pronounced the same condemnation on Whitman as "all preacher."[8] But for the young Yeats, what a teacher taught could make all the difference. One special achievement with which Yeats's elders credited Whitman was the creation of that national literature for which Emerson, as Yeats recognized, had issued the call. Edward Dowden, a friend of Yeats's father and professor of English in Trinity College, Dublin, published in 1871 an article on Whitman that began with the claim that, before Whitman, a truly American literature had not existed.[9] The relevance of this claim to a young man who dreamed of creating an Irish literature is obvious. Whitman taught nationality, whereas Wordsworth taught a morality that was itself part of the English tradition from which Whitman helped Yeats to escape.

Whitman's teaching was further distinguished from Wordsworth's according to the opposition of passion and intellect that Yeats used as a test for pure poetry. "Ireland was perhaps but one side in an argument," Yeats wrote in recollection of the early nineties. "I wished to make it, by good writing, an experience, and to be able to say with Walt Whitman, 'I convince as a sleeping child convinces'" (*Memoirs* 64; see *LG* 218). "Experience" is the term Yeats uses to designate the pole of passion; he is referring to a sense of wholeness that can only be felt, not known. If the image of a nation stemmed not from reason but from passion, the source of poetry, and if a nation was conceived of as something to be created—just as Yeats conceived of the self—then nationalism was not extraneous to poetry in the way that Wordsworth's morality was. Indeed, nationalism and poetry were integrally related. "There is no great literature without nationality, no great nationality without literature," Yeats wrote in the *Boston Pilot* in 1890.[10] Nationality served both Yeats and Whitman as an ordering principle for poetry in place of the literary tradition that both men had rejected. Yet America or Ireland existed for each poet more as an ideal than as a reality, for each created his nationality out of himself.

In addition to teaching that literature should be nourished by nationality, Whitman proved the lesson by his own example and thus encouraged Yeats further in his campaign for Irish literature. In 1892 Yeats told the editor of *United Ireland* that Ireland should be able to produce a national literature such as the Americans had: "Walt Whitman, Thoreau, Bret Harte, and [George Washington] Cable, to name no more, are very American, and yet America was once an English colony. It should be more easy for us, who have in us that wild Celtic blood, the most un-English of all things under heaven, to make such a literature" (*UP* I, 256). When the task proved much less easy than Yeats had hoped, he once again found encouragement in Whitman. In the face of the indifference or hostility shown by his countrymen toward the players of the young Irish National Theatre, Yeats recalled that Poe and Whitman had won recognition in Europe before they were truly accepted in their own country (*Ex* 156-57). The Irish players, then, could look elsewhere for recognition, which they found in fact in England and America.

The germ of this argument is contained in a pair of letters that Yeats wrote to *United Ireland* in 1894. There he used Whitman's case to point the moral: "The true ambition is to make criticism as international, and literature as National, as possible" (*L* 239). Yeats left democracy and even nationalism behind in his dependence on an international elite as an aesthetic tribunal: "Whitman appealed, like every great and earnest mind, not to the ignorant many, either English or American, but to that audience, 'fit though few,' which is greater than any nation, for it is made up of chosen persons from all, and through the mouths of George Eliot, Ruskin and Emerson it did him honour and crowned him among the immortals."[11] What linked the poet of democracy to the cultured elite, in Yeats's view, was a mutual reliance on tradition, whether written or unwritten. Both perspectives opposed "the triviality of emotion" that, as Yeats argued in his essay on "What is 'Popular Poetry'?" in 1901, manifests itself in the work of Longfellow: "Longfellow has his popularity, in the main, because he tells his story or his idea so that one needs nothing but his verses to understand it" (*EI* 6). In contrast, "when Walt Whitman writes in seeming defiance of tradition, he needs tradition for protection," because he is bound to be misunderstood by the rootless middle class that forms the majority of the reading public (*EI* 8). To put the argument in terms of nation rather than class, Whitman needs the recognition of European critics who are steeped in tradition because America, as a nation, is lacking in tradition.

The exception to Europe's monopoly on tradition is, of course, the tradition of the self that Whitman took over from Emerson. Here it was America's turn to offer the criticism. It is appropriate, therefore, that the earliest example of an American poet's reaction to Yeats comes from Walt Whitman. The second article Yeats published, possibly the first he wrote, was entitled "The Poetry of Sir Samuel Ferguson" and appeared in the *Dublin University Review* of November 1886. The article came to Whitman's attention in a copy of the journal probably sent by its editor, T. W. Rolleston. In March 1889, when Whitman was spending much of his time going through the mass of papers he had accumulated over the years, he gave his copy of Yeats's article to Horace Traubel, remarking that it was "very fine."[12] Traubel noticed that Whitman had marked Yeats's article, sometimes in the margin and sometimes by underscoring particular phrases. Whitman confirmed that he had made the marks "at the time," presumably when he first read the article in 1886. The passages Whitman marked, fortunately recorded by Traubel, provide invaluable testimony to the common concerns of the sixty-seven-year-old poet and the twenty-one-year-old poet-to-be.

The subject of Yeats's article was ideally suited to attract Whitman's attention. Sir Samuel Ferguson was the author of English verse adaptations of Ireland's heroic legends, which Yeats valued because "they are the mothers of nations," because "in them is the Celtic heart" (*UP* I, 104). Whitman marked this passage, though probably less out of interest in legends than out of approval of the principle that the soul of a nation should be sought wherever it might be found. The motive for the search was not simple patriotism, of course, but a recognition of the reciprocal relationship between nationalism and literature. Yeats proclaimed this principle in the conclusion of his article by setting up Ferguson as an alternative to "that leprosy of the modern—*tepid emotions and many aims. Many aims, when the greatest of the earth often owned but two—two linked and arduous thoughts—fatherland and song*" (*UP* I, 104). Whitman's underscoring in this passage serves to acknowledge that Yeats had fully absorbed his teacher's lesson, but it serves more immediately as evidence that Whitman found a kindred spirit in the Ferguson that Yeats presented. When Yeats's friend Ernest Rhys visited Whitman in 1888, he delighted Yeats with the news that Whitman was "a great admirer of Samuel Ferguson" (*L* 58). Although Yeats could not know it, his own article had contributed to Whitman's admiration.

Yeats's allusion to the emotions in the conclusion to his article points to another principle he shared with Whitman. The latter saw in Yeats's article corroboration of his belief that the highest art, as Whitman put it, "would seem to demand first of all passion, warmth—not artistic power, deftness of technique, primarily, but human passion."[13] In effect, this exaltation of human passion over poetic craft is Whitman's reply to those critics who were unable to regard him as a poet. Whitman would simply argue that he was a poet of a different sort—indeed, of a higher sort—who received his title not because of what he wrote but because of what he was. Being a poet in this sense extends to a man's life, partly because his poetry depends on his ability to incorporate the essence of his life in his art, partly because his poetry is conceived of as a form of action. His words are judged not by their beauty but by their power, which should be of heroic magnitude. In short, Whitman's image of the poet is that of the bard. It is understandable that he should reaffirm that image in connection with an article on the bardic tales of Ireland.

Although Yeats was a more meticulous craftsman than Whitman, he held a similar conception of the poet's role. Because Ferguson had captured the bardic spirit of his material, Yeats could excuse his lack of formal polish. Yeats declared, and Whitman's pencil endorsed, the doctrine that "the merely pretty is contraband of art" (*UP* I, 92). What should be sought instead was "fine momentum, the sign manual of the great writers" (*UP* I, 99). Approving of this passage, Whitman could also approve of Yeats's principle that "To know the meaning and mission of any poet we must study his works as a whole" (*UP* I, 90), because only such study could measure momentum adequately. The momentum of a body of work was sustained through its passion, whereas the whole broke into fragments under what Yeats in another context called "the corrosive power of the intellect" (*UP* I, 93). Whitman marked that phrase and another passage dealing with the intellect's divisiveness. The poetry of the intellect was "written by students, for students," Yeats wrote, whereas Ferguson's was a "truly bardic" utterance, "appealing to all natures alike, to the great concourse of the people, for it has gone deeper than knowledge or fancy, deeper than the intelligence which knows of difference—of the good and the evil, of the foolish and the wise, of this one and of that—to the universal emotions that have not heard of aristocracies, down to where Brahman and Sudra are not even names" (*UP* I, 101).

Whitman seems to have read Yeats's article in the light of these democratic sentiments. He told Traubel that he commended the article because he approved "anything which tends to keep art, books, writing, poetry, pictures, music, on the level where the people are, without untoward decoration, without haughty academic reserves."[14] The same sentiment, however, lay at the basis of Yeats's later disenchantment with Whitman, first publicly expressed in *The Trembling of the Veil* (1922). In that autobiographical essay, which recalls the period when he was most influenced by Whitman's democratic ideals, Yeats describes how, "Through some influence from an earlier generation, from Walt Whitman, perhaps, I had sat talking in public bars, had talked late into the night at many men's houses, showing all my convictions to men that were but ready for one, and used conversation to explore and discover among men who looked for authority. I did not yet know that intellectual freedom and social equality are incompatible" (*Au* 229). Yeats's confession of his own mistake implies that Whitman was mistaken as well.

The democratic optimism that went sour for Yeats was justified for Whitman by his faith in the goodness not of individual men but of universal man, for "only the good is universal" (*LG* 227). Yeats thus struck at the core of Whitman's democracy when he charged, in *The Trembling of the Veil*, that Whitman and Emerson "have begun to seem superficial precisely because they lack the Vision of Evil" (*Au* 246). In his essay on "Swedenborg; or, The Mystic," a pendant to the Shakespeare essay with which Yeats was familiar, Emerson reminded his readers, "Evil, according to old philosophers, is good in the making. That pure malignity can exist, is the extreme proposition of unbelief" (*Works* 176). The Evil of Yeats's Vision, however, was not pure malignity but rather discord or conflict, the opposition that continually frustrates man's plans in the world. This was a vision that Emerson and, to a greater extent, Whitman could have shared with Yeats, but one that they in turn would have dismissed as superficial when they looked upon man from above or beyond the world. Though Yeats might yearn for that transcendentalist perspective, he never in fact assumed it. He remained convinced that the place for a poet was in the world with all its conflict. "What theme had Homer but original sin?" he asks in "Vacillation" (1932).

Yeats's opinion of Whitman is systematized in *A Vision* (1926), where Whitman represents Phase 6 among the twenty-six incarnations and two disincarnate states of the human soul (*Vision* A, 46-47). Some familiar aspects of Yeats's picture of Whitman are unobscured by the technical jargon with which the system is adorned. For instance, Yeats accuses Whitman of creating a myth "of vague, half-civilised man, . . . all his thought and impulse . . . a product of democratic bonhomie, of schools, of colleges, of public discussion." The qualification "half-civilised" and the reference to the public discussion that Yeats rejected in *The Trembling of the Veil* indicate Yeats's disapproval of Whitman's democratic sentiment. Yeats also recognizes the potential for demagogy when Whitman sets himself up as an image of "perfect health." This is an extreme form of the didacticism for which Yeats condemned Wordsworth and with which, as I have noted, he charged Whitman elsewhere. Here, however, Yeats is content to deflate Whitman's pretension by recalling Thoreau's ironic example of perfect health, "the jaw-bone of a pig that had not a tooth missing," and by concluding that the demagogic potential in Whitman was not realized.[15] Whitman would have become a demagogue had he been "out of phase," but he was not.

The Phase assigned to Whitman in *A Vision* represents a refinement of Yeats's earlier views. The diary entry of 1909 that contrasts Whitman and Wordsworth allows for two categories of men: those who receive their self-image from their surroundings, and those who create an image for themselves. Yeats evidently felt uncomfortable about fitting Whitman into the scheme, for he used Wilde as his principal example of the latter type, to which Whitman "less obviously" belonged. In *A Vision* Yeats uses a tripartite scheme: character and personality correspond to the two types of 1909, and individuality is added as a transition between the two. As Yeats works it out, the scheme clearly favors personality; thus it is no honor for Whitman to represent a preliminary stage of individuality. In that condition, man defines himself solely according to what he is, not according to an image defined by society or invented by his own imagination. The demagogic potential, the tendency to measure all men by oneself, is clearly there in such a self-centered orientation, but for a man true to phase there can be no tyranny because he has not yet learned to distinguish himself from other men. What a man is, as opposed to what he imagines himself to be, is only what he shares with all humanity. As far as it goes, the self thus defined really is the measure of all men.

This new understanding of Whitman's position colors the familiar opposition of intellect and passion, which appears as a contrast of "observed fact" and "experience" in Yeats's discussion of Phase 6. For Whitman, "observed fact" is subordinate to "experience." The latter term is used here to denote a wholeness that embraces not only the individual man but also the community of men. Emotion for the man of Phase 6 must be shared emotion. Whitman's instrument of sharing, and hence of feeling, was the catalogue, Yeats says. There is no more useful distinction between the two poets than the difference in the catalogues each composed. Yeats's catalogues are exclusive: he must list his friends by name in order to distinguish them from the mass of anonymous others, and in turn the friends serve the primary purpose of distinguishing Yeats, who stands in their midst. Whitman's catalogues are inclusive: his lists of diverse men and women remain anonymous and tend to assimilate the poet into their anonymity. The Walt Whitman named in "Song of Myself" is not one man but a corporate entity. Yeats's ultimate objection to Whitman's democracy is that it places the self among circumstances in such a way as to lose a sense of the self as unique.

Although Yeats came to regard Whitman as "one of the errors of our youth,"[16] he did not altogether deny what he had learned from Whitman. Instead, Yeats attempted to retreat where Whitman went too far and to advance where Whitman stopped short. Whitman went too far in letting circumstance that should have defined the self overwhelm it, but his initial impulse had been valid, Yeats implied. For an introduction to a projected edition of his collected works, Yeats wrote in 1937, "I thought when I was young—Walt Whitman had something to do with it—that the poet, painter, and musician should do nothing but express themselves" (*EI* x). The objection lies in the "nothing but," not in a dismissal of the basic proposition or its corollaries. Though Yeats's view of Whitman changed considerably, he never denied the aesthetic principles that Whitman originally seemed to exemplify, the most important being that self-expression entails making the self the poet's subject, not just his point of view. From this proposition, Whitman seemed to derive a paradoxical pair of corollaries: in making his self his subject the poet concedes the artificiality of the self; but at the same time, he asserts the reality of the self by placing (but not losing) the self amid the actual circumstances of the poet's life.

The direction in which Yeats wanted to go beyond Whitman involves a third corollary, that the dimensions of the self expressed in a poem must be larger than those of an individual man, since the poetic self must function as a tradition. Self-expression, Yeats wrote in that 1937 introduction, had seemed the only alternative "when the laboratories, pulpits, and newspapers had imposed themselves in the place of tradition." But now Yeats felt that "a poet is justified not by the expression of himself, but by the public he finds or creates." Whitman had created a public, of course, by identifying himself with America, but he had done so, it finally seemed to Yeats, not by expanding the self but by reducing it to its lowest common denominator. No longer able to accept that democratic ideal,

Yeats wanted the poet to fashion his public by creating images
of "desirable people."

Yeats would no doubt have approved, had he recognized
it as such, the other public that Whitman created, namely, a
body of poets. If it were not for this audience, Yeats's reading
of Whitman would be a much less important moment in lit-
erary history than it is. In the history of Yeats's own devel-
opment, Whitman was a positive example for barely half of
Yeats's long career, and even when Whitman looked most
congenial, Yeats had trouble placing him among the surer
influences of Shelley and Wilde. For the American poets who
read Yeats in the twentieth century, however, his ties to the
nineteenth-century English tradition seemed no less provincial
than his obsession with Irish bardic legend. They could make
use of Yeats's example only where he seemed to have broken
with the nineteenth century or where, as in his connection
with Whitman, he had mined a lode in nineteenth-century
literature that did not appear to have been exhausted and that
was, for Americans, peculiarly close to home. Whether that
closeness was cause for satisfaction or discomfort, the Amer-
ican poets who saw themselves as part of a new movement
in the second decade of this century referred to that movement
as a "renaissance" partly because it involved a reassessment
of Whitman's neglected example. Though they were seldom
aware of the extent to which Yeats had redressed that neglect,
these and later poets inevitably found that in the separate
processes of coming to terms with Yeats and Whitman, or,
indeed, even if they thought they were only coming to terms
with Yeats, they were forced to explore the crucial concerns
that Yeats and Whitman had shared. The strongest link be-
tween Yeats and Whitman, finally, is the public they mutually
helped to create.

III

A Live Tradition:
Ezra Pound

If Yeats's contribution to the tradition of the self was to extend Whitman's example by attempting to create an audience, Ezra Pound's contribution was to define the mode of speech through which the audience was addressed. The speech must sound natural "to give a feeling of the reality of the speaker," the goal that Pound proclaimed in 1915 to be "the first difficulty in a modern poem" (*SP* 418). A respectful quarrel over the meaning of natural speech absorbed the first few years of Pound's friendship with Yeats, after which Pound gradually worked his way back through the other corollaries of the tradition of the self to arrive finally at the generating postulate, that the poet as a "real" man must be the speaker of his poem. Paradoxically, Pound's work came closest to Yeats's version of the tradition only after Pound had reestablished a distance between himself and Yeats in their personal relations. But then, Pound was able to read Whitman only after sailing to Europe in 1908 in search of a tradition that he thought he could not find in America.[1] It is in the nature of the tradition that Pound eventually discovered that one follows the master only by setting a different course for oneself.

Pound announced his new appreciation of Whitman in 1909, in notes that he headed " 'What I feel about Walt Whitman,' " which proposed making Whitman part of a cultural exchange program: "It seems to me I should like to drive Whitman into the old world. I sledge, he drill—and to scourge America with all the old beauty. (For Beauty *is* an accusation) and with a thousand thongs from Homer to Yeats, from Theocritus to Marcel Schwob" (*SP* 146). Which of these European writers

Pound had foremost in mind becomes clear if his affirmation that "Beauty is an accusation" is recognized as a quotation from Yeats's "The Symbolism of Poetry" (1900; *EI* 153). Pound's project, then, was to learn what he could from Yeats while he introduced Yeats to Whitman. Yeats was willing to play the dual role of master and pupil, but he had his own ideas about what he wanted to teach and what he wanted to learn. He looked to the New World for something much newer than Whitman, with whom he was already acquainted.

In his forties when he first met Pound, Yeats was deliberately rounding off the first stage of his career. He had issued his *Collected Works* (1908), and he would shortly begin his memoirs. If he was to go on writing poetry, he needed to do so in a way that would avoid conjuring the ghost of the art he had publicly buried. The solution was to embrace Pound's influence publicly, and he did so, for instance, in a 1914 address to the friends of *Poetry* magazine (*UP* II, 414) that was in effect a proclamation of rebirth. Pound was not merely another poet. Yeats recognized him to be a forerunner of the younger generation with which he wanted to identify at least part of himself. Pound's most important contribution to Yeats was his youth.

Perhaps the only specific instance of Pound's releasing Yeats from the past is Pound's suggestion, probably late in 1915, that the dominant tone of *The Player Queen* might be farcical rather than serious.[2] Yeats thus salvaged the labor of some seven years and produced a play that cast a cold eye on his speculations about the supernatural. Yeats valued tradition too highly, however, to wish ever to break completely with the past. In some cases Pound helped by providing Yeats with traditional sanction for what might otherwise appear as too radical innovation. Pound's work with Ernest Fenollosa's translations of the Japanese Noh, beginning in 1913, thus provided a past for the dramatic form that Yeats perfected in his "Plays for Dancers." As with the influence of Pound himself, the Noh did not initiate but rather announced Yeats's work with that form. *On Baile's Strand* (1903) and *Deirdre* (1907) had already used choric characters to frame the main action. Masks were used in *On Baile's Strand* by 1911. Even the introduction of dance may owe as much to Wilde's *Salome* (1894) as to the Noh.[3]

Like the Noh, Pound's studies in medieval poetry served to give Yeats traditional authority for breaking with traditions closer to home. In 1909, the year Pound became a regular guest at the Monday "At Homes" in Yeats's London flat, Yeats reported to Lady Gregory that "this queer creature Ezra Pound . . . has become really a great authority on the troubadours" (*L* 543). Writing again in 1913, Yeats gave some idea of the troubadours' importance by explaining that Pound "is full of the middle ages and helps me to get back to the definite and concrete away from modern abstraction."[4] He repeated his acknowledgment of Pound's aid in the fight against abstraction at the *Poetry* magazine banquet the following year (*UP* II, 414). Such statements have formed the basis of many accounts of Pound's influence on Yeats. "Abstraction" was Yeats's term, however, representing a general category to which Yeats relegated anything unspecific. Before he met Pound, Yeats rejoiced in revising *The Shadowy Waters* to admit " 'creaking shoes' and 'liquorice root' into what had been a very abstract passage" (*L* 462). The elimination of abstraction was what Yeats wanted to be taught, whereas Pound wanted to teach a different lesson about language, one he claimed to have learned from Whitman.

In " 'What I feel about Walt Whitman,' " Pound compares Whitman with Dante as a pioneer in using the language of his own people in literature (*SP* 146). By using real speech, Whitman had managed to convey a sense of the speaker's reality, Pound's "first difficulty in a modern poem." A few years later, in "Patria Mia" (1913), Pound contrasted Whitman's willingness to commit himself personally as the speaker, "to stand exposed" in his work, with the self-restraint characteristic of the English poets (*SP* 123). He may well have been thinking of Yeats, with whom he differed on this issue in two important respects. Yeats agreed that Whitman was a model, but for his content rather than his speech, which Yeats called "wild" and "irregular" (*UP* I, 216)—exactly the sort of comment Pound would expect from a restrained Englishman. Yeats also agreed on the need for "a speech so natural and dramatic that the hearer would feel the presence of a man thinking and feeling" (*L* 583), but when he first met Pound, Yeats was concentrating on speech from the standpoint of diction ("abstraction"); Pound, on the other hand, stressed rhythm and syntax.

This contrasting emphasis is apparent in the specific revisions that each man tried to introduce in the other's work. Yeats objected to precisely the feature that Pound most clearly shared with Whitman, "unrestrained" diction. In response to Yeats's criticism, Pound tried changing "pot-bellied" to "obese" in "Salutation the Third," but the version that appeared in *Blast* (1914), with "slut-bellied," replaced the unrestrained with the outrageous.[5] The surviving record of Pound's uninvited revisions in Yeats's "Fallen Majesty" (1912), "The Mountain Tomb" (1912), and "To a Child Dancing upon the Shore" (1912) do not reveal a concern with "abstraction."[6] Rhythm is tightened at the expense of meter by deleting "as it were." Parallel syntax is reinforced by adding a second "with." Proving no more agreeable than Pound to suggestions based on alien principles, Yeats tried to undo Pound's revisions. Eventually, Pound concluded that Yeats had simply failed to establish the reality of the speaker. Yeats wrote "the speech of no man," Pound asserted in 1935 (*SP* 435). Despite Yeats's frequent acknowledgment of Pound's influence, the evidence was difficult for even Pound to detect.

There has been much debate about the extent and importance of Yeats's influence on Pound and Pound's influence on Yeats. The importance may be impossible to measure, but the extent is certainly greater in the case of Yeats's influence on Pound.[7] The reason is simply that Yeats, having had more experience, knew exactly what he wanted from Pound and was determined to appear to get it even when Pound did not have it to give. Pound, on the other hand, was a young poet still feeling his way, and he began by absorbing from Yeats much that he later rejected. This pattern, encapsulated in the history of "Salutation the Third," is repeated on a larger scale in many ways throughout Pound's association with Yeats.

Though the indiscriminate nature of Pound's early admiration for Yeats contributed to Pound's later embarrassment at being "drunk with 'Celticism' " (*LE* 367) in the years just before he left America, remarks he made closer to that time seem to betray pride in the influence. In *A Lume Spento*, which Pound had printed in Venice in 1908 and sent to Yeats shortly thereafter, the poem "La Fraisne" is accompanied by a note in which Pound attempts to trace the tradition for the mood the poem invokes. He begins with Janus of Basel and adds, "Also has Mr. Yeats in his 'Celtic Twilight' treated of such, and I because in such a mood, feeling myself divided between myself corporeal and a self aetherial."[8] By appearing directly as the poet in this note, Pound is attempting to assert the historical reality of the poem's speaker, but he expands that reality in his references to earlier writers. The self of the poem includes not only corporeal and etherial aspects but also aspects of Yeats and Janus of Basel. Yeats is one of Pound's *personae*, a mask Pound uses, sometimes in isolation and sometimes in combination with others, to create the self that speaks in his poems. Derived from Browning's technique in the dramatic monologues, Pound's early *personae* suggest dramatic situations that foster a sense of the speaker's reality, thus preparing for Pound's entrance into the tradition of the self, but usually the *personae* also block that entrance through an insistence that the speaker is not the man Ezra Pound. At this period it is unusual for Pound to identify himself with a *persona* as closely as he does in the note to "La Fraisne." On the other hand, Yeats's willingness to impersonate himself helped to make him available as a *persona* to Pound.

Even without Pound's note, Yeats's contribution to the *persona* of "La Fraisne" would be evident. In theme the poem recalls the abdications of Yeats's Fergus and King Goll, and there is a verbal echo of Yeats's "The Madness of King Goll" (1887) in Pound's line, "Naught but the wind that flutters in the leaves." The refrain of Yeats's poem is "They will not hush, the leaves a-flutter round me, the beech leaves old."

Such echoes are disguised under the Provençal dress in which
Pound fits out his poem, and it is to the troubadours, or to
Rossetti's translations of their Italian relations, that the poem
owes its archaisms and inverted phrasing, which can be found
only in the very earliest examples of Yeats's verse. Something
of Yeats masquerades in other poems of *A Lume Spento*, as
in the Italian romance of "Cino," who closes his song with

> I will sing of the white birds
> In the blue waters of heaven,
> The clouds that are spray to its sea.
>   (*CEP* 12)

The final cadence, as well as the birds, can be found in Yeats's
"The White Birds" (1892), which begins, "I would that we
were, my beloved, white birds on the foam of the sea." The
Greek-inspired "Threnos" returns to the Yeatsian "fluttering"
and the characteristic twilight, but the Greek mood allows
Pound to control these elements by rejecting them: "No more
the winds at twilight trouble us" (*CEP* 30). The speakers are
the dead who, unlike Yeats's "Man Who Dreamed of Fairy-
land" (1891), have found comfort in the grave.

Yeats is most evident in Pound's verse whenever there is no
strong counter-influence. In "The Tree," also from *A Lume
Spento*, Pound's allusion to Roman rather than Celtic legend
does not obscure the "mood" derived from Yeats's "He Thinks
of His Past Greatness When a Part of the Constellations of
Heaven" (1898). The degree of rhythmical similarity encour-
ages comparison. Pound begins:

> I stood still and was a tree amid the wood,
> Knowing the truth of things unseen before,
> Of Daphne and the laurel bow
> And that god-feasting couple olde
> That grew elm-oak amid the wold.[9]

Yeats's first lines are:

> I have drunk ale from the Country of the Young
> And weep because I know all things now:

> I have been a hazel-tree and they hung
> The Pilot Star and the Crooked Plough
> Among my leaves in times out of mind.

Although Pound again uses archaism and inversion, the metrical fluidity and the theme of arboreal incarnation make "The Tree" unusually close to Yeats for the poems of *A Lume Spento*. It would not seem at all strange among the poems of *Exultations*, published in London in 1909. Here echoes of *The Wind Among the Reeds* (1899), in which "He Thinks of His Past Greatness" appears, are applied in such a single-minded fashion that we almost miss hearing Pound's voice above Yeats's monotonous chant.

In *Exultations* a sequence of ten poems, under the cumbrous title of "Laudantes Decem Pulchritudinis Johannae Templi," provides a convenient focus for studying the range of devices that contributed to Pound's Yeatsian *persona*.[10] Pound calls attention to the use of a *persona* in the title of Poem IV, "He speaks to the moonlight concerning the beloved," which recalls many post-1906 titles in *The Wind Among the Reeds*. "He Reproves the Curlew" and "He Bids His Beloved Be at Peace" resemble Pound's title even more than "He Thinks of His Past Greatness." The speaker's true beloved in both Pound and Yeats at this period is beauty, of which the woman is only a symbol. The poet is obsessed with beauty so exclusively that the woman is distilled into a few symbolic attributes: hair, eyes, or breast. Pound's Poem IV begins, "Pale hair that the moon has shaken / Down over the dark breast of the sea." Similarly, Yeats's "The Lover Mourns for the Loss of Love" begins by invoking "Pale brows, still hands and dim hair." Hair is specifically "dim" in at least two other poems of the *The Wind Among the Reeds*, and Pound did not fail to follow suit in *Exultations*. "Sestina for Ysolt" boasts, "I praise dim hair that worthiest is of praise" (*CEP* 114), and " 'Fair Helena' by Rackham" celebrates "The soft, dim cloud of her hair" (*CEP* 116). "Shaken" hair, as in Poem IV of "Laudantes Decem," appears in Yeats's "He Reproves the Curlew," although it can also be found in "The Two Trees" from another volume, *The Countess Cathleen and Various Legends and Lyrics* (1892). That volume includes a reference to "the white breast of the dim sea," in "Who Goes with Fergus?" which may have inspired Pound's marine anatomy in Poem IV. A feature of the beloved could be easily transferred to the sea because the poet is concerned with something beyond the existence of any one woman. Pound is in fact unusually specific in referring to "the beautiful white shoulders and the rounded breasts" of the beloved in Poem IV. The rounded breasts are a bit too corporeal for the Yeats of this period, who preferred the word "breast" in the idealizing singular.

Beauty is entirely disembodied in Poem III of "Laudantes Decem," where "The unappeasable loveliness is calling to me out of the wind." Though it abides in a natural element, this loveliness has the same supernatural power as "the unappeasable host" whose call, in a poem that eventually took its title from the phrase, lures mortals in *The Wind Among the Reeds*. The host are the Sidhe, ancient gods of Ireland who are associated with the wind, a suitably dominant image in Yeats's volume. In the title of another poem from that volume, the Sidhe appear as "The Everlasting Voices," similar to the spirits who are represented in the title of Pound's Poem V, "Voices speaking to the sun." In Poem IX they are "The innumerable voices that are whispering / Among you [raindrops] as you are drawn aside by the wind." Somewhere beyond the ethereal wind the beloved receives a new incarnation, purely as a symbol. Though the symbol may be derived from the natural world, all connections with that world are severed. The outstanding example in Yeats's love poetry is the symbol of the Rose, and Yeats's presence in "Laudantes Decem" is nowhere more certain than when the lover laments in Poem II, "I am torn, torn with thy beauty, / O Rose of the sharpest thorn!"

The Rose, the wind, and dim hair contributed little to the development of Pound's imagery, except perhaps to convince him of what he did not want. Yeats employed symbols, not the Image toward which Pound's work was evolving. In 1911 Pound declared, "I believe that the proper and perfect symbol is the natural object, that if a man use 'symbols' he must so use them that their symbolic function does not obtrude" (*LE* 9). The symbolic function of Yeats's Rose obtrudes to the complete exclusion of its natural origin. Pound used the rose more characteristically in the final poem of "Laudantes Decem":

> The glamour of the soul hath come upon me,
> And as the twilight comes upon the roses,
> Walking silently among them,
> So have the thoughts of my heart
> Gone out slowly in the twilight
> Toward my beloved,
> Toward the crimson rose, the fairest.

Although this poem stands as a confession of the spell Yeats has cast over Pound, the roses in the second line are still of the common garden variety. "The crimson rose" that represents the beloved emerges from nature but does not deny it.

A more enduring influence of Yeats on Pound can be demonstrated if the same passage is analyzed not for imagery and diction but for the elements that Pound thought he was teaching Yeats, rhythm and syntax. "Syntactical simplicity is in the pages of 'The Wind Among the Reeds,' " Pound declared,[11] and syntactical simplicity is precisely what we find here. The inversions of *A Lume Spento* have been eliminated, and the underlying metrical scheme has been loosened to such an extent that each line develops an independent cadence. Yeats's "He Thinks of His Past Greatness" produces a similar effect, one that Pound had only begun to approach in "The Tree." A valuable side effect of the rhythmical independence of each line is the syntactical suspension that the poet could exploit to increase tension and ambiguity. Pound allows us to think that his thoughts have "gone out" in the twilight, in the sense of being extinguished, before he supplies the information that the thoughts have "gone . . . toward my beloved." Similarly, in "He Remembers Forgotten Beauty," Yeats's first line deliberately misleads the reader from expecting the abstraction that follows:

> When my arms wrap you round I press
> My heart upon the loveliness
> That has long faded from the world.

Thomas H. Jackson has argued that this type of syntactical suspension formed part of the foundation of Pound's later *vers libre*.[12]

What Pound's devotion to Yeats may have meant at the time is all the more puzzling, considering that the volume *Personae*, also published in 1909, contains such a poem as "Revolt Against the Crepuscular Spirit in Modern Poetry." Here Pound explicitly condemns the twilight mood he sought to evoke in "Laudantes Decem." He asks if dreams are better than action and answers yes, but only if the dreams have life, not

> if men are grown but pale sick phantoms
> That must live only in these mists and tempered lights
> And tremble for dim hours that knock o'er loud
> Or tread too violent in passing them.
>
> (CEP 97)

The last line seems directed at Yeats's "He Wishes for the Cloths of Heaven," from *The Wind Among the Reeds*, where the poet pleads, "Tread softly because you tread on my dreams." Pound was even less obliging in Canto LXXX (1946), where "Your gunmen tread on my dreams" (*Cantos* 496).

If Pound's attitude toward Yeats was consistent throughout one year of his life, it must be assumed that the distance that separates the two men in "Revolt" was no less when Pound wrote "Laudantes Decem," even though that distance is not as easily detected in the latter case. Where it may appear, however, is in the failure of the poem, which may not be entirely unintentional. Both poems result from the poet's adoption of a particular *persona*. Neither *persona* is the poet himself, nor can the *persona* in the case of "Laudantes Decem" be taken simply for Yeats. It is a kind of caricature of Yeats, produced by isolating certain features of Yeats's verse and intentionally exaggerating them toward the point of absurdity.

"Laudantes Decem" is a type of parody more subtle than the satire in "Revolt," because in the former instance Pound does not offer an alternative position to the one he parodies. Such an alternative position is usually educed, through exaggeration, from the work that is parodied, but Pound did not find this possible with Yeats, because Yeats had already claimed for himself his own opposite. Pushed to an extreme, he might become bad Yeats, but never non-Yeats. Because Pound has been anticipated in his criticism of Yeats, "Laudantes Decem" fails even as parody.

Yeats's resistance to parody was interpreted very differently by Pound, who warned not of Yeats's comprehensiveness but of his narrowness. "Mr. Yeats' method is, to my way of thinking, very dangerous," Pound advised young American poets in 1913, "for although he is the greatest of living poets who use English, and though he has sung some of the moods of life immortally, his art has not broadened much in scope during the past decade."[13] This estimation must be understood as a statement about influence, not about Yeats's achievement in itself. Yeats's influence remained narrow precisely because his achievement was so comprehensive. A poet who admitted Yeats into his work found he had room for little else, including himself. The admission of Yeats into *Exultations* had nearly stifled Pound, and he was afterwards concerned primarily for the broadening of his own art, not Yeats's. One method that won Pound some room of his own was the one he applied in "Revolt," that of denying Yeats's position outright. Denial or reversal took the form of what Pound called, in the poems he aimed at Ernest Dowson, the "anti-stave" (*CEP* 50-51, 249). Other antistaves were inspired by Rossetti (*CEP* 26-27), Browning (*CEP* 18-19), and Housman (*CEP* 163-64), but Pound used the strategy most in dealing with Yeats.

The earliest examples of Yeatsian antistaves after "Revolt" date from 1911. In that year Pound published the volume *Canzoni*, including the sequence "Und Drang," which represents in miniature the conflict of attitudes between "Laudantes Decem" and "Revolt." The seventh poem of "Und

Drang," entitled "The Flame," makes an appeal to Yeats's authority:

> And all the tales they ever writ of Oisin
> Say but this:
> That man doth pass the net of days and hours.
> Where time is shrivelled down to time's seed corn
> We of the Ever-living, in that light
> Meet through our veils and whisper, and of love.
>
> (*CEP* 171)

Yeats's tale of Oisin is of course *The Wanderings of Oisin* (1889). The "net of days and hours" was woven in *The Wind Among the Reeds*, where "The nets of day and night" appear in "The Poet Pleads with the Elemental Powers" and "the nets of wrong and right" in "Into the Twilight." The gods are referred to as "the ever-living" in *The Shadowy Waters* (1906; *VPo* 224). Material from Yeats threatens to flood Pound's sequence at this point, but the flood is eventually contained in "Au Jardin," the twelfth and final poem. There, Pound quotes a line from Yeats's "The Cap and Bells," again from *The Wind Among the Reeds*: "The jester walked in the garden." "Did he so?" Pound asks. "Well, there's no use your loving me / That way, Lady" (*CEP* 174). The distance Pound gains from Yeats's tale of romance parallels the estrangement between the lover and the lady in Pound's poem.

A similar estrangement is the theme of another poem from 1911, "The Fault of It," which reverses Yeats's "Reconciliation" (1910). Pound's lovers are not reconciled, though Pound comes very close to Yeats in his poem's opening lines: "Some may have blamed us that we cease to speak / Of things we spoke of in our verses early" (*CEP* 207). Yeats's original version begins: "Some may have blamed you that you took away / The verses that they cared for." Pound seems to have regarded Yeats's fondness for reunions as the sentimental opposite to the mask of worldly cynicism that Pound chose for himself in such poems. On two occasions Pound took issue with another poem from *The Wind Among the Reeds*, "The

Lover Pleads with His Friend for Old Friends," which advises the beloved,

> think about old friends the most:
> Time's bitter flood will rise,
> Your beauty perish and be lost
> For all eyes but these eyes.

Pound's "In Exitum Cuiusdam" (1912) scoffs,

> 'Time's bitter flood'! Oh, that's all very well,
> But where's the old friend hasn't fallen off,
> Or slacked his hand-grip when you first gripped fame?
>
> I know your circle and can fairly tell
> What you have kept and what you've left behind:
> I know my circle and know very well
> How many faces I'd have out of mind.
>
> (*CEP* 182)

"Amities" (1916) takes the phrase "Old friends the most" as its epigraph but proceeds to dismiss all "friends" except the one who "discovered a moderate chop-house" (*Personae* 101).

Pound's antistaves seek to bring Yeats into the world of chop-houses, which may be less beautiful than the garden where the jester walked but is at least, Pound would insist, closer to reality. An undated manuscript poem entitled " 'It is a Shame'—With Apologies to the Modern Celtic School" pretends to speak up for the neglected fairy dog P'ti'cru as a way of intruding the chop-house world into fairyland: "He chases the chickens in the barnyard of the winds" (*CEP* 273). "The Lake Isle" (1916) transforms "The Lake Isle of Innisfree" (1890) into "a little tobacco-shop" (*Personae* 117). Such parodies helped Pound to put Yeats in his place, but, more important, they placed Pound's speaker amid circumstances that usually were explicitly contemporary and thus mark an advance over the earlier *personae* poems toward a fuller embodiment of the tradition of the self.

A similar advance in Yeats's poetry had been signaled by the publication of *The Green Helmet and Other Poems* (1910),

as Pound acknowledged in a 1914 review that especially ad-
mired the absence of "glamour" in "No Second Troy" and
the epigram "To a Poet, Who Would Have Me Praise Certain
Bad Poets, Imitators of His and Mine" (*LE* 379-80). Although
these poems date to the time when Pound first met Yeats, their
disillusionment is better explained by Yeats's bitter quarrels
in the Abbey Theatre than by the unlikely influence of a young
American who had not yet himself developed the style in
question. In fact, similar poems, such as "An Appointment"
and "All Things Can Tempt Me," seem to have been written
before Yeats met Pound. Again, Pound's major influence was
to assist Yeats in declaring a direction he had already chosen.

Yeats continued to write declarations of his new commit-
ment to realism throughout the next decade. His obligation
to Pound seems deepest in two poems that appeared in *The
Wild Swans at Coole* (1917). "The Dawn" and "Lines Written
in Dejection" come closer to Pound's free verse than anything
else Yeats ever wrote. For the most part, however, Yeats's
specific debts to Pound are confined to allusions to authors
whose realism Pound commended: Confucius in the disen-
chanted epigraph to *Responsibilities* (1914), Catullus in "The
Scholars" (1915), and Landor in "To a Young Beauty" (1918).[14]
Meanwhile, Yeats was honing the cynical edge of his realism
to such sharpness that Pound was moved to transfer Yeats's
phrases to his own work without alteration. The sense of
estrangement that Pound had opposed to Yeats's view in ear-
lier poems seemed to be endorsed by Yeats in "The People,"
so that Pound applied Yeats's measure of the fading of a
reputation—"Between the night and the morning"—in "Vil-
lanelle: The Psychological Hour" (1915).[15] The quotation marks
placed around the phrase could have meaning only for Yeats
and Pound, because Pound's poem preceded Yeats's in pub-
lication. A later poem that Pound admired for its caustic tone
was Yeats's "Blood and the Moon" (1928), which Pound
printed in *The Exile*. At least twice in his prose Pound referred
to Yeats's contemptuous designation of the "pragmatical, pre-
posterous pig of a world."[16] Even here, though, Pound found
room to differ with Yeats's estimate that the times were "Half

dead at the top." "My dear William B. Y. your ½ was too moderate," Pound corrected in Canto LXXIX (*Cantos* 487). It would be only fair to say that the satire Pound turned against Yeats was itself partly derived from Yeats's example, yet the question of influence here is different from that in "Laudantes Decem." Yeats did not completely dominate satire, as he did the type of lyric in *The Wind Among the Reeds*. There was still room for Pound to exploit his reading of, for example, Catullus and Propertius.

The evocation of other masters was a second technique, in addition to outright denial of Yeats, that Pound found useful in tempering Yeats's influence. He had used the technique as early as in *A Lume Spento*, where the controlling influences had come from Provence and Greece. After arriving in London, Pound discovered the ideal counter-influence to Yeats embodied in the person of Ford Madox (Hueffer) Ford. "I made my life in London by going to see Ford in the afternoons and Yeats in the evenings," Pound recalled. "By mentioning one to the other one could always start a discussion. That was the exercise. I went to study with Yeats and found that Ford disagreed with him. So then I kept on disagreeing with *them* for twenty years."[17] During the nineteen-tens, however, Pound came to agree more with Ford and less with Yeats. Ford stood for the objectivity of the realistic novel, as opposed to Yeats's romantic subjectivity, which seemed to persist no matter how much Yeats opened his poems to the real world. As early as 1913, Pound had assigned his two mentors to their respective poles: "Mr. Yeats has been subjective; believes in the glamour and associations which hang near the words. 'Works of art beget works of art.' He has much in common with the French symbolists. Mr. Hueffer believes in an exact rendering of things."[18]

Ford's position evidently determined the first principle of Imagism, as formulated by Pound in the same year: "Direct treatment of the 'thing' whether subjective or objective" (*LE* 3). Pound willingly conceded that "Mr. Yeats has set an example (specifically as to the inner form of the lyric or the short poem containing an image)," but Yeats's strength over Ford lay not in the creation of images but in what Pound called "the inner form of the line," the poem's rhythm.[19] Ford's verse might be set to music, according to Pound in 1914, but Yeats had incorporated music within his lines (*LE* 376). As a master of poetic music, Yeats influenced the last principle of Imagism, "to compose in the sequence of the musical phrase, not in sequence of a metronome" (*LE* 3), though Yeats felt that the Imagists' application of this doctrine resulted in "devil's metres" (*LE* 378). From his earliest acquaintance with Pound, Yeats had recognized that the American was working toward the same goal that he himself had sought to approach through his experiments with Florence Farr Emery in "speaking to the psaltery." Pound "has I think got closer to the right sort of music for poetry than Mrs. Emery," Yeats wrote in 1909. "It is more definitely music with strongly marked time and yet it is effective speech" (*L* 543). The musical quality of natural speech was perhaps the one characteristic of that elusive concept on which Pound and Yeats agreed.

Even as attractive a counter-influence as that of Ford Madox Ford could not wean Pound from Yeats entirely, because the opposing temperaments that Pound assigned to his two masters were projections of Pound's own complex temperament. That complexity revealed itself curiously as Pound broadened his interest to include other arts and expanded Imagism into Vorticism. One of the important counter-influences in Vorticism, the sculptor Gaudier-Brzeska, incredulously "said to Yeats at a vorticist picture show: / 'You also of the brotherhood?' " (*Cantos* 504), but Pound had reason to be less skeptical. Before Pound began taking Yeats to Vorticist picture shows, Yeats had taken Pound to séances, and Pound's early use of the term "Vortex" retains the aura of the occult that it took on from such sessions. In "Plotinus," from *A Lume Spento*, where the title character is "one that would draw thru the node of things, / Back sweeping to the vortex of the cone" (*CEP* 36), the vortex is the center of universal creation. Pound noted on his typescript that the theory of the vortex owed less to Plotinus than to Hindu teaching (*CEP* 296), but Yeats was his most likely guide in this obscure realm where sources were as nebulous as doctrine. Empedocles received the credit when Yeats made the vortex the Principal Symbol of *A Vision* (1937).[20]

Pound had tried to distance himself from Yeats's spiritualism by the time the vortex gave its name to an artistic movement, but the spiritualist heritage can be traced in a comparison of two articles by Pound, "Psychology and Troubadours" (1912) and "Vorticism" (1914).[21] In the latter article, Pound divides humanity into two types: those who passively receive impressions from their surroundings, and those who actively participate by "directing a certain fluid force against circumstance" (*GB* 89). The Vorticist, of course, belongs to the latter type, and the mysterious fluid force is the key to the power of the Vortex. In "Psychology and Troubadours," which appeared in the esoteric journal *The Quest,* Pound is more revealing about the fluid force: "We have about us the universe of fluid force, and below us the germinal universe of wood alive, of stone alive" (*SR* 92). After this animistic assertion, Pound goes on to make the same division in humanity that he was to make in "Vorticism." Those who are able to participate in the germinal universe, presumably in such a way as the speakers of "The Tree" and "La Fraisne" were able to identify with trees, "are the more poetic, and they affect mind about them" (*SR* 92-93). Pound does not intend to limit the effect of poetic minds to the mere transmission of ideas. Rather, he is thinking of the power attributed in Yeats's essay on "Magic" (1901) to the forerunners of modern poets, "imagining themselves to be stocks and stones and beasts of the wood, till the images were so vivid that the passers-by became but a part of the imagination of the dreamer" (*EI* 43). The inspiriting of stocks and stones in this passage anticipates Pound's animism.

"Psychology and Troubadours" makes the germinal universe of wood and stone related to, but not identical with, the fluid force. The former is "below us," the latter is "about us." A few paragraphs later, Pound comes closer to identifying what is about us: "when we do get into contemplation of the flowing"—that is, the fluid force—"we find sex" (*SR* 93). The

mystical clouds of Pound's essay seem to disperse here under
the bright beams of Freudian psychology, but Pound is less
interested in exploring libido than he is in probing the super-
natural powers of the troubadours' cult of Amor. "The prob-
lem, in so far as it concerns Provence," he explains, "is simply
this: Did this 'chivalric love,' this exotic, take on mediumistic
properties? Stimulated by the color or quality of emotion, did
that 'color' take on forms interpretive of the divine order?"
(SR 94). Pound is seeking in the troubadours the power he
later assumed for himself in the Cantos, which he designed
to "bust through from quotidien into 'divine or permanent
world' " (PL 210). His belief in that power was supported by
Yeats's conviction, proclaimed in "The Moods" (1895), that
the artist has a special instinct "to discover immortal moods
in mortal desires, an undecaying hope in our trivial ambitions,
a divine love in sexual passion" (EI 195). The "mood" that
Pound claims as the source of "La Fraisne" (CEP 8), the
"mood" that produces myths in "Psychology and Trouba-
dours" (SR 92), and the "race-long recurrent moods" in "Vor-
ticism" (GB 92)—all derive from Yeats's immortal moods.
Because they are immortal, they constitute a tradition linking
the poet with the past. Because they are moods, the poet has
to find them first not in the past but in himself, as Pound
stresses (SR 92; GB 86). The doctrine of the immortal moods
is an occult version of the tradition of the self, but Pound had
yet to work out the implications of that tradition for his poetry.

   Meanwhile, tradition moved in opposite directions for Pound
and Yeats. For Pound, it was the means by which the past
was brought into the present. The present conferred value on
the past; or, rather, the presentness of the past made its value
operative. For Yeats, the past had value in a more absolute
sense, and tradition was a means for withdrawing from the
present into the past. This difference in emphasis led to a
difference in terminology, a matter in which Pound was not
usually so tolerant as he was in "Psychology and Trouba-
dours." There he conceded that the sexual force could be
represented by interchangeable sets of opposites, such as "pos-
itive and negative," "North and South," "sun and moon" (SR

93). Pound preferred "positive and negative," even in the imagery of the medievalist "Psychology and Troubadours," because modern physics recorded the most recent manifestation of the phenomenon he was studying. Yeats preferred "sun and moon" because that opposition was perhaps the most ancient expression of the same phenomenon. In his eagerness to dissociate himself from Yeats, Pound made remarks that could easily be interpreted as a complete rejection of occultism, but in fact his objection was to the terminology or imagery rather than the doctrine, which remained part of Pound's credo to the end of his life.

The process of dissociation from Yeats began as early as 1913. Preparing to spend the first of three winters in Sussex as Yeats's secretary, Pound predicted that "Yeats will amuse me part of the time and bore me to death with psychical research the rest" (PL 25). During that winter, while Yeats was working on his essay "Swedenborg, Mediums, and the Desolate Places," Pound took pleasure in informing him that Swedenborg's belief in the lingering of the soul after death was not original but could be traced to Homer, thus giving priority to a poet rather than a mystic. Yeats added a reference to the belief but acknowledged Porphyry and Philoponus, rather than Pound, for the citation in Homer.[22] The essay gave Pound full credit, however, for interesting Yeats in the Noh drama during their first Sussex winter. Yeats was fascinated by the correspondences he found between the Japanese view of the spirit world and the views of Soho mediums and Aran Islanders (Ex 65, 68). When Pound prepared his 1917 edition of the Noh, he cited the Aran legend but dismissed such "parallels with Western spiritist doctrines" as "an irrelevant or extraneous interest."[23] In the following year Pound dismissed his own work on the Noh, along with Yeats's Per Amica Silentia Lunae (1918), as "all too damn soft" (PL 137).

The divergence of Yeats and Pound after their collaborative study of Noh brought them, as did their interest in tradition, to opposite ends of the same territory. Although Pound continued to look to Asia for inspiration, he focused increasingly on the objective political world of Confucius, whom Yeats now condemned as an eighteenth-century English divine in Chinese clothing.²⁴ Yeats's Asian studies continued in a rediscovery of his early interest in Indian philosophy, which he cited to defend a subjectivity bordering on solipsism. Subjectivity was the root of the "softness" Pound saw in Yeats and the Noh. As Pound presented the distinction in his fullest treatment of it, "The Hard and Soft in French Poetry" (1918), "hard" art concentrates on subject matter (*LE* 285-86). "Soft" art, by implication, begins where hard art leaves off, pursuing the suggestions aroused by the subject matter into territory that grows increasingly distant from the subject's reality. Because of that distance, and because the suggestiveness of an object may differ for different beholders, soft art frequently leads to what Pound calls "muzziness" (*LE* 285). Pound was returning to his earlier distinction between Ford's objectivity and Yeats's subjectivity, only now the latter seemed more objectionable than it had before.

Recognizing the subjective tendency in his own nature, Pound undertook a project of self-purgation in "Hugh Selwyn Mauberley" (1920). The poem at first appears to be Pound's most personal work so far, perhaps the first of his poems clearly written in the tradition of the self. Yeats responded in this way when he hailed the sequence as a document of self-discovery.²⁵ But the self is discovered only to be killed off. Pound commits himself to the sequence by signing his initials in the title of the first poem, "E. P. Ode pour l'election de son sepulchre," and the various *personae* associated with E. P. collectively represent the subjective man who is dismissed in " 'The Age Demanded' " for his ability to produce

> Nothing, in brief, but maudlin confession,
> Irresponse to human aggression
> Amid the precipitation, down-float
> Of insubstantial manna,
> Lifting the faint susurrus
> Of his subjective hosannah.
>
> (*Personae* 202)

The objective artist in Pound wrote "Hugh Selwyn Mauberley" as an anticonfessional poem, not because confessional, soft, subjective art was bad in itself, but because it was fatal in an age that was hostile to all art. Only an objective art that took society into account, as "Mauberley" does with a deliberately Jamesian eye, could respond to the human aggression that had just manifested itself in a world war. Pound felt the cultural consequences of that war directly in the disintegration of the community of artists on which he had depended. Shortly after writing "Mauberley," Pound announced to William Carlos Williams his plans to leave London for Paris, because "there is no longer any intellectual *life* in England save what centres in this eight by ten pentagonal room; now that Rémy [de Gourmont] and Henry [Gaudier-Brzeska] are gone and Yeats faded" (*PL* 158). Along with E. P., Yeats had chosen his tomb by choosing subjective art.

In the winters of 1928 and 1929, Yeats and Pound were reunited in the Italian resort town of Rapallo, but renewed acquaintance brought only a heightened awareness of their differences. Yeats, revising *A Vision*, decided to introduce the new edition with "A Packet for Ezra Pound" (1929) because Pound seemed to fill the role of the antiself or mask that was vital to the system Yeats described. Pound's art was "the opposite of mine," Yeats wrote (*Vision* B, 3). The specific art he had in mind was that which Pound was applying in the *Cantos*. In "A Packet for Ezra Pound," Yeats claimed to present Pound's explanation of his project, but Pound was justifiably annoyed by the impression of muddlement that Yeats's presentation conveys (*Vision* B, 4-5; *PL* 321). The reason for Yeats's dislike of the *Cantos* is expressed more directly in his introduction to the *Oxford Book of Modern Verse* (1936): "There is no transmission through time, we pass without comment from ancient Greece to modern England, from modern England to medieval China; the symphony, the pattern, is timeless, flux eternal and therefore without movement" (*OBMV* xxiv). Pound's insistence that the past is present destroys the distinction of times and thus destroys time. Conceived of in these terms, Pound's art is indeed the opposite of Yeats's, for *A Vision* is an elaborate ordering of time, and the opposition of past and present creates the drama of many of Yeats's poems.

At the end of "A Packet for Ezra Pound," Yeats takes obvious relish in quoting "The Return" (1912) and twisting Pound's meaning, so he thinks, by reading metaphorical gods as literal. In fact, however, Yeats's interpretation is a reminder of the occult interests that he had shared with Pound in London and that were still active in Rapallo. Charles Olson has deduced from his later conversations with Pound that Pound allowed himself, however skeptically, to be made a fourth in table-rapping sessions at Rapallo.[26] Yeats answered Pound's skepticism in his journal for January 1929: "I agree with Ezra in his dislike of the word belief."[27] Yet an artist, Yeats felt, was tempted to assert belief in response to his need to get inside tradition and exploit its poetic power. "I recall a passage in some Hermetic writer," went Yeats's analogy, "on the increased power that a god feels on getting into a statue." As in the case of "Swedenborg, Mediums, and the Desolate Places," Yeats substituted a hermetic writer for Pound, who had written in the *Dial* for March 1928 that "the best Egyptian sculpture is magnificent plastic; but its force comes from a nonplastic idea, i.e. the god is inside the statue" (*LE* 152). In the next paragraph Pound referred to the "non-plastic idea" simply as "the force." He had returned to the terminology of the period when he spoke mysteriously of "the fluid force," when the gods were Yeats's immortal moods.

The image of the god in the statue appears in Pound's essay on the thirteenth-century Italian poet Guido Cavalcanti, a work Hugh Kenner has called "perhaps his most pregnant single prose essay."[28] As an heir of the troubadours, Cavalcanti invited the spiritualist interpretation Pound had applied to the troubadours themselves, but Pound's return to Cavalcanti, whom he had translated as early as 1910, gave him the opportunity to revise his opinion of the sort of spiritualism in which such poets and later spiritualists, including Yeats, were engaged. Although a version of spiritualism took on new interest for Pound in the light of his study of Cavalcanti, his interest in the troubadours declined because "the medieval Italian poets brought into poetry something which had not been or not been in any so marked and developed degree in the poetry of the troubadours" (*LE* 150). In "Psychology and Troubadours," Pound allies Provence with a Greek attitude toward the body, which he expresses in the Latin phrase "mens sana in corpore sano" (*SR* 94). In "Cavalcanti," Pound finds in the Italians "more than the simple athleticism of the *mens sana in corpore sano*" (*LE* 152), and he explicitly opposes the Italian ideal to the "wholly plastic" aesthetic of Greek sculpture. The wholly plastic is inanimate—the god is not inside the statue—though Pound's earlier interpretation of the Greeks and troubadours had made them fully animistic. What is really significant in his new understanding is the source of the animation. Where Pound had once credited the troubadours with a form of nature worship, from which Renaissance humanism had been a falling away (*SR* 93), he now claimed that the medieval Italians perceived "something which requires a human being to produce it" (*LE* 151), thus preparing for Quattrocento sculpture, which "discovered 'personality' " (*LE* 152). The god inside the statue is the spirit of the sculptor.

We cannot know what role Yeats's conversations with Pound at Rapallo played in Pound's shift toward what might be called humanist spiritualism. Yeats reports, however, that they discussed Cavalcanti (*Vision* B, 16), and two images found in Pound's Cavalcanti essay appear later in contexts that prove that Pound associated Yeats with the new trend in his aesthetic. "The god is inside the stone," Pound writes in "Cavalcanti," "*vacuos exercet aera morsus*" (*LE* 152). The Latin is a phrase from Ovid that Pound had used earlier in "Hugh Selwyn Mauberley," where he had translated it as "Mouths biting empty air" (*Personae* 198, 200). In "Mauberley" the image reflects adversely on the insubstantiality of subjective art, but in "Cavalcanti," Pound triumphs in that insubstantiality because the creation of something from nothing, as if from the air, is proof that the artist has been truly creative, that he has created out of himself. Yeats had made that boast in "He Thinks of Those Who Have Spoken Evil of His Beloved" (1898), when he claimed, "I made it out of a mouthful of air," and Pound quoted that line in *Guide to Kulchur* (1938) in connection with the "dynamic form" that animates mat-

ter.[29] Another image of creativity in "Cavalcanti" is that of
the eye projecting as well as receiving impressions, the defin-
itive image of romantic subjectivism. A poet like Cavalcanti
"declines to limit his aesthetic to the impact of light on the
eye" (*LE* 151), the implication being that "light . . . moves
from the eye" (*LE* 153). Pound had been present as Yeats was
composing aloud his claim, in "The Peacock" (1914), to have
"made a great peacock / With the pride of his eye." In Canto
LXXXIII (1947) Pound records Yeats's claim, along with the
judgment, "indeed he had, and perdurable / a great peacock
aere perennius" (*Cantos* 534).

Made out of a mouthful of air, and yet more lasting than
bronze—*aere perennius*, in Horace's phrase—the force that
Pound has discovered is paradoxical. Yet the paradox can be
explained in terms of the tradition of the self. The permanence
of the force confers on it the authority of tradition, as Pound
implies in a passage from Canto LXXXI (1948), where his
imagery of air and eye places him in the tradition of Cavalcanti
and Yeats:

> To have gathered from the air a live tradition
> or from a fine old eye the unconquered flame
> This is not vanity.
>
> (*Cantos* 522)

At the same time, the force, or flame, cannot be derived solely
from tradition, but must be discovered in the self, as proof of
the self's creative power:

> and that certain images be formed in the mind
>   to remain there
>   *formato locho*
>   Arachne mi porta fortuna
> to remain there, resurgent ΕΙΚΟΝΕΣ
> and still in Trastevere
> for the deification of emperors
> and the medallions
>   to forge Achaia.
>
> (*Cantos* 446-47)

Two allusions in this disjunctive passage from Canto LXXXIV (1948) have special relevance in this context. The Italian phrase "formato locho," which Pound earlier translated as "that forméd trace" (1934; *Cantos* 178), is from Cavalcanti's canzone "Donna mi prega," the poem that led Pound to reverse the interpretation he had given to Ovid's phrase in "Mauberley." The last line, "to forge Achaia," shows Pound reversing "Mauberley" once again, for in that poem he had feared that he might be "lacking the skill / To forge Achaia" (*Personae* 198).

The *Pisan Cantos* (1948), from which I have been quoting, represent not only the new understanding of subjective vision that is discernible in Pound's study of Cavalcanti but also, as a consequence of that understanding, a view of the self that is radically different from that which produced "Hugh Selwyn Mauberley." Once again, "Cavalcanti" needs to be compared with "Psychology and Troubadours." Both essays assume the projection of the self into its surroundings, but where the earlier essay views that projection as an "exteriorization of the sensibility" (*SR* 94), the Cavalcanti essay refers to an "interactive force" (*LE* 152) and explicitly treats what is "exteriorized" as a lesser sensation (*LE* 151). The distinction becomes clearer when translated into the opposition of "objective" and "subjective" that was so important in Pound's relation to Yeats. According to Pound's early view, when the self is projected, subject becomes object, "I" becomes "tree." In "Cavalcanti" subject and object interact so that the distinction becomes meaningless. Only at this point does Pound truly come within reach of what Robert Langbaum describes as "a poetry of experience which is at the same time both subjective and objective in that the poet talks about himself and other things, finding his meaning in neither but evolving it through an interchange and final fusion between the two."[30] Yeats had such a poetry in mind when he described the subordination of "observed fact" to "experience" in Whitman, and Pound thought he found signs of revolutionary ideas in Cavalcanti's appeal to what is "postulate / Not by the reason, but 'tis felt" (*LE* 156, 159). In Cavalcanti, Pound explained, "The conception of the body as perfect instrument of the increasing intelligence pervades" (*LE* 152). No longer "divided between myself corporeal and a self aetherial," Pound had moved from the Yeats of *The Celtic Twilight* to the Yeats of "The Thinking of the Body" (1907; *EI* 292), where the corporeal and the etherial are one.

"Cavalcanti" posits theoretically an abandonment of the related distinctions of body and spirit, external and internal, object and subject, that becomes a reality in the *Pisan Cantos*, where Pound dismisses any attempt to categorize his visionary moments. In Canto LXXXI "there came new subtlety of eyes into my tent, / whether of spirit or hypostasis"—it does not matter (*Cantos* 520). The most important practical consequence of this attitude is that Pound is able to put himself into his poem more fully than he had ever done before, to develop "personality" as Quattrocento sculpture had developed from Cavalcanti. The speaker in the lines just quoted is clearly the man Ezra Pound, writing in his tent in the Disciplinary Training Center near Pisa. The attendant confessional tone explains why the *Pisan Cantos* became a key text in the confessional school of poetry that grew out of the nineteen-forties. A year after Pound's work was published John Berryman observed, "The *Cantos* have always been personal; only the persona increasingly adopted, as the Poet's fate clarifies, is Pound himself" (*FP* 268). Berryman's statement accurately expresses the synthesis of subjectivity and objectivity that clarified the Poet's fate. The self in the *Pisan Cantos* is objectified, it is a *persona*, and yet it remains, as a self, subjective. Pound wrote "Hugh Selwyn Mauberley" before he had conceived of such a synthesis, and, as a result, objectification of the self meant death, a ceasing to be self. The initials "E. P." in the title of the first poem of the sequence are the sepulcher that the title describes E. P. as choosing.

The *Pisan Cantos* can be further compared with "Mauberley" from the point of view of the circumstances from which each work arose. Each was written at the end of a world war, when the community on which Pound had based his hopes, first that of Vorticists and later that of Fascists, had been shattered. In the absence of community the writer has no one to turn to but himself. In "Mauberley," Pound sacrifices a part of himself as if to atone for the loss of community. In the *Pisan Cantos*, on the other hand, Pound makes a new commitment to himself and, through that commitment, rediscovers community. Gaudier-Brzeska, Wyndham Lewis, W. B. Yeats, and many others return to Pound in his memory under their real names, not fictionalized like the various *personae* of "Mauberley." Yeats had appeared, usually anonymously, as one of Pound's *personae* in his earliest poems. Now, however, Pound no longer speaks *through* Yeats, as a mask, but *for* "William who dreamed of nobility," in the first of the *Pisan Cantos*, and for the entire community of which Pound has made Yeats a member: "these the companions" (*Cantos* 432-33). Pound's voice is correspondingly enlarged. From the air, or, as he might also have said, from himself, he has gathered a tradition.

In his reaction to the *Pisan Cantos* John Berryman placed Pound in the tradition of the self by comparing him with Yeats, who wrote of "himself-as-himself" (*FP* 263). Berryman also singled out Pound's contribution to the tradition by claiming a major role for Pound in Yeats's move toward more natural speech (*FP* 254), but by the time of the *Pisan Cantos*, Pound's achievement within the tradition went far beyond that issue. Pound had learned that "to give a feeling of the reality of the speaker," the speaker as well as the speech must be real; at the same time, the speaker could retain the artificiality that derived from his privileged place in a poem. As part of that privilege, the speaker could assume a voice larger than that of any one man; he could speak for a community, provided that community had its foundation in himself.

The trouble was that such a community existed only as an ideal. The real world would not be reformed by a mere act of self-assertion, as Pound humbly acknowledged when he wrote, "I cannot make it cohere" (1962; *Cantos* 796). What would not cohere were the real and the ideal worlds, the objective and subjective visions, which fell into disunion once again for Pound after the momentary coherence achieved in the *Pisan Cantos*. Pound returned to his insistence that subjective vision was made valid only by becoming objective, that an imagined paradise had to become an earthly paradise, but since this could not be, either the subjective or the objective vision had to give way. In Pound's case the subjective vision gave away, though he retained a sense of the value of what he had lost. At the end of the *Cantos* as a whole he confessed, "I lost my center / fighting the world" (*Cantos* 802).

The experience of having lost the self as an organizing principle is alien to the tradition of the self, but it suggests yet another way in which Pound served to connect Yeats with a poet like Berryman, whose view of the self forced him also to confront Yeats from outside the tradition. In the course of his long career, Pound took up all the major positions occupied by various younger poets during the four decades after Pound's struggle with Yeats had begun.

IV

NATURAL SPEECH:
THE NINETEEN-TENS

THE ROLE PLAYED by Ezra Pound in transmitting a version of Yeats to America is most clearly discernible in the work of those poets whom Pound introduced to Yeats during the nineteen-tens. The introductions were personal if the poet visited London, as William Carlos Williams and Robert Frost did. Many more poets, however, were led to Yeats through the pages of the American magazines, starting with *Poetry*, for which Pound wrote and for which he secured contributions from Yeats. Whatever form the introduction took, the attention of Pound's compatriots was first directed to the extent to which Yeats's poetry had moved toward natural speech, a direction signaled in *The Green Helmet and Other Poems* (1910) and confirmed in *Responsibilities* (1914). Pound was interested in Yeats's efforts in this direction because they helped to establish the reality of the speaker, but another advantage emerged as American poets sought to reaffirm the independence from England that Whitman had earlier declared. Natural speech was natural only to a particular region. By identifying with the region through its speech, poets could establish the locality as well as the reality of the speaker.

MIDWESTERN RHETORIC:
Poetry MAGAZINE AND VACHEL LINDSAY

Although committed to self-imposed exile, Pound maintained a hope for America that is characteristic of even the most disillusioned natives of that country. "One is always looking to America for signs of a 'renaissance,' " Pound wrote in 1914 (*LE* 218). Not content with merely looking for signs, Pound

actively stumped for a renaissance from a number of plat-
forms, most notably his position as "foreign correspondent"
for the newly founded *Poetry* magazine, in which his statement
about an American renaissance originally appeared. The first
task Pound undertook in fulfillment of his new assignment
was soliciting poems from Yeats in order to "set the tone"
(*PL* 10) of *Poetry*. In the third issue (December 1912) Yeats
published five poems, slightly altered by Pound, all making
their first appearance in print. The total represented as many
first printings of poems by Yeats as had appeared in all Amer-
ican periodicals prior to that time. In the next issue of *Poetry*
Pound told his readers that, among contemporaries, Yeats was
"the only poet worthy of serious study."[1] That study was
essential for the renaissance Pound hoped to see. Yeats's ex-
perience in Ireland had made him, as Pound had acknowl-
edged in 1911, a "specialist in renaissances" (*CEP* 313).

   Poetry generated an excitement among American writers
that seemed to herald the arrival of a true poetic renaissance.
The editors' consciousness of past writers, particularly Whit-
man, from whom *Poetry* took its motto, helped to define the
movement as a rebirth and not a first occasion. The elements
of rebirth had been present for at least a decade before 1912,
but they could not be recognized until *Poetry* had given them
a regional focus centering on Chicago, the capital of the Mid-
west and, so the argument ran, a cultural capital more truly
American than those Eastern cities whose gaze was fixed on
Europe. In notes for a lecture, *Poetry*'s founder, Harriet Mon-
roe, suggested a similarity between *Poetry* and the Irish Na-
tional Theatre,[2] and in no respect is there greater similarity
between the two projects than in their emphasis on locality.
On their first American tour in 1912 the Abbey players stim-
ulated interest in the regional theater in Chicago. An imme-
diate result was the founding of Maurice Browne's Little Thea-
ter, which headed its repertory with works by Synge and Yeats.[3]
Another playwright of the Irish theater, Padraic Colum, de-
clared Yeats to be the forerunner of the poets who rallied
around *Poetry*. In a review of Yeats's *Selected Poems* in the
Dial in 1921, Colum declared that, "by his [Yeats's] insistence

upon the importance of local life, local speech, and local tra-
dition, he created in English-speaking countries the movement
to which is due John Masefield in England, and Edgar Lee
Masters and Vachel Lindsay in America."[4]

Colum's reference to local speech isolates the area in which
Yeats's example proved most fruitful, perhaps because nat-
uralness of speech concerned even those writers and critics
who were not especially interested in the local. In a 1915
review of Forrest Read's critical study of Yeats, Lawrence
Gilman quoted Yeats's "When You Are Old" (1892) as an
example of "poetry, almost a quarter of a century old, that
is as spare, as direct, as unadorned, as unrhetorical, as any
that Edgar Lee Masters can show us."[5] Yeats presented the
lesson personally in 1914, during his third trip to America,
when he spoke in Chicago at a banquet organized in his honor
by *Poetry*. He described the struggle in which he and his fellow
members in the Rhymers' Club had engaged to free their verse
of rhetoric, and he expressed disappointment at opening an
American magazine and finding all that the Rhymers had
struggled against. Yet, at the same banquet, Yeats acknowl-
edged the help of an American, Ezra Pound, as a symbol of
Yeats's intention to go even farther in removing rhetoric from
his verse (*UP* II, 414).

The meaning of rhetoric for Yeats is thrown into some
doubt by his praise at the *Poetry* banquet for another Amer-
ican, Vachel Lindsay, whose poetry seems often deliberately
rhetorical in the conventional sense of being florid in imagery
or diction. Lindsay was present at the banquet to read his
new poem "The Congo" after Yeats's talk, and Harriet Mon-
roe had made sure that Yeats was acquainted with "General
William Booth Enters into Heaven," which had appeared in
Poetry in January 1913 and as the title poem in Lindsay's first
book. To some degree, then, Yeats could hardly avoid paying
Lindsay a compliment. Yet the phrase Yeats chose when he
described "William Booth" as "stripped bare of ornament"
(*UP* II, 412) comes too close to a principal area of his concern
to be dismissed as mere courtesy. A phrase Yeats used im
mediately after the one about ornament helps to make his

meaning clearer. There was "an earnest simplicity" in "General Booth," Yeats found. In other words, the poem seemed sincere.

A poet's sincerity was an ambiguous issue for anyone who placed as much value in posing as Yeats did, but a poem might be judged sincere if the speaker, to return to Ezra Pound's formulation, was felt to be real. Rhetoric, for Yeats, was a function not of a poem's diction but of its *persona*. If the sentiment expressed in a poem, no matter how simply, seemed to have descended from social opinion rather than having arisen from individual experience, the poem would be rhetorical. On the other hand, any words, no matter how extravagant, would have the ring of sincerity if the poem suggested an individual character who might plausibly speak them. The conventions underlying Lindsay's poems immediately establish such a character because they derive from an oral tradition, that of soapbox oratory and the sidewalk sermon, rather than the printed page. The evocation of revival meetings supplies a mundane base for the most visionary imagery in "The Congo": "And some had visions, as they stood on chairs, / And sang of Jacob, and the golden stairs" (*LCP* 183). Such curious mixtures of the real and the visionary help the poet to establish his own singularity, the goal of "the American orator-poet," according to Harold Bloom, who gives Emerson that title.[6] A similar goal led Yeats to admire "fine oratory" (*UP* II, 355), as opposed to rhetoric, and to commend Lindsay for, in effect, achieving natural speech.

Ideally, oratory would incorporate another of Yeats's concerns that might seem to conflict with the goal of natural speech, that is, the goal of bringing out the music in poetry. That he saw no contradiction in his aims is indicated by his belief that he had found the two combined in Pound, whose verse was "definitely music" yet "effective speech" (*L* 543). Lindsay's verse seemed to promise a similar combination. After praising Lindsay for stripping away ornament, Yeats asked him privately, "What are we going to do to restore the primitive singing of poetry?" which Lindsay took to refer to "the old Greek precedent of the half-chanted lyric."[7] Yeats's chants had been accompanied by the psaltery, whereas Lindsay called for bass drum and banjo in performance of "General Booth" and "The Congo." Yet each man recognized the initial impulse that united them. Lindsay's recognition had come long before the *Poetry* banquet, at least as early as 1906, when he chose Yeats's poems as suitable for recitation on the first of his celebrated tramps through America.[8]

For his third tramp, in 1912, Lindsay prepared a pamphlet of his own poems, *Rhymes to Be Traded for Bread*, which included a poem that he came to regard as a prophecy of his meeting with Yeats.[9] Entitled "The Perilous Road," the poem recalls Browning's mechanical rhyme and metrics in "Love Among the Ruins," but the situation is similar to that of Yeats's "The Blessed" (1897). A youth approaches a hermit for instruction: "Teach me, the while I kneel, a curious prayer / To rule the air." Such an attitude of reverent discipleship ensured that Lindsay, after his meeting with Yeats, would dutifully carry out his master's instructions. Specifically, Yeats advised Lindsay to modulate the tone of his chanting, advice Lindsay first applied in "The Santa Fé Trail," a poem written shortly after his meeting with Yeats.

While writing "The Santa Fé Trail," Lindsay told Harriet Monroe, "I have tried hard to take Yeats' advice and put something *under* it—and have over-tones and minor strains and whispers."[10] Another reader entered Lindsay's thoughts, however. The poet Sara Teasdale, with whom Lindsay was in love, had been an admirer of Yeats from her youth, and Lindsay promised her that, for her sake, his poem would include "tiny flutes and fairy whispers and Yeatsy quietnesses and twilights."[11] The fairy whispers are audible at the end of the poem: "Listen . . . to . . . the . . . whisper . . . / Of . . . the . . . prairie . . . fairies" (*LCP* 158). But the result of Yeats's advice is most fully displayed in the structure of the poem as a whole, which contrasts the opposing tones of nature and machines. One turning point in particular illustrates Lindsay's inability to manage contrast with Yeats's adeptness:

But I would not walk alone till I die
Without some life-drunk horns going by.
And up round this apple-earth they come
Blasting the whispers of the morning dumb.

(*LCP* 154)

Yeats usually managed to keep one term implicit when he made its opposite explicit, but Lindsay opposes terms only to annihilate one of them.

"The Santa Fé Trail" appeared in *Poetry* for July 1914, accompanied by other "Poems to Be Chanted" ("The Firemen's Ball," "The Black Hawk War of the Artists") and a note by Lindsay reporting Yeats's remark about the primitive singing of poetry. In the following year Lindsay extended Yeats's lesson beyond poetry when he published *The Art of the Moving Picture*. He proposed the Abbey Theatre as a model for regional film companies, and he named Yeats specifically in a list of "Prophet-Wizards" who taught the standards by which future wizards might be recognized. "Yeats has bestowed upon us The Land of Heart's Desire, The Secret Rose, and many another piece of imaginative glory," Lindsay wrote. "Let us hope that we may be spared any attempts to hastily paraphrase his wonders for the motion pictures. But the man that reads Yeats will be better prepared to do his own work in the films, or to greet the young new masters when they come."[12] Lindsay was clearly thinking of the greeting he received in America and, for the first time, in Britain from those who respected Yeats's opinion,[13] yet he must have begun to wonder if he would ever hear again from Yeats himself. By 1917, with Yeats still to be heard from, Lindsay was bitterly convinced that Yeats's praise had been little more than "polite taffy," as he told Harriet Monroe. In the same letter he decided it was more important to have the esteem of Monroe and her circle "than that I should have been praised on one evening by a mysterious stranger who has since disappeared."[14]

Although Lindsay felt personally estranged from Yeats, he retained a fondness for Yeats's poetry. In his home town of

Springfield, Illinois, he would read poems such as "Red Hanrahan's Song About Ireland" (1894) and "He Wishes for the Cloths of Heaven" (1899) to the young people who gathered around him.[15] For one of these young people, Robert Fitzgerald, Lindsay wrote a letter of introduction to Yeats, in which he looked back seventeen years to view the 1914 banquet as "the literary transformation scene of my life" and assured Yeats that Lindsay and his circle in Springfield "read your every line devoutly."[16] Robert Fitzgerald never made use of Lindsay's letter, but he was able to make use of Lindsay's readings from Yeats. Critics have noted that the freedom of imagery and the "grand oratorical style" of some of Fitzgerald's translations from Greek drama are also features of Yeats's versions of Sophocles.[17] If Fitzgerald's work cannot be called regional, it continues the delight in oratory that the Midwestern poets had shared with Yeats.

In December 1931, two months after writing to Yeats, Lindsay committed suicide. Although his estrangement from Yeats could not have been nearly as painful as the fear of failure that led Lindsay to take his life, the two problems can be traced to the same root. As "The Perilous Road" indicates, Lindsay desperately wanted to have a master and thought for a time that Yeats would be willing to play that role, but Yeats's long silence proved otherwise. The desire to claim a master was a desire to be one of a company, to be part of a tradition, to be read in a context within which one's work might be understood. Lack of understanding was the greatest cause of Lindsay's despair as well as the reason behind his attempt to assimilate popular tradition along with the literary tradition represented by Yeats. Neither tradition proved open to Lindsay as a poet, however. He found himself facing the task that American poets inevitably face, not that of inventing new things to say in an inherited language, but rather that of inventing the language itself.

"The task for the American poet is twice as difficult as it is for his continental brother," wrote Alice Corbin Henderson, *Poetry*'s assistant editor, in her reaction to Yeats's talk at the 1914 banquet.[18] Despite the difficulty of the task, Henderson saw it not as a cause for despair but as a stimulating challenge. She objected to Yeats's advice that American poets look to Paris for models. If there was to be any model, she insisted, it should be Whitman. Yet Whitman and other American writers such as Poe and Hawthorne defied would-be imitators: "So individual is the creative structure reared by these men that imitation seems almost to bear upon its face the stigma of plagiarism." For an American poet, success was achieved through the bold individuality that Lindsay displayed in "The Congo"—a sharp contrast with the examples that Yeats offered. "All the poems that he read except his own," Henderson observed, "however simple and explicit in diction, portrayed poetic fixities, or took their root in past tradition."

The exception of Yeats's own poems is an important one. Yeats had read "September 1913" (1913), proclaiming that "Romantic Ireland's dead and gone." He had always known that Ireland's past was "gone," but now he feared that it was "dead" in the sense of having no meaning to Irishmen of the present, even if past forms were revived. The impulse for revival that Yeats had once felt correspondingly waned, and the movement he had built around that impulse left him behind in an isolation that called for a considerable readjustment in his outlook. Faced with a similar isolation after the *Poetry* movement had lost its initial energy, Vachel Lindsay was unable to adjust. One explanation may lie in the difference between the elegiac mode, which allowed Yeats to write after hope was lost, and the prophetic mode, on which Lindsay's hope depended. More important, Yeats looked to himself; Lindsay looked to others, as he looked to Yeats. Ironically, Yeats was better prepared than Lindsay to endure the extreme of individualism that Alice Corbin Henderson described as uniquely American.

NEW ENGLAND RETICENCE:
ROBERT FROST

Ezra Pound's self-appointed role as Yeats's American champion proved to be a mixed blessing in the case of Robert Frost. Although Pound introduced Frost to Yeats in 1913, he remained an obstacle in the way of anything more than an introductory acquaintance. The fact that a compatriot eleven years his junior should have already gained the favor of the man whom Frost agreed was the greatest living poet was galling to Frost's jealous temperament.[19] Moreover, Frost was less willing to tolerate Pound's interference than Yeats was. Frost claimed to be present on one occasion when "Pound said to Yeats: 'You're too full of adjectives and expletives. Let's wring you dry.' He then proceeded to take some of Yeats's poems and, as he put it, wring them dry."[20] The story is too neat to be taken for fact. It is probably modeled on Yeats's own account of Pound's influence on him, yet it adequately represents the threat Pound posed to Frost. After a few instances in which the threat seemed to be realized, Frost decided it was time to sever relations with Pound. Since Frost had no independent avenue to Yeats, however, that relationship suffered as well. On 24 October 1913 Frost wrote to Thomas B. Mosher, "I am out with Pound pretty much altogether and so I don't see his friend Yeats as I did" (FL 96).

A major source of the friction between Frost and his two new acquaintances was Frost's first book of verse, A Boy's Will, published in London in April 1913, some eight months after Frost had moved with his family to England. Both Yeats and Pound thought highly of the book, but, where Yeats said too little about it, Pound said too much. A letter written by Elinor Frost at this period reflects the family attitude in the former instance: "Yeats has said to a friend, who repeated the remark to Robert, that it [A Boy's Will] is the best poetry written in America for a long time. If only he would say so publicly, but he won't, he is too taken up with his own greatness" (FL 78). On the other hand, Pound had begun writing a review of A Boy's Will on the day he met Frost, according to the latter, but when the review appeared in Poetry, Frost was upset to find the poem "In Neglect" set in the personal context that Frost had confided to Pound in a spitefully distorted version.[21]

Yeats's and Pound's approval of A Boy's Will was partly predetermined by Frost's obvious use of The Wind Among *the Reeds* as one of his models. The original table of contents of *A Boy's Will* glosses all but two of the poems with such phrases as "He is happy in a society of his choosing" and "He is in love with being misunderstood."[22] Similar titles in Pound's "Laudantes Decem" sequence had been inspired by many of Yeats's titles in *The Wind Among the Reeds*. By thus identifying a series of poems with a single speaker, Yeats, Pound, and Frost transform the speaker from the mere voice of a poem to a character in a continued romance. Endowed with this fuller life, the speaker approaches more nearly the poet himself, whose consciousness is the real unifying force in the poems. To an extent, the speaker is the poet, but he is the poet reconceived as a dramatic character who is conscious of playing a role. According to the gloss of "A Late Walk," Frost's *persona* deliberately "courts the autumnal mood" and may have been inspired to do so by Yeats's doctrine of "The Moods" as set forth in the poem of that title in *The Wind Among the Reeds*. Appropriately, the dramatic setting for Frost's mood includes the "reeds" of "In a Vale" (*PRF* 15) and "the shallow waters aflutter with wind" of "A Line-Storm Song" (*PRF* 27). Frost's waters recall the "leaves a-flutter" of "The Madness of King Goll" (1887), from another of Yeats's volumes.

A work that perhaps left an even deeper impression on *A Boy's Will* than *The Wind Among the Reeds* is Yeats's play *The Land of Heart's Desire* (1894). There the supernatural wind is specifically "withering" (*VPl* 194), which helps to account for the suggestion that the "withered tree" in Frost's "My November Guest" (*PRF* 6) and the "withered weeds" in "A Late Walk" (*PRF* 8) have not suffered merely from changing seasons. In another poem from *A Boy's Will*, "Love and a Question," a mysterious stranger arrives to challenge precisely "the heart's desire" of a bride, just as the Faery Child disturbs the bride in Yeats's play.[23]

Frost discussed *The Land of Heart's Desire* with Yeats on one of his first visits to Yeats's flat and reported the discussion with the observation that Yeats "is the big man here in poetry of course, though his activity is largely dramatic in late years"

(*FL* 70). The distinction was not merely academic for Frost. In 1910 he had had his students at the Pinkerton Academy in New Hampshire produce a series of five plays, including *The Land of Heart's Desire* and *Cathleen ni Houlihan* (1902). To publicize the productions, Frost wrote a release for the local newspaper in which he described Yeats as a contemporary of special relevance: "Yeats is head and front of that most interesting of recent literary movements known as the Celtic Renaissance; most interesting of course to the Irish but hardly less so to the rest of us who speak the same tongue. He is the exponent of the lyrical drama, in which kind The Land of Heart's Desire is the best thing he has done."[24]

The lessons Frost learned from *The Land of Heart's Desire* are most clearly set forth in a letter Frost wrote from England in 1913 to Sidney Cox. The letter contains the fullest statement on Yeats that Frost ever wrote:

> Some one the other day was deriving all the Masefield and Gibson sort of thing from one line of Yates' [sic] Land of Hearts Desire:
>
> "The butter's at your elbow, Father Hart."
>   (*FL* 93)

Although Frost used such natural speech in his poetry to identify himself with New England, he found models for such speech in the Georgian poets of old England and in Yeats. That Yeats was the earlier of these models to influence Frost is suggested from his involvement, before he went to England, in the production of plays, the same experience through which Yeats had worked out a satisfactory relation of speech and poetry.

When Frost produced *The Land of Heart's Desire*, he simplified the text, as he did for the other plays. It is probable that he retained lines like the one quoted in his letter to Sidney Cox but eliminated passages where the syntax was less direct or the diction more elaborate, according to criteria which he later outlined: "There are the speaking passages and the rhetorical passages to choose from. When I think of successful poetic drama I think of the speaking passages. They are the best of Shakespeare to me—lean, sharp sentences, with the give and take, the thread of thought and action quick, not lost in a maze of metaphor or adjective."[25] Yeats, too, edited *The Land of Heart's Desire* in 1923 so that it might "sound simple and natural" (*VPl* 212) in amateur performance, but his more extensive experience in the theater had taught him that the simplest lines demand the most accomplished actor. He deleted not only lofty verses such as "Or where stars walk upon a mountain-top" (*VPl* 184) but also the most lowly, including "The butter is by your elbow, Father Hart" (*VPl* 190).

Frost's encounter with Pound, however unpleasant, may have encouraged Frost to incorporate the simple diction of Yeats's plays into his own poetry, a project that makes its first noticeable impression in the poems of Frost's second volume, *North of Boston* (1914). Even if many of these poems were efforts from an earlier period, they were clearly assembled by a man whose sense of natural speech had been recently sharpened. Just as Yeats had replaced primroses and a red nasturtium with the folksier quicken wood in *The Land of Heart's Desire* (*VPl* 185, 192), so the "thousand orchises" of "Rose Pogonias," from *A Boy's Will* (*PRF* 13), are transformed in "The Self-Seeker" to the Yellow Lady's Slipper that is "too *common*" (*PRF* 97). "After Apple-Picking" has the earthy flavor of a passage from the original version of Yeats's *The Countess Kathleen* (1892):

> His apples are stolen. Pruning time,
> The rounding and ripening of his pears and apples
> For him's a long heart-moving history.
>
> (*VPl* 52)

The contraction in the last line, similar to "the butter's by your elbow" in the version of *The Land of Heart's Desire* known to Frost (*VPl* 190), contributes to a syntactical informality that complements the informal diction employed by both Yeats and Frost. The first line of "After Apple-Picking" reads, "My long two-pointed ladder's sticking through a tree"

(*PRF* 68), and in "The Mountain" the narrator objects, "a lake's different. What about the spring?" (*PRF* 43). That the lake in question is "Somewhere in Ireland on a mountain top," perhaps an allusion to Yeats's account of Clooth-na-Bare (*VPo* 801), points to a difference between Frost and Yeats. As Richard Ellmann has observed, Frost learned "the art of sinking" from Yeats,[26] but because the basic tone of Frost's poetry was established at a lower level, what was sinking in Yeats often appears to be rising in Frost. The "little silver trout" in Yeats's "The Song of Wandering Aengus" (1897) brings natural simplicity to a visionary poem, but "the little silver cloud" marks the visionary high point of Frost's naturalistic "The Death of the Hired Man" (*PRF* 40).

As the evidence in *A Boy's Will* would suggest, the supernatural vision, no less than the natural language, attracted Frost to *The Land of Heart's Desire*. In his letter to Sidney Cox, Frost mentioned that play along with *The Shadowy Waters* (1900), *Cathleen ni Houlihan*, and a number of lyrics as examples of Yeats's ability to "make the sense of beauty ache" (*FL* 93). He described the line "Who dreamed that beauty passes like a dream?" from "The Rose of the World" (1892), as one that "fairly weeps defiance to the unideal." Frost's concern with a speech stubbornly down to earth obscures his concern for the ideal, but the two concerns are not in direct contradiction. No language, however exalted, could express the ideal as Frost conceives of it. The ideal is "ineffable," a term Frost associated with Yeats. "Yeats was always saying that the true poet would never publish a poem—the silence deep in the soul," Frost recalled. "That's this 'ineffable', you know—you mean something that you just come up to the edge of."[27] The choice of natural speech was a sign of stoic resignation in the face of the inexpressible.

The sentiment Frost attributed to Yeats in recollection is similar to the moral of Yeats's story about the opium eater who composed poems in his dreams but never wrote down more than the titles (*Au* 485). Yeats, however, tells the story to exemplify "the only happy poet," not the true poet. The true poet, as in "Vacillation" (1932), rejects the silence imposed on the saint who is "Struck dumb in the simplicity of fire." For Yeats, the poet cannot shun the task of expressing the ineffable. Yeats's voyages to Byzantium may be compared with Frost's repeated journeys to the edge of the woods, in "Into My Own" (1913), "Stopping by Woods on a Snowy Evening" (1923), and "Come In" (1941). Frost always turns away from the woods, and, because they are dark, or ineffable, we are never quite sure what he has turned away from. In both "Sailing to Byzantium" (1927) and "Byzantium" (1932), Yeats ends by symbolically turning back to the natural world from which he has sailed, but in the course of each poem we are given a detailed description of the Byzantine artifice that is opposed to the natural world. If Byzantium is rejected, Yeats's willingness to describe it leaves no doubt that he is aware of the sacrifice he is making.

The difference between Yeats and Frost concerning what can be expressed arises from a difference in what each man was willing to believe. Both were skeptics, but Yeats's skepticism was affirmative, Frost's negative. Yeats saw no reason why he should not believe; Frost saw no way he could. Frost had a firsthand example of Yeats's suspension of disbelief during an evening at Woburn Buildings. "I had a chance to see and hear the other night how perilously near Yates [sic] comes to believing in fairies," Frost wrote in his informative letter to Sidney Cox. "He told with the strangest accent of wistful half belief of the leppercaun (spell it) two old folks he visited had had in a cage on the wall" (FL 94). Captivity proved unhealthy for the leprechaun, and his benevolent keepers had to let him go to join a little friend who lingered nearby. Frost's reaction is illuminating: "Yates I could see, was in a state of mind to resent being asked point blank what he thought of such a story. And it wouldn't have been best for anyone to go on the assumption that he told it to be amusing." Like Frost, Yeats knows the value of silence, but Yeats uses silence to protect belief, whereas Frost uses it to disguise unbelief. Furthermore, Yeats's silence is less restricting than Frost's. Frost can say nothing without implying belief; Yeats, who does not mind that implication, can tell a story, whether it be about Byzantium or leprechauns. The stories Frost tells violate his own principles, and he knew it.

Frost openly took issue with Yeats's opposing attitude toward belief when he wrote "A Masque of Mercy" (1947) in part as a reply to Yeats's play *The Resurrection* (1931). "A Masque of Mercy" contains a direct allusion to *The Resurrection* and is close to it in form, involving a set of characters, distantly analogous to the allegorical figures of Jacobean masques, who represent different theological positions. Each work consists largely of a discussion arising from the characters' differing views and ends with a miraculous event that is intended somehow to resolve the argument. In *The Resurrection* the debate between Greek, Hebrew, and Syrian is resolved when the Greek touches the side of the resurrected Christ and his skepticism dissolves in terror: "The heart of a phantom is beating!" (*VPl* 929). What seemed impossible is revealed as a concrete reality. In "A Masque of Mercy," Jesse Bel, My Brother's Keeper, and Paul receive a paradoxical demonstration of the need for mercy through an unmerciful act, the slamming of the cellar door through which Jonah had been about to pass into enlightenment. The presence of mercy itself is not felt, nor is there an increase in knowledge. Frost's miracle reveals only the absence of true revelation. The reader is thrown back on Jesse Bel's earlier plaint, "Still what we need / Is something to believe in, don't we, Paul?" (*PRF* 515). Just as Frost refuses to enter the woods, so he denies entry to the equally dark cellar to Jonah, whose most positive statement of belief, like Frost's, is an evasion: "You ask if I see yonder shining gate, / And I reply I almost think I do" (*PRF* 513).

The lines from *The Resurrection* that are alluded to in "A Masque of Mercy" come from the closing lyric of Yeats's play:

> In pity for man's darkening thought
> He walked that room and issued thence
> In Galilean turbulence;
> The Babylonian starlight brought

> A fabulous, formless darkness in;
> Odour of blood when Christ was slain
> Made all Platonic tolerance vain
> And vain all Doric discipline.
>
> (*VPl* 931)

In "A Masque of Mercy," Paul warns Jonah against Keeper and Jesse Bel:

> Don't you be made feel small by all this posing.
> Both of them caught it from Bel's favorite poet,
> Who in his favorite pose as poet-thinker
> (His was the doctrine of the Seven Poses)
> Once charged the Nazarene with having brought
> A darkness out of Asia that had crossed
> Old Attic grace and Spartan discipline
> With violence.
>
> (*PRF* 511)

Paul goes on to argue that Greece was already violent and that Christ's real revolution was in the introduction of mercy. He has forgotten that Yeats's Christ, too, walked "in pity."

Paul's accusation of affectation was perhaps Frost's earliest complaint about Yeats. Elinor Frost's comment that Yeats was "too taken up with his own greatness" has already been noted. In the letter in which Frost took so much care to praise Yeats to Sidney Cox, he adds one qualification: "Let him be as affected as he pleases if he will only write well. But you can't be affected and write entirely well" (*FL* 94). Much later Frost told Louis Mertins that he considered Yeats to be "the world's first egotist," though he conceded, after having met Yeats again in Ireland in 1928, that Yeats was also the world's greatest conversationalist.[28] That concession was a large one for Frost, who knew himself to be a contender for the title.

The title of "poet-thinker" that Paul dismisses as a sham in "A Masque of Mercy" might also be claimed for Frost. He assumed that very "pose" as he wrote Paul's words and thereby attacked himself as he attacked Yeats. Frost did not always attack a scapegoat. At the end of "New Hampshire" (1923), for instance, he deflates his own myth of the rustic bard:

> I choose to be a plain New Hampshire farmer
> With an income in cash of, say, a thousand.
> (From, say, a publisher in New York City).
> It's restful to arrive at a decision,
> And restful just to think about New Hampshire.
> At present I am living in Vermont.
>
> (*PRF* 172)

Many of the poses Frost assumed, however, went unchallenged by either the poet or his audience. Frost was able to persuade most of his readers that he wrote poems such as "Stopping by Woods on a Snowy Evening" "at one stroke of the pen," as he liked to put it. Lawrance Thompson has pointed out that the manuscript evidence does not support this contention.[29] Yeats, in his own way, also discouraged this particular myth. At Frost's first meeting with Yeats, the younger poet boasted that he could tell that Yeats had written "The Song of Wandering Aengus" at one stroke of the pen, but Yeats corrected Frost, saying that he had written the poem out of a long struggle with his anguished heart.[30]

Yeats was delighted to pose at other times, of course, and Frost borrowed Yeats's pose as early as his deliberate assumption of the autumnal mood in *A Boy's Will*. But Frost could not be happy with Yeats's pose because even his own poses made him uncomfortable. In a letter to Louis Untermeyer in 1916 Frost expressed his discomfort, reckoning the number of his poses not at the master's seven but at a humbler four: "The poet in me died nearly ten years ago. Fortunately he had run through several phases, four to be exact, all well-defined, before he went. The calf I was in the nineties I merely take to market. I am become my own salesman" (*FL* 201). Frost describes here precisely that tradition of the self in which Yeats discovered an authority that was unavailable elsewhere. In his poems Frost appeals to that authority, but he does not believe in it. Belief is again the issue that divides these two poets. Yeats could believe in his pose because it had a reality beyond himself. It existed as his opposite even when he did not assume it, but to assume it meant to expand the range of reality that the self embraced by expanding the number of selves. For Frost, a man had only one self, whose edge was the edge of the woods, where silence began. To say anything about what lay beyond the very limited range of the individual's experience was to assume a pose that falsified that silence. Even the most natural speech of Frost's poems can be counted, then, as one of the poses that Frost learned in part from Yeats, but Frost's disbelief in all poses implies a radical doubt in the value of Yeats's lesson.

AMERICAN RHYTHM:
WILLIAM CARLOS WILLIAMS

After Pound had conceived of Yeats as a scourge for American poets, William Carlos Williams was one of the first to feel the lash. In 1909 Williams issued his privately printed *Poems*, revealing a shortsighted obsession with Keats for which Pound was quick to prescribe a cure: "If you'll read Yeats and Browning and Francis Thompson and Swinburne and Rossetti you'll learn something about the progress of Eng. poetry in the last century." And for poetic theory, Pound advised, "Read Aristotle's *Poetics*, Longinus' *On the Sublime*, De Quincey, Yeats' essays" (*PL* 8). Pound and Williams had met in late 1902, when the two men were students at the University of Pennsylvania, but apparently they did not speak much of Yeats then. Williams recollected that Pound knew of Yeats slightly while in America, "but to my knowledge did not become thoroughly acquainted with Yeats's work until he went to London" (*WL* 210).

Williams visited Pound in London in March 1910 and was duly conducted to Woburn Buildings to meet the man he had heard Pound call "the greatest living poet" (*PL* 7-8). Williams was impressed by the performance, but he had reservations about the play: "It was a studio atmosphere, very hushed. We tiptoed in. Yeats, in a darkened room, was reading by candlelight to a small, a very small gathering of his protégés, maybe five or six young men and women, members of the Abbey Theatre group. He paid no attention whatever to us as we entered and seated ourselves, but went on reading; reading, of all things, Ernest Dowson's 'Cynara'—in a beautiful voice, I must say, but it was not my dish."[31] Having been taken to Yeats to be modernized, Williams must have been annoyed with the older man's reverence for friends from his past, but Yeats spoke of little else in Williams's presence.

Later in the same week Williams went to the Adelphi Club to hear Yeats speak on the younger Irish poets, but Yeats digressed from his topic to make excuses for the decadence of his friends in the Rhymers' Club, of which Dowson had been a member. Williams watched indignantly as Sir Edmund Gosse, the chairman for the evening, "whammed his bell" to silence Yeats.[32] No matter how little sympathy Williams had for the Rhymers, he had less for Gosse's closed mind. Years later Williams remembered the incident while preparing a lecture on the short story. "We get fixed in squirrel cages of thought," Williams wrote in his notes. "Everyone does. Drink, drugs—anything you can think of is practiced to escape. The Yeats story about his London lecture."[33] Fixed in his squirrel cage, Gosse was intolerant of Yeats's friends, the Rhymers, who had tried to escape through drink.

The image of the squirrel cage suggests not only fixity but also redundancy, the turning of a wheel that moves nowhere. Gosse objected to the Rhymers, Williams suggests, not because their ideas were immoral but because they were new. To be new, for Williams at this time, meant to be individual, like no one else who had come before. He valued this quality to the degree that he condemned the opposite trait: "our prize poems are especially to be damned not because of superficial bad workmanship, but because they are rehash, repetition."[34] In this passage from his prologue to *Kora in Hell* (1920), Williams's examples are Eliot and Pound, "men content with the connotations of their masters." Among the charges against Pound are his "early paraphrases from Yeats" and his decision to seek his fortune in London, in the Old World, rather than to explore the possibilities of the New. This argument hit a

sore point with Pound, who was just then feeling profoundly
disillusioned with London as well as with Yeats. Yeats had
"faded," Pound told Williams in a letter that expressed some
violent objections to the prologue to *Kora* (*PL* 158).

Although harsh in his condemnation of those who had not
broken with the past, Williams was conscious of the difficulty
of the task.

> How easy to slip
> into the old mold, how hard to
> cling firmly to the advance,

as he wrote in Poem V of *Spring and All* (1923).[35] This poem,
in a sense, begins with Yeats and ends with Pound, two of
the old molds that threatened Williams's advance. The poem
begins:

> Black winds from the north
> enter black hearts. Barred from
> seclusion in lilies they strike
> to destroy.

The destructive power of the imagination is represented by
the "black wind" of Yeats's "Red Hanrahan's Song About
Ireland" (1894), an image Pound had singled out for its
suggestiveness (*SR* 159). Six lines from the end of Williams's
poem there is explicit reference to Pound's "Song of the Bow-
men of Shu" (1915). Williams writes:

> The grief of the bowmen of Shu
> moves nearer—There is
> an approach with difficulty from
> the dead—the winter casing of grief.

The poet has not yet succeeded in escaping the "dead," but
he has made a start by acknowledging their presence so openly.

Such openness represents a first step toward the parody
through which Pound attempted to escape Yeats. The cul-
mination of Williams's escape through parody is the poem
that Corydon reads to Phyllis in Book IV of *Paterson* (1951).
In two sections of Corydon's poem Williams juxtaposes Eliot's

aversion (IV, i, pp. 164-66) and Yeats's attraction to the foul-
ness of love, and at the same time manages to poke fun at the
slippery nature of Yeatsian echoes:

> Come with me to Anticosti, where the salmon
> lie spawning in the sun in the shallow water
>
> I think that's Yeats
>
> —and we shall fish for the salmon fish
>
> No, I think *that's* the Yeats   .
> (IV, i, p. 167)

Williams's conception of the importance of parody is under-
lined in a letter to Reed Whittemore in 1939: "The book in
which the poem 'Lilian' [sic] will appear and of which it is
an essential part is to be called *Detail and Parody*. The Lilian
piece is a parody of Yeats' Down by the Salley Gardens."[36]

Detail and Parody never appeared, but the poem "Lillian"
was published in *American Prefaces* for summer 1943 and
under the title "The Gentle Negress" in Williams's volume
The Wedge (1944):

> Wandering among the chimneys
> my love and I would meet
> I with a pale skin
> she as brown as peat
>
> Her voice was low and gentle
> and full of surprise
> that I should find her lovely
> and would search her eyes
>
> with a longing hard to fathom
> from what she said
> as I sat to comfort her
> lying in bed.[37]

In a situation that anticipates the "Beautiful Thing" episode
of *Paterson* (1949; III, ii, pp. 124-28), Williams has trans-
formed Yeats's concern with time into a more lighthearted

attention to setting. The reader is expected to be just as sur-
prised as Lillian that the same gentleness to be found down
by the salley gardens is still possible among the chimneys.
Gentleness also informs the relation between authors here.
The poem is not directed against Yeats in the sense that Pound's
parodies are. Yeats's theme simply becomes Williams's with-
out any sign of struggle. Another product of this process is
Williams's poem "Cuchulain" (1949), which shuns even the
metrical imitation of Yeats attempted in "The Gentle Ne-
gress."[38]

As Williams came to deal with influences more openly, he
also came to recognize the reciprocal nature of influence among
contemporaries. In 1944 Williams told Robert McAlmon that
Pound was "a one sided bastard if there ever was one, who
has borrowed from everybody, including myself in the old
days, but he's done a good job, surpassingly good. And I've
borrowed from him much more than I've given. Everyone has
who has followed him. Yeats especially" (WL 220). This is a
long way from Williams's earlier condemnation of Pound for
"paraphrases from Yeats" and other masters. In fact, in most
of Williams's later accounts it is Yeats who appears as the
pupil, and if he has failed to absorb Pound's lessons, it is only
because of the difficulty of breaking old molds. After telling
Richard Eberhart in 1953 that Pound's influence was evident
in much of Yeats's best work, Williams continued tolerantly,
"But the style of the older man had been set long and if, as
you say, he reverted to the use of inversions in an abnormal
contour of the phrase in his last work you can put it down
to the dominance of a measure to which he had become ac-
customed and which he did not find it easy to escape" (WL
320).

In the next paragraph of his letter to Eberhart, Williams
begins to develop what for him was the decisive distinction
between himself and his immediate predecessors: "What Pound
did not realize, nor Yeats either, is that a new order had
dawned in the make-up of the poem. The measure, the actual
measure, of the lines is no longer what Yeats was familiar
with. Or Pound either, except instinctively." The poet's task
is a matter of realization rather than invention, because the

new order, Williams implies, has its origin outside of poetry. Something had happened to the English language as it was spoken; by developing the new measure, poetry was readjusting itself to natural speech. Although Williams did not claim to have created the new measure, his contention to have discovered it was his way of asserting his unique poetic identity. The new measure was the New World in poetry and was in fact identified with the historical New World that Williams had chided Pound for ignoring. In syntax and diction, the analogue to the new measure was what Williams now called "the American idiom."[39]

Yeats's inclusion in Williams's letter to Eberhart is something of a compliment, for he appears, along with Whitman, Pound, and Hopkins, as one of the patriarchs who pointed the way to the new measure, although none of them reached the promised land. Since the promised land was specifically America, however, it is difficult at first to understand how Williams interpreted the relevance of Yeats's prophecy. Yeats's role in founding a movement for regional speech is a partial explanation, even though the region was Ireland rather than America. The difference meant little to Williams when he wrote his early play *A September Afternoon* and made characters of the American Revolutionary period speak in the folk dialect of the Abbey Theatre: "It's this we've been fearing the two weeks now they've been camping beyond the hills."[40] Even more important to the development of the new measure, however, was Yeats's tendency, overemphasized by Williams, to flout traditional metrical rules. In this regard, Williams might have seen Yeats as continuing the work of Hopkins, the other non-American who had prepared the way for Williams's discovery.

Like Pound, Williams acknowledged Yeats as a master of rhythm, and as such he taught a lesson to which Williams felt he could attend with impunity. In 1913 Williams wrote to Harriet Monroe, "Surely if Yeats teaches anything that can be learnt—that is, anything that it would not be copying to take to one's self—he teaches what can be done with the three-syllable foot by dropping the last syllable in the foot every time but once or twice in the entire poem. Witness 'The Mountain Tomb' in your own *Poetry*" (*WL* 24). One assumes that a three-syllable foot missing one syllable would look very much like the two-syllable foot that has been standard in English verse since the time of Chaucer. In fact, "The Mountain Tomb" is written in iambic pentameter, but a closer look at the poem provides some clues to what might have led Williams to read it as he did.

Following an allowable practice in metrical convention, Yeats used three-syllable feet as substitution, most notably in the line, *Pull dówn | the blínds, | bring fíd | dle and clár | i o nét.* But aside from this line, there is only one other three-syllable substitution in the poem, also an anapest. Williams acknowledged that there were few genuine anapests in "The Mountain Tomb." What he saw instead were anapests with the last foot dropped, which would produce a conventional pyrrhic. Yeats's poem contains a fair number of pyrrhics, eight in the twelve lines, including that in the refrain: *Our Fá | ther Rós | i cróss | is in | his tómb.* By counting the pyrrhics along with the anapests, and adding a certain amount of his own willfulness, Williams arrived at the conclusion that Yeats's meter was anapestic rather than iambic. He read the substitution as if it were the norm.

As Willliams pursued his metrical investigations, he elevated what began as an observation on a particular poem by Yeats to the status of universally applicable doctrine. His essay on "Measure," drafted in 1958, declared, "In all iambics in worthy hands there lurks a triple beat that transforms them into anapests when they are read with a subtle understanding of their true nature."[41] This subtle understanding involved preference for the irregular rather than the regular that was characteristic of Williams. The very fact that anapests do not occur as expectedly as iambs in most English poetry made the anapests more interesting. A similar preference informed Williams's understanding of the "variable foot," in which the principle of variability is introduced into a concept that most metrists would consider invariable by definition. Yeats's late work, however, was available to encourage Williams by the time he developed his theory of the variable foot in the nine-teen-forties.

The new metric that Yeats approached in his last plays resembles the variable foot in principle. A line may vary in number of unstressed syllables but is fixed to a definite number of stressed syllables—in Yeats's case usually four, in Williams's, three. In practice the results were very different. Williams tended to understress, as his preference for anapests suggests, whereas Yeats tended to overstress, sometimes writing four-syllable lines where each syllable is stressed. Yeats had arrived at his solution through experimentation with the system of variable stress that Gerard Manley Hopkins called "sprung rhythm." An advantage of the system, as Yeats saw it, was that "it enables a poet to employ words taken over from science or the newspaper without stressing the more unmusical syllables, or to suggest hurried conversation where only one or two words in a sentence are important, to bring about a change in poetical writing like that in the modern speech of the stage where only those words which affect the situation are important" (*OBMV* xxxix). Williams had seen the variable foot, too, as a vehicle for common speech: "It gives resources to the ear which result in a language which we hear spoken about us every day" (*WL* 327).

Yeats quickly decided that the disadvantages of sprung rhythm outweighed the advantages. While working on his play *The Herne's Egg* in 1935, Yeats wrote to Dorothy Wellesley, "I am writing in short lines, but think that I shall not use 'sprung verse'—now that I am close to it I dislike the constant uncertainty as to where the accent falls; it seems to make the verse vague and weak. I like a strong driving force. If there should be a subtle hesitating rhythm I can make it. I do not want it as part of the metrical scheme" (*L* 845-46). To paraphrase the last two sentences, if there is to be variation, let it appear as variation; substitution is not to become the norm. In the final version of *The Herne's Egg* and in *Purgatory* (1939), Yeats continued to vary the number of unstressed syllables but sought also to preserve what he called, borrowing a term from Robert Bridges, "the contrapuntal structure of

the verse" (*EI* 524). As Hopkins himself had observed, "strict
Sprung Rhythm cannot be counterpointed" because the rhythm
becomes so irregular that the underlying meter is no longer
heard.[42]

Williams's reading of "The Mountain Tomb" demonstrates
the emphasis he placed on metrical substitution; yet he did
not want to destroy counterpoint. He wrote in the closing
lines of *Paterson* (1958),

> We know nothing and can know nothing
> but
> the dance, to dance to a measure
> contrapuntally,
> Satyrically, the tragic foot.
>
> (V, iii, p. 239)

Clearly, the foot referred to here is not solely a measurement
of verse. The relation between Yeats and Williams on the issue
of metrical counterpoint can be applied to the counterpoint
that creates the rhythm of life. For Williams, what Yeats looked
upon as substitution and norm reverse their roles, but neither
element obscures the other, as was the case with sprung rhythm.
Yeats's norm is ideal reality, Williams's is ordinary reality. In
a world of fleeting appearances, Yeats's regular meter repre-
sents the realm of ideal permanence, but for Williams, ap-
pearances, however unattractive, are the abiding reality, and
the ideal is established only briefly at best. *Paterson* moves
from Book I, where "the / language stutters" (1946; I, ii, p.
22), toward "the unfaltering / language" of Book III (III, i, p.
108). The language reaches a climax in the lyric of Sappho
in Book V, but the lyric contains within it the plaint, "my
voice falters, my tongue / is broken" (V, ii, p. 217). Stuttering
is analogous to the halting gait of the cleft-foot satyr. As an
art of shortcomings, Williams's verse is "satyric," punning on
"satiric." Parody is its essential mode.

Unlike the anti-idealist parodies of Pound, and unlike the
ironic shortcomings of Frost, poised at the edge of the inef-
fable, the dance of Williams's satyrs incorporates the ideal
within the limitations of the dance itself. We can know nothing

but the dance, says Williams, but the dance is a mode of knowledge, "the embodiment of knowledge," as Williams phrased it in the title of an unfinished book. In notes for that book, written in 1928, Williams acknowledged Yeats's efforts to express the theme: "One does not need to be young. Hell with that. One might know it at the brink of destruction. Yeats had tried his best to say it recently. Usually do realize it at the brink."[43] When Yeats was at the brink, three weeks before his death, he summed up his philosophy in the phrase, "Man can embody truth but he cannot know it" (L 922). He was still a long way from the brink in 1928, but in that year he published *The Tower*, which contained at least two poems about the embodiment of knowledge, "Leda and the Swan" and "Among School Children." In the latter poem the dance is proposed as compensation for the limits of man's knowledge, about which Yeats was just as skeptical as Williams. "How can we know the dancer from the dance?" Yeats asks. We cannot know intellectually, but it is only intellect that insists on such distinctions. In experience, temporal dancer and ideal dance form an inseparable whole.

The image of the dance was part of the symbolist inheritance shared, in this rare instance, by Yeats and Williams, but the meaning of that image, the elevation of experience over intellect, derives from an inheritance within which Yeats and Williams could find much more common ground: the territory mapped out by Walt Whitman. Whitman "wrote the way he felt," without studying the effects he produced, Williams declared approvingly.[44] The feature of Whitman's poetry that Williams must have approved most strongly, however, was the intimate connection between what the poet felt and where he lived. Williams made that connection progressively tighter in his own work as he narrowed the range of circumstances that he found relevant, from the vaguely defined America that featured in Williams's early quarrel with Pound, to the richly particularized Paterson of Williams's American epic, and, finally in the late work, to the family of the individual man, William Carlos Williams, the *persona* having gained in particularity as his circumstances registered a similar gain. In

delineating Williams's contribution to the confessional poetry
of Robert Lowell, Steven Gould Axelrod has finally been able
to do justice to the confessional quality of such poems as
Williams's "To Daphne and Virginia" (1954), addressed to
the poet's daughters-in-law, and "Asphodel, That Greeny
Flower" (1955), celebrating Williams's love for his wife.[45]
Axelrod stresses that such poems are based on a technical
achievement, the development of a natural speech in which
the poet's only discipline is "the discipline of his own voice,"
as Williams described Whitman's method.[46] In dealing with
Yeats as with Whitman, Williams would allow himself to
imitate only that technical achievement, but such imitation
admitted him to a tradition in which he fully embraced his
masters when he most fully expressed himself.

V

ARTIFICIAL LIVES:
THE NINETEEN-TWENTIES

HOWEVER NATURAL THE SPEECH, the speaker of a poem in the tradition of the self must be artificial, if for no other reason than that the self is remade as a tradition. This artificiality provided an entrance into the tradition for those poets who insisted that poetry must be impersonal. To get any further in the tradition, however, these poets, like Pound, had to struggle with Yeats's example. Pound needed to be convinced that the self could become a *persona*, could enter fully into literature, without ceasing to be self; the poets of impersonality, on the other hand, doubted whether a *persona* could become the self, could descend from literature into the life of the poet, without ceasing to be serviceable as a *persona*. Though stressing different terms, the two questions are really the same, and both could be answered by an art in which subjectivity and objectivity are united, an art such as Pound outlined in his essay on Cavalcanti and achieved in the *Pisan Cantos*. Distinctive versions of such an art proved possible for three poets who shared an aesthetic of impersonality, Wallace Stevens, T. S. Eliot, and Robinson Jeffers. Each discovered a fruitful approach to Yeats through his theater, especially the mode of symbolist theater that Yeats perfected under the influence of the Japanese Noh and collected, in 1921, as *Four Plays for Dancers*.

The theater as a medium guaranteed the objectivity of the *personae* it presented. Witnessing a conflict between characters who were given physical embodiment by actors, an audience was not encouraged to interpret the characters merely as expressions of their author. On the other hand, symbolism as a mode of theater pushed that medium in the direction of more subjective art by creating a dominant mood in which the audience was invited to interpret what was outwardly presented as symbolic of an inner world, a world that, with little difficulty, could be identified with the author's consciousness. Having tested, through the writing of plays, the equilibrium of subjectivity and objectivity exemplified in Yeats's drama, a poet who sought impersonality could be confident of maintaining a similar equilibrium in his poems, confident that even surprisingly personal *personae* would still be more than "merely oneself."

THE RACIAL SELF:
WALLACE STEVENS

When Yeats returned to America in 1920, another *Poetry* magazine banquet in his honor reflected some of the changes that had taken place in the six years after the first one. Carl Sandburg and Edgar Lee Masters were called on to read their poems in the place that Vachel Lindsay, now bitter at Yeats's neglect, had been delighted to occupy in 1914. Yeats chose to speak not on poetry but on poetic drama, an expression of his own recent experiments with the Noh drama, but also perhaps a recognition that, since about 1915, America had begun to witness a new burst of activity in experimental theater as well as in poetry. The subject of Yeats's talk reminded Harriet Monroe of one experiment in particular, that of Wallace Stevens's play *Three Travellers Watch a Sunrise*, written in 1916 but produced in New York just a month before Yeats's talk. Much about that production, in Monroe's opinion, met the conditions Yeats outlined: "there was the small audience (over fifty, perhaps, but under one hundred) of the presumably elect. . . . There also was the small stage, almost as informal as a drawing-room, upon which artists had thought out a not too elaborate setting. And there, in Wallace Stevens' play, was the Poetic Drama."[1]

The setting was much more responsible for making the drama poetic than was the verse. *Three Travellers* is the only one of Stevens's three plays to be written in verse, and the verse as such is negligible. Visual effect, on the other hand, is unusually important because it objectifies for the audience an experience that would remain highly subjective were it to be suggested only by the characters' words. Stevens was working in the mode of the symbolist theater, whose basic premise is the embodiment of spirit. Yeats had helped to introduce the mode to English-speaking audiences, and in two of his "Plays for Dancers," *At the Hawk's Well* and *The Only Jealousy of Emer*, he found the definitive representation of the symbolist premise in the possession of a mortal's body by a god. In *Three Travellers* a Chinese sage sings a love ballad that becomes reality when the dead body of one of the lovers is revealed at the back of the stage (*OP* 139). The body is real, yet it has become a symbol, possessed by the significance of the ballad. As Stevens wrote much later in "A Quiet Normal Life" (1952), "his actual candle blazed with artifice" (*SCP* 523). That is in fact the central symbol of another of Stevens's plays, *Carlos Among the Candles* (1917), in which the only action consists of the lighting and extinguishing of rows of candles by a ridiculous middle-aged dandy.

The "rarefied atmosphere or mood" of Stevens's symbolic theater has led Denis Donoghue to assert that "*Three Travellers Watch a Sunrise* may be 'explained' as the result of Mr. Stevens's inordinately pious reading of Yeats's poems up to *The Green Helmet*."[2] Yeats certainly provided a potent stimulus, though there seems to be no reason to assume that Yeats's poems were the source rather than his plays, since there is little biographical evidence of Stevens's pious reading of either. Stevens, however, would want to deny that even Yeats's plays could "explain" his own, because the conclusion of each of Stevens's plays ironically limits the mood that has been evoked. After the departure of the three Chinese in *Three Travellers*, the audience is left with the sight of a Negro servant and the sound of a whip applied to a horse, reminders of the world of ordinary reality that the Chinese regard as an intrusion (*OP* 143). Carlos, at the end of his play, exits through a window exclaiming, "Oh, ho! Here is matter beyond invention" (*OP* 150). The opening stage directions of Stevens's third play,

Bowl, Cat and Broomstick (1917), prescribe a setting whose symbolic, antinaturalistic colors are reminiscent of those specified in the opening stage directions of Yeats's *The Green Helmet* (1910; *VPl* 148), but Stevens's play concludes with an irony that is especially revealing in the light of Stevens's reluctance to follow Yeats's lead toward an autobiographical poetry. Bowl and Cat spend most of the play developing an ideal image of a young poetess out of her portrait and her volume of poems, only to be disillusioned by Broomstick's discovery in the preface that the author is in fact fifty-three (*PEM* 34).

One of Stevens's poems from 1918, "Le Monocle de Mon Oncle," offers a realistic undercutting of symbols that can be traced specifically to Yeats's play *At the Hawk's Well*, published one year earlier. The tenth stanza of Stevens's poem begins:

> The fops of fancy in their poems leave
> Memorabilia of the mystic spouts
> Spontaneously watering their gritty soils.
> I am a yeoman, as such fellows go.
> I know no magic trees, no balmy boughs,
> No silver-ruddy, gold-vermilion fruits.
>
> (*SCP* 16-17)

The emblems that Stevens associates with his "fops of fancy"— "miraculous water" (*VPl* 404) and a magic tree—are central symbols of *At the Hawk's Well*. In opposition to them, Stevens presents another tree and well, whose alternative status is somewhat blurred by their indebtedness to certain outstanding characteristics of Yeats's images. Yeats's tree is barren except for a brief blossoming when water flows into the ordinarily dry well. Stevens conveys a comparable sense of suddenness by compressing the natural cycle of his tree into one line: "It comes, it blooms, it bears its fruit and dies" (*SCP* 16). As for the well, though Stevens has in mind "A deep up-pouring from some saltier well" (*SCP* 13), he has some difficulty in distinguishing that flow from Yeats's. He attempts such a distinction by explaining, "The honey of heaven may or may

not come, / But that of earth both comes and goes at once"
(*SCP* 15). The implication is that Stevens's uncle is devoted
to the honey of earth, whereas Yeats's "mystic spout" yields
the honey of heaven, but in fact the functioning of the two
wells is remarkably similar. "When it comes / The water has
scarce plashed before it is gone," Yeats's Old Man explains
(*VPl* 405).

The similarity in Yeats's and Stevens's accounts of decidedly
different phenomena can be explained by the similarity in the
perspective each poet adopts. Though Yeats's characters seek
the eternal, they do so within the temporal world, the same
world to which Stevens's *persona* commits himself. In each
case the passage of time is calculated numerically. Stevens's
uncle betrays his age in his plans to "celebrate the faith of
forty" (*SCP* 16), and Yeats's Old Man is said to have waited
by the well for fifty years (*VPl* 401). The characters to whom
these numbers apply are lent a degree of reality not only
because they are located in time but also because they are
identified with their authors, whose ages the numbers repre-
sent.[3] The author's age, which had served a special purpose
in directing *Bowl, Cat and Broomstick* toward realism, com-
bines with the claim of relationship in the title of "Le Monocle
de Mon Oncle" to identify the author with his *persona*. Yeats's
lyrics had recently begun to incorporate the poet in his poems
by introducing specific details from the poet's life. An out-
standing example is the introductory poem to *Responsibilities*
(1914), in which T. S. Eliot found "the naming of his age in
the poem" especially noteworthy (*PP* 300). Eliot's discovery
"that Yeats is pre-eminently the poet of middle age" (*PP* 301)
had been anticipated by Stevens, who accordingly wrote his
poem of middle age with Yeats in mind.

Having approached Yeats in his identification of poet and
persona, and having gone even further than Yeats in his com-
mitment to the temporal world, why did Stevens not go on
to develop a poetry that would locate the poet himself amid
autobiographical circumstance, the sort of poetry that is char-
acteristic of the tradition of the self? As it turns out, Stevens
does write a poetry of the self, but because the self has a

different meaning for him than it has for Yeats, Stevens's poetry seems more impersonal in content than Yeats's. The different meaning of the self for each poet is a reflection of their different interpretations of the world in which the self is located, which in turn resolves into a basic difference in temperament. Although each poet identifies himself with an aging *persona* in *At the Hawk's Well* and "Le Monocle de Mon Oncle," Yeats could not reconcile himself to the fact of his aging as Stevens could. Yeats's preference in his play is clearly for the young Cuchulain. The Old Man is cheated and left to rage impotently, "That there should be such evil in a shadow" (*VPl* 411). The shadow is the Woman of the Sidhe, a spirit representing the world of spirit, an image representing the imagination. Because she is of another world, the immortality she offers is made available to the temporal world only rarely and briefly. For Stevens's uncle, in contrast to Yeats's Old Man, the shadow, or shade, that represents the permanence of imagination appears as a constant within the impermanent things of the temporal world. The Old Man's statement of rage is revalued in the last line of "Le Monocle de Mon Oncle," which records the lesson "That fluttering things have so distinct a shade" (*SCP* 18). That shade, the "universal hue" of the imagination, suffuses the "ephemeral blues" of life's fluctuations (*SCP* 15), as the function of the imagination suffuses all individual acts of imagining.

Stevens's disagreement with Yeats over the location of the imagination is reflected in each poet's symbolic geography. In *At the Hawk's Well*, the alien nature of the Woman of the Sidhe, which causes the Old Man to turn away in terror when she approaches, contrasts with the domesticity of the world that Cuchulain renounces by choosing to pursue the Woman. The desolate landscape haunted by the Sidhe is given a voice to express the opposition:

> 'The man that I praise,'
> Cries out the empty well,
> 'Lives all his days
> Where a hand on the bell

Can call the milch cows
To the comfortable door of his house.'
(*VPl* 413)

The alternative fulfillment that Cuchulain seeks can never be achieved while he is alive, because the imagination is incompatible with the world of ordinary reality. In keeping with his romantic heritage, the world of imagination remains the normative ideal for Yeats, as comparison of his work with that of William Carlos Williams makes clear, but it is an ideal, like Yeats's ideal Byzantium, which a living man can only sail toward. "Sailing to Byzantium" (1927) longingly depicts the condition Yeats might achieve "Once out of nature."

Because Stevens saw no incompatibility between nature and the imagination, he was able to pursue the romantic ideal without renouncing domestic comforts, without the frustration of travel. If Stevens travels at all, it is toward home, away from the grandeur of imaginative transcendence. "Home Again," written as early as 1908 but not published until 1914, describes this movement:

Back within the valley,
Down from the divide,
No more flaming clouds about,
O! the soft hillside,
And my cottage light,
And the starry night.[4]

In a letter to his fiancée in 1909, Stevens observed that "the cottage," the ultimate goal in "Home Again," "has been the youthful ideal of all men" (*SL* 120). He was commenting on Yeats's "The Lake Isle of Innisfree" (1890), from which he had just quoted some lines. A. Walton Litz has used this letter to argue that the theme of "Home Again" is Yeatsian, but it must be added that Stevens has given the Yeatsian theme some important twists.[5] The cottage is home in Stevens's poem, whereas in "Innisfree" it is a distant dream. Moreover, Yeats seeks that dream as an escape from "the pavements grey" of the real world; Stevens, on the other hand, seeks home as an escape from the "flaming clouds" of the realm where Yeats sought the imagination.

As in the case of "Le Monocle de Mon Oncle," it is likely that Stevens's transformation of the cottage motif was a deliberate response to Yeats, one further elaborated in three poems of 1922 that refer to "cabins," the specific term that Yeats used in "Innisfree." The most important of the three poems is "The Comedian as the Letter C," in which the protagonist, Crispin, repeats the movement from imaginative splendor to domestic contentment outlined much more briefly in "Home Again," the only difference being that Crispin comes home not "again" but for the first time. In Part V of the poem, entitled "A Nice Shady Home," Crispin's earlier dreams are contrasted with his present situation: "he built a cabin who once planned / Loquacious columns by the ructive sea" (*SCP* 41). Another poem, "Frogs Eat Butterflies . . . ," offers a further gloss on what Crispin has given up:

> the man who erected this cabin, planted
> This field, and tended it awhile,
> Knew not the quirks of imagery,
>
> (*SCP* 78)

including, presumably, such quirks as "flaming clouds." To understand what Crispin has gained, as opposed to what he has given up, we must turn to the third poem of the cabin series, "Hymn from a Watermelon Pavilion," which addresses the "dweller in the dark cabin, / To whom the watermelon is always purple" (*SCP* 88). In the final section of "The Comedian as the Letter C," Crispin learns that the world's "ancient purple" cannot be finally "daubed out" (*SCP* 45). He has discovered the "universal hue" of "Le Monocle de Mon Oncle," which represents the permanent aspect of the imagination that can be found in the "ephemeral blues" of nature but that contrasts with the unpredictable "quirks" of "the honey of heaven." This permanent imagination is that which is always with us; like Coleridge's primary imagination, it exists not in what we see but in the act of seeing itself. As Stevens asserts in another passage of "Hymn from a Watermelon Pavilion," our sleeping and waking states are both dreams, if dream is the imaginative mode. The compatibility of the real and the imaginative for Stevens is an identity. There is no need to seek the imagination in a transcendent world because the "real" world itself is a function of the imagination.

This understanding of the imagination made it all the easier for Stevens to adapt "Innisfree" to his own purposes. He could go Yeats one better by moving into the cabin, yet he did not have to deny the atmosphere of daydream that Yeats conferred on the place. Stevens's clearest acknowledgment of "Innisfree" as a dream comes in the late poem "Page from a Tale" (1950), where lines quoted from "Innisfree" represent the difference between man's world of meaning and the meaningless sounds of nature,

> between sound without meaning and speech,
> *Of clay and wattles made* as it ascends
> And *hear it* as it falls *in the deep heart's core.*
>
> (*SCP* 421)

On a larger scale, the pastoral world of Innisfree is contrasted with the hostile arctic environment in which a ship has become icebound. The crew plan to walk across the ice to land, but they are "afraid of the sun: what it might be" (*SCP* 422). It might be a symbol of the imagination as the antinatural "honey of heaven," capable of destroying both the dreamy complacencies of Innisfree and the apparent solidity of the "real" world by revealing that world to be no less fictional but considerably less powerful than the world of transcendence. This revelation will emerge if the sun comes "nearer than it / Had ever been before" (*SCP* 422), near enough to dazzle the observer with the brilliance of its images. Stevens would prefer, as he wrote in "Imagination as Value" (1948), "to live in the mind with the imagination, yet not too near to the fountains of its rhetoric, so that one does not have a consciousness only of grandeurs."[6]

Though more eager for grandeurs, Yeats, too, occasionally found it necessary to keep them at a distance, as in the equiv-

ocating invocation "To the Rose upon the Rood of Time"
(1892):

> Come near, come near, come near—Ah, leave me still
> A little space for the rose breath to fill!
> Lest I no more hear common things that crave.

Stevens may have had these lines in mind when he wrote the
passage just quoted from "Imagination as Value." An even
closer resemblance, however, can be found in his poem "To
the One of Fictive Music" (1922). Close resemblance is pre-
cisely the point here, provided it is not too close:

> Yet not too like, yet not so like to be
> Too near, too clear, saving a little to endow
> Our feigning with the strange unlike.[7]

It is commonly accepted that this poem, like "To the Rose
upon the Rood of Time," is an invocation to the Muse. Yet
Stevens again keeps his distance from Yeats by selecting as
Muse not the transcendent imagination, represented by Yeats's
Rose or the Sun in "Page from a Tale," but the natural imag-
ination through which we perceive the world. For Stevens's
Muse, "No crown is simpler than the simple hair" (SCP 87).
Nevertheless, the poet ends by requesting that the Muse adorn
her hair with "A band entwining, set with fatal stones" (SCP
88), because there is a danger, for Stevens, in limiting the
imagination solely to reality.

"To the Rose upon the Rood of Time" and "To the One
of Fictive Music" illustrate Yeats's and Stevens's common
concern for keeping the imaginative ideal at a distance. This
distance maintains a distinction, in the terms of Stevens's poem,
between "perfection" and "our imperfections," thus preserv-
ing the sanctity of the ideal but, more important, also pre-
serving the individuality of the poet. The poet must prevent
the imagination from writing his poem for him, or, to view
the matter from the reader's perspective, the poem must pre-
serve some sense of having been written by a particular man,
not by man in the abstract. The danger of such abstraction
was much less for Yeats than it was for Stevens. Despite Yeats's

occasional claim that all of existence was a product of man's imagination, experience told Yeats that the imaginative world and the natural world were in conflict. Accordingly, Yeats perceived the Muse, the embodiment of the imagination, to be separate from his natural self, as demon or antiself. His principal task was to reduce that separation as much as possible, knowing that it could be overcome entirely only in death. Stevens, for whom the imagination and the natural world were one, assumed a corresponding identity between the Muse and the self. The One of Fictive Music is one "in whom / We give ourselves our likest issuance," and Stevens's principal task is to establish some separation so that the likeness will be "not too like." Since *personae* are the ones in whom the poet gives himself issuance in poems, Stevens's *personae* must maintain a touch of "the strange unlike," of the uncommon or the extraordinary, in order to remain distinct from the imagination that constitutes the ordinary world. This means, further, that the *personae* remain distinct from the poet who lives in the ordinary world, but impersonality is a price that Stevens is willing to pay for individuality.

Because Yeats's Muse is the transcendent rather than the natural imagination, he maintains the individuality of his *personae* through contact with the ordinary, with the "common things" that the speaker does not want to give up in "To the Rose upon the Rood of Time." The poet himself can appear in his poem as a common man, but, Yeats insisted, that appearance depends on a crucial transformation. He made it a "first principle" that the poet in a poem is a "phantasmagoria": "he is never the bundle of accident and incoherence that sits down to breakfast; he has been reborn as an idea, something intended, complete" (*EI* 509). Agreement on the artificiality of the *persona* formed the common ground that was essential if Stevens was to confront Yeats at all. Without the "phantasmagoria," one is faced with "the desolation of reality" of Yeats's "Meru" (1934) or of the graveyard where Stevens discovered "the reality that time and experience had created here, the desolation that penetrated one like something final."[8] The protagonist of Stevens's "The Man on the Dump"

(1938) sits in a graveyard of worn-out images of the self, among "Bottles, pots, shoes and grass" (*SCP* 203), and considers what it means to "Be merely oneself," apart from an image. Yet the adverb indicates that he is no more happy in that position than Yeats was to be a year later among the "Old kettles, old bottles, and a broken can" of "The Circus Animals' Desertion" (1939).[9] The only reason for putting up with such indignities is that the discarding of old images makes room for new ones. As Stevens explains:

> One feels the purifying change. One rejects
> The trash.
>   That's the moment when the moon creeps up
> To the bubbling of bassoons.
>
> (*SCP* 202)

One poet's fresh images will of course be trash to another. Thus, in "Memorandum" (1947), Stevens revises the lines just quoted to throw Yeats on the dump: "the American moon comes up / Cleansed clean of lousy Byzantium."[10]

America in "Memorandum" represents not a political entity but a type of imagination, the natural type as opposed to the transcendent; the Yeatsian contrast is Byzantium, not Ireland. Stevens's concern here is not merely with individuality, the poet's uniqueness, but with essential selfhood, the poet's imagination. In this context, the identity of self and Muse is fully acknowledged as the limits of the self are expanded beyond the dimensions of the individual. This expansion is manifest in the debate over the poetess in *Bowl, Cat and Broomstick*, during which Bowl points out "a group of poems in which she studies herself—not the individual Claire Dupray, but the racial Claire" (*PEM* 30). True selfhood, in fact, seems to depend on such an identity, for Bowl insists that Claire Dupray meets the standard of "being one's self in one's day" (*PEM* 29), a standard that Stevens rigorously applied in his own case. Ironically, Stevens claimed to have learned the importance of being oneself "from Yeats who was extremely persnickety about being himself" (*SL* 575). In the tradition of the self, this is the only lesson that one poet can legitimately pass on to another.

Usually Stevens's intention to be himself as an individual remains behind the scenes in his poetry. The *personae* may be shaped according to that intention, but as a whole each poem is about that larger self that is the imagination. The one image in which these two notions of self overlap and through which Stevens's poetry comes closest to sounding like Yeats's is that of the poet as hero (cf. *EI* 193; *OP* 208). When Yeats's body was ceremonially removed from France to Ireland in 1948, Stevens drew the moral: "The meaning of the poet as a figure in society is a precious meaning to those for whom it has any meaning at all" (*SL* 618). In contrast to Yeats, who was a poet in everything he did, Stevens approached society as a poet only through his poems. The poems, more than the age stated in "Le Monocle de Mon Oncle" or the places named throughout his work, are the circumstances of his life that defined Stevens as he wished to be defined. In the late apology "As You Leave the Room" (1954), the retrospective catalogue of poems is modeled on that in Yeats's "The Circus Animals' Desertion," but Stevens refuses to follow Yeats beyond the poems into the "heart-mysteries" that inspired them.[11] Instead, the poems appear as their own and their poet's justification:

> That poem about the pineapple, the one
> About the mind as never satisfied,
>
> The one about the credible hero, the one
> About summer, are not what skeletons think about.
>
> (*OP* 117)

The references are too general to identify specific poems, though "Someone Puts a Pineapple Together," "The Well-Dressed Man with a Beard" ("It can never be satisfied, the mind, never"), "Examination of the Hero in a Time of War," and "Credences of Summer" readily come to mind. "Credences of Summer" (1946), one of Stevens's favorite poems (*SL* 778), helps to define its author as poet partly by offering

his clearest presentation of his relation to Yeats. Seeking to
"comfort the heart's core" (*SCP* 372), Stevens returns to the
pastoral mood of "The Lake Isle of Innisfree" from which he
had drawn his early cabin images and from which he was to
quote, in "Page from a Tale," Yeats's line about "the deep
heart's core." Stevens now finds a home not in a cabin but in
another Yeatsian symbol, a tower. The *persona* who repre-
sents both the author and the imagination,

> is the old man standing on the tower,
> Who reads no book. His ruddy ancientness
> Absorbs the ruddy summer and is appeased,
> By an understanding that fulfils his age,
> By a feeling capable of nothing more.[12]

Again Stevens has turned to Yeats to help him depict the age
he has reached, but as in the contrast of "Le Monocle de Mon
Oncle" and *At the Hawk's Well*, Stevens's contentment in
"Credences of Summer" distinguishes him from the Yeats of
"The Tower," who is plagued by "fantastical imagination"
and by senses that "expected the impossible." Because Stevens
favors the natural over the transcendent imagination, "what
is possible / Replaces what is not" (*SCP* 376), yet the imagi-
native aspect of the possible is acknowledged in terms that
echo Yeats: "It is a mountain half way green and then, / The
other immeasurable half" (*SCP* 375). In Yeats's "Vacillation"
(1932), it is a tree "that from its topmost bough / Is half all
glittering flame and half all green." As "Vacillation" proves,
Yeats has his moments of contentment, when the imagination
and reality stand in equilibrium, but they are moments, not
seasons.

The last section of "Credences of Summer" begins with a
dramatic metaphor that recalls the interest in theater that
Yeats and Stevens shared: "The personae of summer play the
characters / Of an inhuman author" (*SCP* 377). Stevens rec-
ognized the importance of *personae* in Yeats and drew on that
recognition to develop *personae* of his own—the speaker of
"Le Monocle de Mon Oncle," the "One of Fictive Music,"
the old man on the tower—each sharply differentiated from

its Yeatsian original. But Stevens also found that he could adapt, to continue the dramatic metaphor, Yeats's scenery as well as his characters. To this discovery we owe the symbolic colors of *Bowl, Cat and Broomstick,* the well and tree of "Le Monocle de Mon Oncle," the several cabins, and the tower. Scenes as well as characters must be counted among Stevens's *personae,* because the Muse in whom they are conceived is the natural imagination that is our means of perceiving the world. In "To the One of Fictive Music" the entire earth, "By being so much of the things we are," becomes "Gross effigy and simulacrum" (*SCP* 87). All objects are part of the grand subject that contemplates itself. The range of circumstances that defines the self for Stevens is much greater than it is for Yeats, because Stevens is defining, in the most individual manner, a self that is universal, or at least universally American. His poems are intended as the record not of a man imagining but of that "inhuman author," the imagination.

THE TRADITIONAL SELF:
T. S. ELIOT

As "the American moon" guided Wallace Stevens, "the mind of Europe" led T. S. Eliot to the "Impersonal theory of poetry" set forth in "Tradition and the Individual Talent" (1919; *SE* 6-7). With allowances for geographical differences, each poet was designating an imaginative force greater than the particular author, which consequently demands, in Eliot's words, "a continual extinction of personality" as sacrifice (*SE* 7). The geographical difference perhaps accounts for the major disagreement between Stevens and Eliot over the manner in which one comes in touch with the imagination. Stevens, who never liked to admit that he had read a potential rival, found America within himself. Eliot insisted that the mind of Europe spoke through the great writers of the past, through literary tradition, as the term is conventionally understood. By combining these approaches, Yeats's concept of the tradition of the self was able to bridge two cultures.

Tradition is no more an unearned inheritance for Eliot (*SE*

4) than it is for Yeats, but where Yeats embraces tradition through a poetic act of the will, Eliot can only expose himself to tradition through a critical act of reason. The rest, the entrance of the predecessors into a new poem, must take place in the unconscious, or else the self will interfere. The difference between the conscious and unconscious stages in the process is illustrated in Eliot's relationship to Yeats as an ancestor. Eliot went to England in 1914 as part of his program of consciously exposing himself to tradition. In the same year, he met Ezra Pound, who in turn introduced him to Yeats. Eliot had already decided that Yeats was not one of his ancestors, and personal acquaintance did nothing to change his mind.[13] Nevertheless, Eliot's continued contact with Yeats over the years prepared the ground for Yeats to enter his poetry and claim him as a successor.

Although at the time of their first meeting Yeats seemed preoccupied with "George Moore and spooks," Eliot cannot have been as bored as he recalled for Richard Ellmann in 1947.[14] An unsigned review of *Per Amica Silentia Lunae* in 1918, Eliot's first published statement on Yeats, noted tolerantly, "as there is no one else living whom one would endure on the subject of gnomes, hobgoblins, and astral bodies we infer some very potent personal charm of Mr. Yeats's."[15] The charm was that of a foreigner from a land so distant that his ways offered no comparison, and hence no threat, to the customs of home, as Eliot made clear in "A Foreign Mind" (1919), his review of *The Cutting of an Agate*.[16] Yeats's mind seemed so different from "ours," Eliot wrote, that it must be "in some way independent of experience." The important qualifier, "our experience," is understood, as is the implication that the experience in question has a historical dimension. Eliot is speaking from within a tradition that does not, in his view, include Yeats.

Throughout the early years of his career, Eliot's criticism continued to place Yeats outside the tradition in which Eliot saw himself. The simple explanation for their difference, tentatively suggested in the review of *The Cutting of an Agate*, was that Yeats was Irish whereas Eliot, by choice and ancestry, was English. Eliot's birth and upbringing in America were crucial because they made him aware of his separation from a tradition he could prepare himself to rejoin, whereas a native of modern England, no less separate from tradition, might be unaware of that separation. Attempting to trace the continuance of seventeenth-century wit in his essay on "Andrew Marvell" (1921), Eliot remarked, "among contemporaries Mr. Yeats is an Irishman and Mr. Hardy is a modern Englishman—that is to say, Mr. Hardy is without it and Mr. Yeats is outside the tradition altogether" (*SE* 252). At an earlier date Yeats might have been gratified at this recognition of a position he sought to achieve, but more recently, as in the poem "To a Young Beauty" (1918), he had sought to join the company of Donne, from which Eliot would exclude him. He was still excluded in 1922, when Eliot designated English, Irish, and American literature as "The Three Provincialities." During a recent barren period, Irishmen, principally Yeats and Synge, had filled a vacuum in England, but their work, according to Eliot, remained "foreign matter" that English literature was too weak to assimilate.[17]

Being outside the tradition did not always mean the same thing to Eliot. Within the rigid structure of his religious and social criticism there was room for no more than one tradition. Whatever lay outside was heresy. In *After Strange Gods* (1933) Eliot saw Yeats's "crystalgazing and hermetic writings" as an attempt "to fabricate an *individual* religion" (Eliot's emphasis) and to repeat Matthew Arnold's heretical attempt to replace religion with poetry.[18] Yeats's journals for 1929 and 1930 indicate that he was quite prepared to accept Eliot's charges, though he would argue that he had greater claim on tradition than his accuser. "I feel as neither Eliot nor Ezra do the need of old forms, old situations that, as when I re-create some early poem of my own, I may escape from scepticism," Yeats wrote in January 1929.[19] The reference to recreating an early poem is a clue to the sort of tradition Yeats had in mind. Earlier in the same entry he affirmed, "I have felt when rewriting every poem—'The Sorrow of Love' for instance that by assuming a self of past years, as remote from that of today as some dramatic creation, I touched a stronger passion, a greater confidence than I possess, or ever did possess." Yeats's tradition was the tradition of the self, which depended on the individual in precisely the way that Eliot considered heretical.

Yeats gladly confessed to heresy in a diary entry in October 1930: "to-day the man who finds belief in God, in the soul, in immortality, growing and clarifying, is blasphemous" (*Ex* 334). These beliefs were "growing and clarifying" only if they were felt as "free powers," free of the dogma that Yeats suspected in "T. S. Eliot's revival of seventeenth-century divines" (*Ex* 334). Dividing Yeats and Eliot on the question of belief is the same issue that separated them in their poetry. Eliot placed the ancestors foremost, where Yeats placed the self, assuming for the self the prerogative of remaking the ancestors if necessary. "Free power is not the denial of that past," Yeats explained, "but such a conflagration or integration of that past that it can be grasped in a single thought" (*Ex* 335). Curiously, Yeats was allowed to call for such thought in the pages of the *Criterion*, under Eliot's editorship, though the title of the essay was tamed from its original "The Need for Audacity of Thought" to "Our Need for Religious Sincerity" (1926). It was probably not Yeats's audacity but rather his attack on censorship that won Eliot's approval. In his "Commentary" for the *Criterion* in December 1926 Eliot drew attention to "an admirable essay" by Yeats in the September *Spectator* on the subject of Irish censorship.[20]

In contrast to his religious and social criticism, Eliot's literary criticism not only tolerated the existence of alien traditions but, at times, demanded their fertilizing influence as well. Eliot diverged from his main concern in *After Strange Gods* to admit that Yeats had made a praiseworthy attempt to rid his poetry of the clutter of mythologies, with the result that "the austerity of Mr. Yeats's later verse on the whole, should compel the admiration of the least sympathetic."[21] Much more than grudging sympathy was displayed in "A Commentary" in the *Criterion* for July 1935, on the occasion of Yeats's seventieth birthday and the appearance in that issue of Yeats's introduction to the Mandookya Upanishad.[22] Eliot

hailed Yeats as "the greatest poet of his time" and acknowl-
edged that that time was the present. Because it produced only
imitators, Yeats's influence in Ireland had been disastrous,
according to Eliot, but in England it was welcome. Influence
could be healthy so long as it came from outside, because in
the struggle to translate an alien influence a poet inevitably
created a new style. Eliot specified two areas in which Yeats
had proved particularly useful to English poets. He had "kept
poetry in the theatre," and he had provided a model for the
expression of a distinctive national rhythm in verse.

Both of the contributions singled out by Eliot are ways in
which Yeats provided a link with tradition. He is praised for
having captured not a personal but a national rhythm. To be
sure, Yeats's nation was still different from the one with which
Eliot identified himself, and Eliot warned against any attempt
to ignore such differences. To hear Yeats read Blake, Eliot
reported in "The Music of Poetry" (1942), was "more aston-
ishing than satisfying" (*PP* 24). On the other hand, only Yeats's
"Irish way of speech" could exploit the full beauty of his own
poetry. Eliot hoped that English poets would write verse with
a similar reliance on their native idiom.

In the case of poetic drama, Eliot's remarks on Yeats's
achievement often imply that Eliot and Yeats shared one id-
iom, one tradition. If Yeats "kept poetry in the theatre," as
Eliot claimed in his *Criterion* "Commentary," then Yeats pre-
served tradition. Eliot repeated the claim in an early version
of his lecture on "Poetry and Drama" (1951), published in
1949, in which he praised Yeats and Hugo von Hoffmannsthal
because they had "kept alive, in a period given over to prose
theatre, the ancient traditional relationship between poetry
and the stage."[23] It seems odd that Eliot, who placed so much
stress on national traditions in his exclusion of Yeats, should
feel gratitude to two foreigners for maintaining this particular
tradition. Two explanations seem possible, and both are prob-
ably applicable, though to different degrees. One explanation
is that Eliot saw poetic drama as an international tradition.
The second, and more important, explanation is that in this
case Eliot desired to place himself outside the tradition because

the tradition of poetic drama in English included Shakespeare, who blocked the path of any follower. Yeats seemed to offer a way of avoiding that obstacle by moving in an entirely different direction. Through Yeats's plays, then, Eliot came to his first recognition of the value of Yeats as an ancestor.

Although a literary ancestor need not be dead to assume that role, Eliot's public acknowledgment of his personal debt to Yeats came shortly after Yeats's death, in a lecture simply entitled "Yeats" and delivered at the Abbey Theatre in 1940. Here Yeats is finally admitted into the same tradition as Eliot when the latter concedes that "Yeats was born into the end of a literary movement, and an English movement at that" (*PP* 306). The movement Eliot has in mind in this passage is Pre-Raphaelite aestheticism, but he is equally concerned elsewhere in the lecture with Yeats's inheritance of Shakespearean drama. In each instance, Eliot admires Yeats for his ability to avoid the disadvantages of his inheritance, as Eliot himself wished to avoid the burden of Shakespeare (*PP* 304). The methods of avoidance that Eliot attributes to Yeats are, with respect to the Pre-Raphaelites, the development of a personal poetry (*PP* 299) and, with respect to Shakespeare, the abandonment of blank verse (*PP* 304) and a special handling of myth (*PP* 305). The evidence of Eliot's career suggests that his interest in Yeats's plays and his own experiments in the theater brought him to an appreciation of all three of these methods.

Yeats's attempt to abandon blank verse must have been apparent to Eliot as early as 1916, when Ezra Pound took Eliot to see the first performance of *At the Hawk's Well*.[24] Although the principal actors in the play speak a loose blank verse, the Musicians punctuate the dialogue by singing lyrics composed mainly in trimeter and provide a strongly accented rhythm for the play as a whole by beating on a drum (*VPl* 1304-05). This last element especially drew Eliot's attention, for the beating drum, by reinforcing artifice and ritual, signaled a break with the naturalistic iambic pentameter that kept the verse dramatist imprisoned within the Shakespearean tradition. In 1923 Eliot published an article entitled "The

Beating of a Drum," in which he condemned modern drama principally for its lack of rhythm.[25] To demonstrate what was lacking, he began work on a play in rhythmic prose, "perhaps with certain things in it accentuated by drum beats."[26] The play seems to have evolved into *Sweeney Agonistes*, for which Eliot specified the accompaniment of "light drum taps" in a letter to Hallie Flanagan, who produced the *Sweeney* fragments at Vassar College in 1933.[27] Eliot further specified the models on which Flanagan should base her production: "The action should be stylized as in the Noh drama—see Ezra Pound's book and Yeats's preface and notes to *The Hawk's Well*." In addition to "the accompaniment of drum taps," Yeats's preface to *Four Plays for Dancers*, which includes *At the Hawk's Well*, mentions other elements of stylization that Eliot wanted for the Vassar production of *Sweeney Agonistes*: the stiff movement of actors—"like marionettes," in Yeats's phrase— and the wearing of masks (*VPl* 1304-05).

Even more directly related to verse rhythm than the accompaniment of drums, the lyrics sung by the Musicians further remove *At the Hawk's Well* from dependence on blank verse. In his 1940 lecture Eliot commented on the advance over Yeats's earlier plays achieved by the development of "the lyrical choral interlude" (*PP* 304), and in "Poetry and Drama" (1951) he specified the plays he had in mind by describing the *Four Plays for Dancers* as "poetic prose plays with important interludes in verse" (*PP* 82). Yeats's development in verse drama, as Eliot outlines it, closely parallels Eliot's development in the same genre. After leaving *Sweeney Agonistes* uncompleted, Eliot sought in his next plays to evolve a suitable choral structure (*PP* 85-87). His progress, culminating in *The Family Reunion* (1939), shows an increasing integration of the chorus into the main action of the play. But choral verse, no matter how smoothly integrated, still did not solve the problem of verse structure in the principal speeches. Yeats's experiment had gone beyond the "Plays for Dancers," however, and Eliot gratefully followed him. "It was only in his last play *Purgatory*," Eliot explained in "Poetry and Drama," "that he solved his problem of speech in verse, and laid all his successors under obligation to him" (*PP* 82-83).

The logical place to look for proof of Eliot's obligation to Yeats is in *The Family Reunion*, where Eliot felt he had arrived at the verse form of his later plays (*PP* 88). As Margaret Lightfoot has pointed out, however, it is difficult to see that play as a successor to *Purgatory*, since the first draft of *The Family Reunion* seems to have been completed some months before the first, prepublication performance of *Purgatory* in 1938.[28] A version of the opening scene of *The Family Reunion*, which E. Martin Browne dates to November 1937, already employs the variable four-stress line that is the most common verse form in the final version. In the first draft Mary reflects:

> Surely it is necessary to stay in one place
> To acquire the rhythm of recurrent seasons
> Which strengthen both hope and resignation.[29]

The problem with *The Family Reunion* as it finally evolved is that, although this verse form is the most common, it is by no means the norm in a play sorely needing the unification that a rhythmic norm could bring. What should be modulation is heard as abrupt change, as in the shift to Agatha's reverie in the passage concerning the summoning of Dr. Warburton:

GERALD: He can talk to Harry, and Harry need have no suspicion.
         I'd trust Warburton's opinion.
AMY: If anyone speaks to Dr. Warburton
         It should be myself. What does Agatha think?
AGATHA: It seems a necessary move
         In an unnecessary action.
         Not for the good that it will do
         But that nothing may be left undone
         On the margin of the impossible.

(*CPP* 237-38)

The problem with this passage is not the reverie itself but the mode in which it is expressed. Agatha, with at least one line of two stresses in contrast to earlier lines with a possible six, seems to be in an entirely different world from that of her family. This is the flaw Eliot had in mind in his own criticism of *The Family Reunion*; he regretted "the introduction of passages which called too much attention to themselves as poetry, and could not be dramatically justified" (*PP* 89). Yeats handles the problem more skillfully at the beginning of *Purgatory*, which also juxtaposes the practical concerns of one character and the reverie of another:

BOY: Half-door, hall door,
            Hither and thither day and night,
            Hill or hollow, shouldering this pack,
            Hearing you talk.
OLD MAN: Study that house.
            I think about its jokes and stories;
            I try to remember what the butler
            Said to a drunken gamekeeper
            In mid-October, but I cannot.
            If I cannot, none living can.
                                        (*VPl* 1041)

Alliteration, caesura, and end-stopping give the Boy's lines a weightiness in strong contrast to the quick flight of the Old Man's daydream. Yet both speeches belong to the same metrical world, a basically tetrameter line, now tightened, now loosened, according to the mood of the speaker. As a rhythmic norm, Yeats's tetrameter line is elastic enough to express almost any mood while still tying that mood to others in the play.

Eliot applied the lesson of *Purgatory*, as Margaret Lightfoot argues, in the play that followed *The Family Reunion*, *The Cocktail Party* (1949).[30] Here, a passage such as those we have just examined, contrasting surface emotion with more profound reflection, succeeds because the two moods are united by a common rhythmic structure:

CELIA: But what will your life be? I cannot bear to think
            of it.

> Oh, Edward! Can you be happy with Lavinia?

EDWARD: No—not happy: or, if there is any happiness,
Only the happiness of knowing
That the misery does not feed on the ruin of
loveliness,
That the tedium is not the residue of ectasy.

(*CPP* 326)

The development of a verse norm in his later plays is the specific debt that Eliot owes to *Purgatory*. More generally, that play stood not as an example of method but as an encouraging reminder of achievement in a field in which Eliot also wished to succeed. Eliot admired *Purgatory*, as he said in his lecture, for "the virtual abandonment of blank verse metre" and for its corollary, the "purging out of poetical ornament" (*PP* 304), but he had formulated those goals on his own and achieved them in his own way, a way that Yeats did not entirely approve.

Yeats recognized Eliot's desire for "modernness in language and metaphor" and thought it qualified Eliot for inclusion in a project for verse drama, which never materialized, at the Mercury Theatre in London.[31] Associating himself and Eliot in the same project did not seem strange, for "I too have tried to be modern," as Yeats claimed after linking himself with Eliot in his *Oxford Book of Modern Verse* (1936; *OBMV* xxxvi). When an essay by Joseph Hone was rejected by the *Criterion* in 1932, Yeats sided with Eliot in explaining that Hone should not have used words such as "ocean" or "main" instead of "sea": "If you were a poet not a prose writer you would not use these words because you would feel very acutely that we are in a frenzy of reaction against all the old conventions. I should have warned you that Eliot, who is himself the most typical figure of the reaction, would refuse the essay on that account. Think of his bare poetry" (*L* 792). Yeats and Eliot parted company, however, over the issue of just how bare poetry should be. The "rhythmical animation" that Yeats considered to be an essential of good poetry seemed to him to be lacking in Eliot, except "in the dramatic poems" and the short lines of "The Hollow Men" and *Ash Wednesday* (*OBMV* xxii). In prose, too, Eliot had given up "momentum," as Yeats told Thomas McGreevy. Compared with McGreevy's prose, Yeats claimed, "Eliot is dancing among eggs."[32]

Fearful that the moderns might be giving up too much, Yeats was pleased to see one traditional element of poetry, myth, returning after a long absence. In the work of Eliot, Joyce, and Pirandello, Yeats wrote in the first edition of *A Vision*, "It is as though myth and fact, united until the exhaustion of the Renaissance, have now fallen so far apart that man understands for the first time the rigidity of fact, and calls up, by that very recognition, myth—the Mask—which now but gropes its way out of the mind's dark but will shortly pursue and terrify" (*Vision* A, 212). This passage seems to imply that the restoration of myth was not part of the moderns' intention, though in fact the opposite is true. Yeats's method of handling myth in the *Four Plays for Dancers* was, along with the advantage in eliminating blank verse, one of the qualities that Eliot singled out for praise in his 1940 lecture. The legendary figures of Yeats's early work belong to "a different world from ours," conceded Eliot (*PP* 305), who could not entirely shake off his impression of Yeats's foreignness. But Eliot went on to argue that in the dance plays, with the exception of *Calvary*, "the myth is not presented for its own sake, but as a vehicle for a situation of universal meaning" (*PP* 305).

This universal meaning was developed by bringing the myth into the modern world, thereby revealing the relevance of the myth beyond the world in which it originated. Eliot was more interested, however, in the effect this transference would have on the world into which the myth was brought. Yeats, in Eliot's opinion, had discovered the method that Joyce had extended to prose through the "parallel use of the Odyssey" in *Ulysses*, a method that was no less than "a step toward making the modern world possible for art."[33] Among the "Plays for Dancers," only *The Dreaming of the Bones* derives its universal meaning specifically through the conjunction of modern fact and ancient legend that Joyce employs in *Ulysses*.

Diarmuid and Dervorgilla, whose adulterous love first brought the English into Ireland, return as ghosts to plead forgiveness from a man who has fought to expel the English in the Easter Rising of 1916. In his lecture on Yeats, Eliot makes an exception for this play in his argument because he feels that the story, since it does not derive from prehistory, cannot properly be counted myth. Nevertheless, he claims that "these two lovers have something of the universality of Dante's Paolo and Francesca" (*PP* 305)—high praise indeed from Eliot—and he goes on to explain the more mythic plays in terms of the universality that he finds in *The Dreaming of the Bones*. Eliot's special interest in this play may account for the fact that, among the various dates he chose at one time or another to mark the birth of his enthusiasm for Yeats, 1919, the year in which *The Dreaming of the Bones* was published, is the date cited in his Abbey Theatre lecture (*PP* 296).

The first and most famous product of Eliot's use of mythic parallel as a structural device is *The Waste Land*, published in the same year as *Ulysses*, 1922. The likelihood that the structure of *The Waste Land* was influenced by *The Dreaming of the Bones* is reinforced by the play's contribution to the setting of Eliot's poem. Although its ultimate source is the Grail legend, The Perilous Chapel of the final section, with its "tumbled graves" (*CPP* 49), is also Yeats's ruined Abbey of Corcomroe, "amid its broken tombs" (*VPl* 280). The "white road" leading to the Abbey (*VPl* 277) becomes the "white road" of the journey to Emmaus (*CPP* 48), and the cock that supplies the repeated metaphor of Yeats's play crows from the rooftree of Eliot's chapel (*CPP* 49).

By 1925 Eliot had begun another exploration of myth and modern fact in the drafts for *Sweeney Agonistes*. Eliot's comments on the play indicate that he was constructing his fable of modern spiritual desolation on the ritual pattern of the death and resurrection of a god, as set forth in F. M. Cornford's *The Origin of Attic Comedy*.[34] All of Eliot's plays confront modern man with the legendary past in some way. *The Rock* (1934) presents tableaux of the history of the Church while a modern church is constructed. The Knights in *Murder in the Cathedral* (1935) address the audience directly. Each of the later plays has a specific analogue in Greek tragedy: *The Family Reunion* in *The Eumenides, The Cocktail Party* in *Alcestis, The Confidential Clerk* (1954) in *Ion,* and *The Elder Statesman* (1958) in *Oedipus at Colonus.* The mythic method he found in Yeats thus enabled Eliot to go past Shakespeare toward the roots of the Western dramatic tradition. The age of Shakespeare, according to Yeats, had severed myth and fact; Yeats, according to Eliot, had reunited them.

Yeats led Eliot to Shakespeare, rather than past him, with respect to the third achievement for which, in his 1940 lecture, Eliot admired Yeats: the creation of a personal poetry. For Eliot, the interest in the poet's personality aroused by Yeats's later poetry distinguished Yeats from his minor ancestors, the Pre-Raphaelites, and confirmed him in the noblest poetic lineage. Eliot was aware of the anomaly that he, who had become famous for his "Impersonal theory of poetry," should attempt to explain Yeats's greatness in terms of personality. To preserve the basic principle, Eliot distinguished two categories of impersonality and included the personality of Yeats's poetry in the second: "that of the poet who, out of intense and personal experience, is able to express a general truth; retaining all the particularity of his experience, to make of it a general symbol" (*PP* 299). The end result is not impersonal *as poetry.* The second type of impersonality is distinguished from the first precisely in that poetry belonging to the second type retains "the particularity of experience" as the essence of personality. Though experience did not need to be quite as particularized as it was in Yeats's autobiographical poems, Eliot was far from condemning the results Yeats obtained by that practice. The crucial requirement was that the *poet* become impersonal by transforming what was once his particular experience into universal experience. The poet's subjective experience is preserved; yet, at the same time, it is made objective so that the reader might enter into it. Poet and reader alike have the sensation of "Knowing myself yet being someone other," as Eliot describes it in a section of *Little Gidding* that is haunted by Yeats's ghost (1942; *CPP* 141). In this process distinctions such as subject and object, particular and general, or personality and impersonality are ultimately rendered meaningless.

What Eliot is describing in Yeats is a process he had already attributed to Shakespeare in his early essay on "Philip Massinger" (1920): "the transformation of a personality into a personal work of art" in such a way that we are excited by the poet's personality as it has been incorporated in the work and are willing to ignore the poet as he exists apart from the work (SE 192-93). This transference of life to a work of art has its paradigm in the creation of dramatic characters, where the "work" is actually a new personality. It was natural, therefore, that in the Massinger essay Eliot would speak of a personal work of art with respect to drama at the same time that he was advocating impersonal poetry in "Tradition and the Individual Talent." It was also natural that Eliot's own work in the drama would bring him to a new understanding of the same principle, which he formulated as "the third voice" in "The Three Voices of Poetry" (1953). Eliot's playwrighting had shown him that "the third voice," that of a dramatic character, will succeed only if the author identifies himself with the character, though he must not identify the character with himself (PP 99). Something of the character is the author, but something else is not. "The Three Voices of Poetry" concludes that, at its best, as in the work of Shakespeare, poetic drama presents "a world in which the creator is everywhere present, and everywhere hidden" (PP 112). This is the paradox of personality and impersonality that Eliot faced in his lecture on Yeats, probably for the same reason: Eliot had approached Yeats as a dramatist.

If Eliot tolerated the presence of a man named Yeats in poems written by Yeats, it must be because Eliot recognized that the Yeats in the poems was a dramatic character who both was and was not the author. Thus transformed, Yeats as a dramatic character was available to Eliot for use in the last of the Four Quartets, Little Gidding. Yeats's appearance there is anticipated by less personal allusions in earlier Quartets. In Part I of Burnt Norton (1936) the sudden rush of water into a dry pool revives images from *At the Hawk's Well* (*CPP* 118). A stage blackout—another link between Eliot and Yeats forged through the theater—symbolizes a moment of vision in Part III of *East Coker* (1940; *CPP* 126), as it did in Yeats's "Lapis Lazuli" (1938). "The prayer of the bone on the beach" in Part II of *The Dry Salvages* (1941; *CPP* 131) was sung by "a bone upon the shore" in Yeats's "Three Things" (1929). Yeats considered the bones in Eliot's poetry to be typical of his modernism, and, as Yeats asserted, he too was modern.[35]

In the year that *The Dry Salvages* was published, Eliot was at work on the first drafts of *Little Gidding*, trying to strengthen the poem by providing as a submerged foundation "some acute personal reminiscence."[36] Perhaps Yeats's ability to build just such a foundation suggested to Eliot that he make use of his experience with Yeats, transforming that experience into symbol by having Yeats, now dead, appear as a ghost to Eliot as he watches for fires in the streets of London, a situation based on Eliot's wartime service as an air raid warden. In the ghost's face Eliot sees "the sudden look of some dead master / Whom I had known" (*CPP* 140). The shock felt at this recognition doubtless recalls the moment when Eliot, for the first time, recognized Yeats as an ancestor. The autobiographical thrust of Eliot's "I" in this passage confirms the inheritance.

Although the ghost that appears in Part II of *Little Gidding* is "compound" (*CPP* 140), Eliot has told at least three correspondents that he had Yeats in mind.[37] Early drafts of the conclusion to Part II support that acknowledgment by presenting Yeats even more specifically than in the final version.[38] The foreignness that Eliot stressed in his early criticism of Yeats reappears in the ghost, who is claimed by "alien people with an archaic tongue," but Eliot's later admission of Yeats into the English tradition is reflected in the ghost's knowledge of "the strength and weakness of the English tongue." The same draft attempts to weave the ghost into the evolving pattern of fire imagery in *Little Gidding* through an allusion to the "political fire" that was part of Yeats's Irish experience. Another identity explicitly attributed to the ghost at this stage is that of Dante's Brunetto Latini, the sodomite of *Inferno* XV. Eliot decided to generalize his original references to both Yeats and Brunetto, partly because, as he told John Hayward, he did not wish to transfer to Yeats the taint of Brunetto's sin.[39] Since the tone of the final version retains the reverence with which Dante treated Brunetto, Eliot obviously did not mind transferring that treatment to Yeats.

In the final version of *Little Gidding*, specific passages still tie the poem to Yeats. Grover Smith has suggested that Part II opens with the cadence of Yeats's "Nineteen Hundred and Nineteen," Part V (1921). Certainly the reversal of the ballad pattern of alternating four-beat and three-beat lines that gives Eliot, "Ash on an old man's sleeve / Is all the ash the burnt roses leave" (*CPP* 139), is unusual enough to recall Yeats's, "Come let us mock at the great / That had such burdens on the mind." Eliot told Kristian Smidt that the ghost that appears in the next section of Part II has left his "body on a distant shore" (*CPP* 141) because Yeats, who died in France, still lay buried there in 1942. The ghost reveals "the laceration / Of laughter at what ceases to amuse" (*CPP* 142) as one of the gifts reserved for age. Although John Hayward suggested the word "laceration" with the Latin of Swift's epitaph in mind, Eliot would have accepted the suggestion because the allusion to Yeats's translation of "Swift's Epitaph" (1931) would enrich the compound nature of the ghost while preserving the Yeatsian foundation.[40]

The scene of Eliot's meeting with the ghost, derived primarily from Dante, represents Hell to the senses but Purgatory to the mind that knows salvation may be the reward for present pain. As poets, Eliot and his master have been concerned with a special goal of purgation—as the ghost puts it, "To purify the dialect of the tribe" (*CPP* 141). This translation from Mallarmé's "Le Tombeau d'Edgar Poe" reveals another element of the "compound ghost" but by no means excludes Yeats, whose concern for the Irish dialect was made explicit in early drafts and whose "purging out of poetical ornament" had been an important example to Eliot. Eliot may have thought of Yeats more particularly, however, as the ghost turns from

the purgation of language to remorse for past sins, the first
step in purgation of the soul. The memory of "things ill done
and done to others' harm" (*CPP* 142) is part of the ghost's
legacy, as Yeats in "Vacillation" was haunted by "Things said
or done long years ago, / Or things I did not do or say."[41]
Yeats had written a play called *Purgatory*, which Eliot could
not forget, though he had admired it more for its technique
than for its doctrine. The trouble with the latter, Eliot found
in his 1940 lecture, was that Yeats had not allowed for release
from purgation into salvation (*PP* 302). No longer attending
passively on tradition, Eliot made up for the deficiency of
Yeats's play in the last words of the ghost in *Little Gidding*:

> From wrong to wrong the exasperated spirit
> Proceeds, unless restored by that refining fire
> Where you must move in measure, like a dancer.
> (*CPP* 142)

The dancer and the fire, two of Yeats's principal symbols,
have an aesthetic as well as a spiritual meaning in *Little Gid-
ding*, for they represent the process of purgation that created
Eliot's poem. The dancer becomes the dance, as Yeats illus-
trates in "Among School Children" (1927). The artist's per-
sonality, contingent on the complex circumstances of his life,
is refined by the impersonal flame into the self-sufficient per-
sonality of the work of art. Art is itself the refining flame,
process as well as product, as Yeats suggests in "Byzantium"
(1932) when he has the complexities of "blood-begotten spir-
its" refined in the self-sufficiency of "flames begotten of flame"
and then has the spirits become dancers that move like flames:

> Dying into a dance,
> An agony of trance,
> An agony of flame that cannot
> singe a sleeve.[42]

"Any one who has observed one of the great dancers of the
Russian school," Eliot wrote in "Four Elizabethan Drama-
tists" (1924), "will have observed that the man or the woman
whom we admire is a being who exists only during the per-

formances, that it is a personality, a vital flame which appears
from nowhere, disappears into nothing and is complete and
sufficient in its appearance" (*SE* 95). Again Eliot uses the term
"personality" to include "impersonality," in the paradoxical
sense that his study of Yeats helped him to clarify. Personality
was needed to make a work "vital," as Eliot had tried to do
when he incorporated his experience of Yeats in *Little Gid-
ding*. Impersonality was needed to make the work a "flame"
that would rekindle in the work of later poets in the tradition.

THE INHUMAN SELF:
ROBINSON JEFFERS

In theory, Robinson Jeffers takes the doctrine of impersonal
poetry to its farthest extreme. Stevens celebrates the imagi-
nation as the "inhuman author" who composes the world,
but that figure is at home in the mind of the human author
who composes particular poems. Eliot places greater distance
between the poet and the source of his inspiration by locating
the latter in the work of predecessors, but that tradition is
still within the bounds of humanity. These are the bounds
that Jeffers would like to exceed. Jeffers seeks inhumanity not
simply in abstraction from particular men, as Stevens does,
but in the negation of humanity represented by nature, the
not-human. In the "Epilogue" to Jeffers's first volume, *Flagons
and Apples* (1912), the poet insists:

> I, that have lived, and sorrowed, and sinned
> Have spoken no word of my life as it is;
> Have spoken only the ocean's abyss,
> Only the open waves, that kiss,
> And climb on the cliff, and fall, and climb.
>
> (*FA* 45)

Jeffers found Yeats's example applicable even at this extreme
of impersonality, which, because it was an extreme, proved
very difficult to achieve in practice. Nevertheless, Jeffers's phi-
losophy would not permit him to accept, as a practical for-
mula, the paradoxical combination of personality and imper-
sonality that Stevens and Eliot arrived at. Jeffers's impersonal

stance had to break down entirely before he could recognize the value of personality. Once that had happened, Jeffers took full advantage of Yeats's example in writing a poetry more openly personal than anything Stevens or Eliot produced.

The "Epilogue" to *Flagons and Apples* that makes such emphatic claims for the inhumanity of the volume also makes the concession to humanity that Jeffers made most frequently in his later verse. Though a *persona* might be inhuman in origin, it seemed best to make it recognizably human in form, though still impersonal. Jeffers claims to have written of,

> loves of fools, forlorn and forgot,
> And loves of men that witches have caught,
> And loves enough, God wot; but not
> The loves I have lived, nor the life I could write.
>
> (*FA* 45-46)

The impersonality of Yeats's early poetry was based on a similar practice, that of being "shaped by nature and art to some one out of half a dozen traditional poses . . . lover or saint, sage or sensualist, or mere mocker of all life" (*Au* 87). These poses were, as Yeats says, traditional. Thus, Jeffers's adoption of the lover's pose certainly cannot be charged as a debt to Yeats specifically, though the motivation to pose as a means of tapping some fundamental existence derives from a narrower range of influence that includes the early Yeats. The likely influences are even fewer in the case of Jeffers's depersonalizing of the beloved in *Flagons and Apples*. Here it is almost certain that Yeats was the model Jeffers had in mind.

Love of the entrapping witch is exemplified in Jeffers's "To Helen About Her Hair," where the woman is a witch only in her ability to entrap her lover in the beauty of her hair. "Beware when you are combing it," he pleads,

> In the nights and mornings,
> Shaking its splendor out.
>
> I bid you comb it carefully,
> For my soul is caught there,
> Wound in the web of it.
>
> (*FA* 8)

Such obsession with a single aspect of the beloved transforms her from a woman into a symbol, as Ezra Pound had learned only a few years before in his study of Yeats's *The Wind Among the Reeds* (1899). Evidently Jeffers had undertaken a similar study. In *The Wind Among the Reeds* it is the stars, in "He Wishes His Beloved Were Dead," that are "bound and wound" in the hair, but Yeats's soul is caught in other webs, such as the cloths in "He Wishes for the Cloths of Heaven." Drawing further on that poem, Jeffers asks his beloved to comb gently, where Yeats asked his to "Tread softly because you tread on my dreams." The hair imagery stayed with Jeffers into his third volume, *Tamar* (1924), where a lover in the poem *Fauna* cries, "I'll own, / Witch, that you've wound me up in your bright hair."[43]

Yeats followed *The Wind Among the Reeds* with *In the Seven Woods* (1903), in which he took a major step toward humanizing both lover and beloved by admitting the effects of age. There is a momentary hope that such change might make the beloved more approachable, as the friend suggests in "The Folly of Being Comforted":

> One that is ever kind said yesterday:
> 'Your well-belovèd's hair has threads of grey,
> And little shadows come about her eyes;
> Time can but make it easier to be wise. . . .'

Jeffers acknowledges the passage of time in "Something Remembered," another poem from *Flagons and Apples*, which begins:

> The shadow of an old love yesterday
> Went by me on the street. —Oh, far away
> And faint as thro' a veil I saw her face
> Shorn of the old miracle that gave it grace.
>   (*FA* 7)

Despite the disillusioned tone of these passages, each poem goes on to celebrate the triumph of beauty over time. Yeats proclaims that the nobleness of his beloved can only increase as her physical beauty wanes, and Jeffers declares his devotion to a new love who makes former loves pale by comparison and who, since she is compared with a goddess, presumably shares in the goddess's immortality. The real gain in humanity, and the true point of similarity in these passages, lies in the weariness of the *personae*, as reflected in the rhythm of their lives. Jeffers, who later wrote most of his verse in a free long line, evidently studied quite closely the freedom that Yeats could achieve by a few well-placed irregularities, such as the spondee in the penultimate foot of the first line of each passage just quoted, the initial trochee of the fourth line, and the three-syllable word isolated amid monosyllables, also in the fourth line. To stress the weariness of age further, Jeffers uses the word "old" in this one poem with the same insistence Yeats did in the volume in which "The Folly of Being Comforted" appeared.

Although their *personae* as lovers became humanized, Yeats and Jeffers found symbolic treatment of the beloved a difficult habit to unlearn. As late as 1935, in *At the Birth of an Age*, for which Jeffers rewrote a line from Yeats's "His Phoenix" (1916), "I knew a phoenix in my youth" becomes "I knew an eagle in my youth" (*SPRJ* 528), thus making the beloved less mythical, perhaps, but hardly more human. Myth was cultivated in *Flagons and Apples* through Jeffers's practice of addressing several of his poems to Helen, as in "To Helen About Her Hair." For Jeffers, Helen is the name not of a woman but of an impersonal, destructive force embodied in women, including not only the "witch" of *Flagons and Apples* but also the ghostly Helen whose incestuous love seals Tamar Cauldwell's fate in *Tamar* (1924); Helen Thurso in *Thurso's Landing* (1932), who brings death to those who love her; and the legendary Helen of *At the Fall of an Age* (1933), who is escorted by the shades of men who died for her at Troy. In *The Green Helmet and Other Poems*, which first appeared in a private edition in 1910, Yeats had begun to develop a parallel between the destructive beauty of Helen and that of his own beloved, which very likely helped to stimulate Jeffers's use of the myth. The first trade edition of *The Green Helmet* was published in 1912, the same year as *Flagons and Apples*,

making Jeffers appear Yeats's contemporary more than he
would ever seem again. Yeats stands out as the only contem-
porary in a list, including also Shelley, Wordsworth, Milton,
and Tennyson, that Jeffers later drew up to show the poets
whom he had imitated in his early work and whom he still
found "most satisfying."[44]

The first edition of *The Green Helmet* must have been brought
to Jeffers's attention by Una Kall Kuster, who inspired the
love poems of *Flagons and Apples* and who became Jeffers's
wife in 1913. Una had begun a lifelong enthusiasm for Yeats
when a friend had read to her *The Shadowy Waters* (1900).[45]
From the time of her first meeting with Jeffers in 1905, she
seems to have conducted a campaign to shape the poet in her
life in accordance with the poet in her library. It has been
claimed that Una went so far as to arrange for Jeffers to dress
like Yeats, and it is known that she planned equivalent sur-
roundings.[46] After their house near Carmel, California, had
been completed in 1920, Una suggested that Jeffers build a
tower, clearly inspired by Yeats's reports of the tower he was
restoring in Ireland.

Yeats's tower finally enabled him to explore fully the con-
sequences of the tradition of the self. He had been incorpo-
rating autobiographical detail into his poetry for at least a
decade, but that detail had for the most part been given and
thus did not express the self as fully as the tower, which was
chosen or even created. It was created with the understanding
that, in order to become its own tradition, the self required
a heroic dimension. If one was to write of one's home, that
home had better have some outstanding feature, such as the
tower, that offered not only domestic security but also poetic
authority. Such authority would appear to be traditional, but
actually it would derive from a new source. In "A Prayer on
Going into My House" (1918), one of the first poems to refer
to the tower, Yeats values the place for its ability to put him
in touch with the men of the past and the "norm" their lives
have developed. As Yeats's detractors have been fond of point-
ing out, Yeats is claiming ancestors that were not in fact his,
but such criticism misses the point. Yeats is celebrating the

claim itself, not its historical validity. He has discovered that
he can make tradition out of himself and thereby discover
new "norms":

> should I dream
> Sinbad the sailor's brought a painted chest,
> Or image, from beyond the Loadstone Mountain,
> That dream is a norm.

Although Jeffers had announced in the "Epilogue" to *Flag-
ons and Apples* that he intended to reach beyond himself to
the inhuman authority of nature, he was unable, when he
wrote poems about his own house and tower, to avoid the
responsibility that Yeats had placed on the self when he de-
veloped the theme. When Jeffers asserts, in "To the House"
(1924), "I am heaping the bones of the old mother / To build
us a hold against the host of the air" (*SPRJ* 82), he is echoing
Yeats in more than the title phrase from "The Host of the
Air" (1899 version). Jeffers means to point out the refuge to
be found in the earth, whose bones are the stones he uses in
building, but it is the act of building that produces the refuge,
just as it is Yeats's claim to tradition that creates the tradition.
The value Jeffers discovers in nature has its origin in himself.

Jeffers acknowledged that the poet might be the source of
the land's value after he took several trips to Ireland, during
which he found that the country had been made "magical"
by "Yeats and a few others." Places "have the added signif-
icance of the poetry," he wrote.[47] On his first trip in 1929,
Jeffers and his wife visited Yeats's tower, though Yeats was
not home at the time. The visit inspired an attempt by Jeffers
to use his tower to project himself consciously into the sur-
rounding countryside. As Yeats, in "The Tower" (1928), had
moved from himself—"I pace upon the battlements and stare"—
to a review of the stories of Mrs. French, Mary Hynes, and
Hanrahan, so Jeffers "recalls" the story of "Margrave" (1932)
from an analogous position: "I lean on the broad worn stones
of the parapet top" (*SPRJ* 365). By projecting himself into
the landscape, Jeffers seems to accomplish that fusion of sub-
ject and object that could allow the poet to identify his *persona*

with his autobiographical self without violating the standard
of impersonality. Jeffers did not view the enterprise in this
way, however, as is clear from the misgivings expressed within
"Margrave" itself: "I also am not innocent / Of contagion,
but have spread my spirit on the deep world" (*SPRJ* 371). To
avoid contaminating the pure inhumanity of nature, Jeffers
typically eschewed the sort of poem he had produced in "Mar-
grave," keeping its elements separated into either lyric med-
itations on landscape that remains detached from the observer
or long narratives concerning fictional characters. The latter
poems avoid human contamination because they are about
the destruction of humans who, in being destroyed, break
through into a mode of existence that is, in Jeffers's view,
larger, more essential than humanity.

Jeffers's narratives reveal their author's attention to Yeats
principally in their establishment of a specific locale, the locale
announced in the title of Jeffers's second volume, *Californians*
(1916). Jeffers is one of several American poets, including
Williams, Frost, and Lindsay, to have found encouragement
for their regionalism in Yeats's example. Formal echoes of
Yeats, like those that can be detected in some of the poems
of *Flagons and Apples*, diminish in Jeffers's later poems, lyric
as well as narrative, as Jeffers explores the possibilities of the
free long line. Although Yeats provided Jeffers with a form
suited to the larger-than-life characters Jeffers depicted in his
narratives, Yeats's form was dramatic. Consequently, during
the nineteen-twenties Jeffers's interest in Yeats shifted to the
latter's work for the theater and manifested itself in Jeffers's
plays, or dramatic poems.

The major line of Jeffers's dramatic work begins with *The
Tower Beyond Tragedy* (1925), which, though introduced as
a poem, was produced professionally in 1950. This reinter-
pretation of the story of Orestes commenced a series of plays
modeled on Greek tragedy, including *At the Birth of an Age*,
Medea (1946), and *The Cretan Woman* (1954). Yeats has
some relevance here. Una Jeffers compared Yeats's versions
of Sophocles with her husband's version of Euripides' *Medea*,
and that play employs the Yeatsian image of the "wild swan"

that also appears in some of Jeffers's poems.⁴⁸ But Yeats's influence is much more significant in Jeffers's experiments with the Noh play, notably in *Dear Judas*, which was published in 1929 but not produced as a play until 1947.

In Jeffers's opinion, *Dear Judas* was too subtle for the stage, but Michael Myerberg had insisted on attempting a production, "attracted perhaps by 'the fascination of what's difficult,'" Jeffers wrote in the *New York Times* at the time of the production.⁴⁹ The allusion to the title of Yeats's poem about theater work (1910) prepares for Jeffers's confession that *Dear Judas* was modeled on the Japanese Noh plays; as Jeffers acknowedged in private correspondence, he had in mind particularly the Noh as interpreted by Pound and Yeats.⁵⁰ Of the elements of the Noh that Yeats stressed in his essay on "Certain Noble Plays of Japan" (1916), the dance is conspicuously absent in *Dear Judas*. Masks are employed, however, or at least persons identified as "maskers" (*DJ* 10), and the repeated image of the net represents "a playing upon a single metaphor," as Yeats described the practice (*EI* 234). An attribute of the Noh in which Jeffers admitted particular interest in his *New York Times* article is the depiction of a place haunted by spirits historically associated with it. Yeats had employed this strategy in *The Dreaming of the Bones* (1919) and more pertinently in another of the *Four Plays for Dancers*, *Calvary* (1921). Centuries after the tragedy, Yeats's characters haunt the road to Calvary, just as Jeffers's characters haunt the Garden of Gethsemane. The main characters, Jesus, Judas, and Lazarus, appear in both *Calvary* and *Dear Judas*, though Jeffers typically adds Mary as the woman who has been the source of the tragedy.

In the year he wrote *Dear Judas*, Jeffers commended to a correspondent Yeats's *The Unicorn from the Stars* and Franz Werfel's *Goat Song* for the original conceptions that formed the groundwork of each play, and he deemed it "better to fail with such a conception than succeed with a common one."⁵¹ The form of *Calvary*, then, would have been of less concern to Jeffers than its underlying ideas, which prove to have been crucial to the foundation that Jeffers laid for *Dear Judas*. Yeats conceived of *Calvary* as an illustration of a basic distinction in his visionary psychology between objective men, who exist in relation to others, and subjective men, who must exist only for themselves (*VPl* 789). The basic distinction between communal and solitary men fitted neatly into Jeffers's philosophy as it had already been formulated, although Jeffers could not accept Yeats's correlation with objectivity and subjectivity. For Jeffers, communal man was absorbed in mankind and was thus subjective, whereas solitary man was objective, open to the inhuman, to nature. Hence, the use of birds in *Calvary* as symbols of solitude had a quite different meaning for Jeffers than it did for Yeats, but a meaning that nevertheless seemed appropriate. "God has not died for the white heron" (*VPl* 780) is the refrain of Yeats's opening chorus. Jeffers made use of this imagery in his narrative *The Women at Point Sur* (1927), where human beings are "the animals Christ was rumored to have died for," in contrast to "the hawks and gulls [who] are never breakers of solitude."[52] In *Dear Judas*, the contrast between pitying love and possessive love that Jeffers intended to represent in the conflict between Judas and Jesus can be better understood in terms of the distinction between solitary and communal man.[53] Judas, who betrays Jesus because he pities the masses who might submit to Jesus' rule, is communal man; Jesus, who seeks to separate himself from humanity by becoming a god, is solitary. Yeats's Judas responds to Jesus' communal pity with the rebellion of the solitary, betraying Jesus in order to free himself, not others. Jeffers attempts to establish the originality of his conception by reversing the orientation of the two principal characters.

Another uncommon conception that can be traced back from *Dear Judas* to *Calvary* is the theme of consciousness persisting after death. This theme appears in Jeffers's work as early as *Fauna* (1924), but it is especially noticeable around the time *Dear Judas* was written, in "Post Mortem" (1926) and in *Cawdor* (1927). The theoretical justification presented in *Dear Judas*—that "the great passions life was not wide enough for are not so easily exhausted, / But echo in the wood for certain years or milleniums" (*DJ* 42)—probably owes something to the description of the Dreaming Back in Yeats's *A Vision* (*Vision* A, 226-28), though the specific embodiment that Jeffers gave the theme clearly derives from *Calvary*. *Calvary* offered a clarification in dramatic form of a conception of character that Jeffers had been employing in his narratives, the same conception that hindered Jeffers from entering his narratives himself. The central characters of Jeffers's narratives are distinguished by their possession of passions that life is "not wide enough for," that have some existence beyond the life of the individual. To portray such passions, Jeffers needed to move away from ordinary life, not toward it, as he would seem to be doing if he treated himself as one of his characters. Even with the distance provided by fiction, Jeffers could usually convey a sense of inhuman passions only indirectly, through their destructive effect on the personalities that failed to contain them. *Calvary* showed a way of beginning a story after the destruction has occurred, so that we might confront directly the inhuman essences that have been released. "Humanity is the mould to break away from, the crust to break through, the coal to break into fire," Jeffers writes in *Roan Stallion* (1925; *SPRJ* 149). The breakthrough can be accomplished through various means:

> Tragedy that breaks man's face and a white
> fire flies out of it; vision that fools him
> Out of his limits, desire that fools him out of his limits,
> unnatural crime, inhuman science,
> Slit eyes in the mask.

In *Dear Judas*, Jesus is fooled out of his limits by the vision that tells him he is a god. He appears in the play, if not as a god, at least as something inhuman, something at "an immeasurable height above men" (*DJ* 14).

The notion expressed in *Roan Stallion*, that humanity is a mask concealing a more basic inhumanity that occasionally flashes out, suggests the thematic relevance of an important stage device of Yeats's Noh plays: the appearance of actors wearing masks. Jeffers took up the suggestion in *The Bowl of Blood* (1941), which, unlike *Dear Judas*, is a true dance play, with a Dance of Death as its climax. Three Maskers function as a chorus in the manner of Yeats's Musicians, and they put on masks as they assume the roles of various spirits conjured by a medium at the request of Hitler, who wants to question the dead about the success of his ambitions. The conjured spirits, Frederick the Great, Napoleon, and, in ironic contrast, an old army comrade of Hitler's named Ernst Friedenau, represent the larger-than-life passions portrayed in the central characters of *Dear Judas*. Through his use of the chorus of Maskers, however, Jeffers has gone even further toward embodying an inhuman perspective. Their perspective is anonymous, detached from the action, and collective, thus larger than that of any one person, and they speak for impersonality by making the mask the repeated metaphor of the play. Humanity's role in the world, played out through the cycle of life and death, is said to be "only the on and off of a mask" (*BAS* 75). From such distance, Hitler's ambitions seem of little consequence, yet the fact that Jeffers was concerned enough to write a play about Hitler shows that his perspective, though he may regret it, is a human one.

The volume in which *The Bowl of Blood* appears, entitled *Be Angry at the Sun*, is one of Jeffers's most dramatic because his impersonal aesthetic and his personal feelings, which Jeffers as yet could not reconcile, come into open conflict. "Poetry is not private monologue, but I think it is not public speech either; and in general it is the worse for being timely," Jeffers writes in his prefatory note. But he continues, "Yet it is right that a man's views be expressed, though the poetry suffer for it." As I shall show in the next chapter, Yeats's work had been assigned to both poles of Jeffers's argument, the private and the public, often by the same reader at different times. For Jeffers, Yeats had arrived at a happy medium between the two poles, as Jeffers outlined in an essay written in 1948. A great poet must write for some audience, Jeffers argued, but he must not write for either the aesthetes (the private pole) or the average man (the public pole). One contemporary example offered a possible alternative: "There has been a great poet in our time—must I say comparatively great?—an Irishman named Yeats, and he met this problem, but his luck solved it for him."⁵⁴ Events in Ireland had given Yeats the opportunity to write not just for a country but for a nation. Jeffers is assuming, as Whitman did, that when a poet writes for a nation he also writes for himself.

It did not seem likely to Jeffers that America would offer him the opportunity that Ireland had offered Yeats, yet Yeats's example remained of practical importance. *Be Angry at the Sun* shows Yeats returning to Jeffers's poetry, as distinct from his plays, with greater relevance than at any other time since *Flagons and Apples*. One point in common was a vision of the approaching chaos. To Jeffers the signs of the times were as palpable as the animated sphinx, "moving its slow thighs," of Yeats's "The Second Coming" (1920). "We saw them with slow stone strides approach, everyone saw them," writes Jeffers in "Battle (May 28, 1940)" (*BAS* 130). Jeffers echoes Yeats's lines—"The best lack all conviction, while the worst / Are full of passionate intensity"—with those of Bruce Ferguson in "Mara": "All that's good's crippled; every bad thing / Has big hands and strong heart and wings like a hawk" (*BAS* 51). Personal utterance rather than historical vision, however, is Jeffers's greatest debt to Yeats, particularly the late Yeats, in this volume. Crazy Jane, "tired of cursing the Bishop" in "Crazy Jane on the Mountain" (1939), bequeaths her vehemence to Drunken Charlie, the titular hero of a poem in which Jeffers returns to the short, nearly rhyming line:

> I curse the war makers, I curse
> Those that run to the ends of the earth
> To exalt a system or save
> A foreign power or foreign trade.
> (*BAS* 148)

For Jeffers's recognition of Yeats's full achievement, however, fictional characters are less important than autobiographical *personae*, for instance, the old man distracted by a young girl. The opening of "I Shall Laugh Purely"—"Turn from that girl / Your fixed blue eyes" (*BAS* 96)—recalls Yeats's "Politics" (1939), which also deals with the conflict of public and private concerns and the torture of young lusts in an old body. These tensions erupt when Jeffers bursts out, "Why may not an old man run mad?" (*BAS* 97), as Yeats asked in "Why Should Not Old Men Be Mad?" (1939). The tension of Jeffers's entire volume, foreshadowed in the prefatory note and reiterated in the poem "Great Men," is that of the poet who feels compelled to speak at a time when he had "Better been mute as a fish" (*BAS* 127). Yeats had wished, in "All Things Can Tempt Me" (1909), to be "Colder and dumber and deafer than a fish."

In his postwar volume, *The Double Axe* (1948), Jeffers reaffirmed his belief in what he called in his preface the philosophy of "Inhumanism." But in 1950 his wife died, and his philosophy finally collapsed. The pain from which Jeffers could readily abstract himself when it involved man in general now invaded his personal life, and he was forced to confront that life in his art. With "Hungerfield" (1952), which resembles the earlier "Margrave" in its juxtaposition of personal meditation, based on Una's death, and fictional narrative, Jeffers begins a series of poems that assess in detail the circumstances of his life. This project is confessional in the strictest sense, because it expresses Jeffers's conviction of his own inadequacy, his inability to live up to his own philosophy. In "The World's Wonders," from the *Hungerfield* volume (1954), Jeffers concedes, "Humanity has its lesser beauty, impure and painful; we have to harden our hearts to bear it. / I have hardened my heart only a little" (*HOP* 108). It seems likely that Jeffers's sense of vulnerability is not new, for that sense helps to account for the urgency with which he insists that he is not writing about himself in the "Epilogue" to *Flagons and Apples*. What is new at the time of "Hungerfield" is the absence of the defenses Jeffers built around himself and formalized in his doctrine of Inhumanism. Thrown back on himself, Jeffers discovers a new line of defense in a dimension of the self he had not considered before—the same strength Yeats discovered when he looked into himself. The themes employed by Yeats and by Jeffers in his late poetry seem inevitable consequences of that discovery.

The mixture of despair and hope in Jeffers's confessional project is clearly revealed in "The Deer Lay Down Their Bones," also from *Hungerfield and Other Poems* (*HOP* 114-15). Jeffers expresses his predicament by specifying his age, as Yeats did in several poems, and explaining the circumstance of his wife's death. These causes of despair feature in several other poems of the volume, but here Jeffers finds amidst them a possible source of hope in the thought of his granddaughter. Descendants, living embodiments of the tradition of the self, were celebrated as such by Yeats in poems like "A Prayer for My Daughter" (1919). There, the poet is continued not only in the blood of his descendant but also in the world he wishes for her, which is essentially his creation. Jeffers makes a similar prayer for his "Granddaughter" in the poem of that title, published in the posthumous volume *The Beginning and the End* (1963) as part of a group of poems entitled "Autobiographical." "I hope she will find / Powerful protection and a man like a hawk to cover her," writes Jeffers, depending on readers familiar with his poetry to recognize his Yeatsian image of himself.[55]

Jeffers's ability to protect is reasserted in "But I Am Growing Old and Indolent," from the same posthumous volume, where he recalls a pledge from thirty years ago to "Make sacrifices once a year to magic / Horror away from the house."[56] The sacrifices are the doomed characters of Jeffers's narratives—Tamar, Cawdor, and Helen Thurso—whom Jeffers now regards very differently from when he created them or when he recorded his pledge of sacrifice in "Apology for Bad Dreams." In that poem the characters were regarded as substitutes for the self. "Imagine victims / Lest your own flesh be chosen the agonist" was Jeffers's self-admonishment (*SPRJ* 175). Now, having grown old, Jeffers sees his characters as extensions of himself: "my pain, my blood, / They were my creatures." He has grown indolent because, from this perspective, imagination seems pointless; any pain that is to be suffered and any defense against that pain lie within the actual self. Still, by enumerating his *personae*, after the manner of Yeats in "The Circus Animals' Desertion" and Stevens in "As You Leave the

Room," Jeffers is acknowledging that there is a dimension of the self that is imagined. Like Jeffers's granddaughter, for whom he imagined a protected life, Tamar and other *personae* serve as descendants who extend Jeffers into the future.

Thus extended, Jeffers becomes the source of a tradition. But what of that other direction of tradition, the past, that we often consider the only direction? If Jeffers has descendants, does he also have ancestors? In the *Hungerfield* volume he refers to himself as "The Old Stonemason" who thirty years ago "pulled me / Out of the tide-wash" along with the stones that he used to build his tower (*HOP* 110). The obvious intention is to claim the sea, the great mother from which all life sprang, as ultimate, and inhuman, ancestor. But there is another implication here, of which Jeffers is more aware than he was when he wrote "To the House" at the time of building. "The Old Stonemason" speaks not of a biological but of an imaginative origin; the man Robinson Jeffers already existed, but he had not conceived of himself until the time he describes, and he, not the ocean, did the conceiving. He owes the ocean only the blocks from which he builds both his tower and himself. Jeffers thus completes the tradition of the self by making himself his own ancestor, extending himself into the past as well as the future.

In conceiving of himself as a tradition, Jeffers in fact preserves the impersonal aesthetic that he feared he had abandoned. Tradition, as a dimension of the self, is a larger-than-life dimension such as Jeffers had sought to incorporate in the characters of his narratives and plays. As in his early lyrics, Jeffers is still playing a role, presenting a self that has been made, not born, but it is a role based on his own life in a way that the roles of *Flagons and Apples* were designed to avoid. Both types of roles, the personal and the more purely impersonal, could be found in Yeats, but Jeffers eventually decided, as Yeats had, that the personal role was the one that best defended against the threats posed by the modern world. It is appropriate that Jeffers's first intimation of that role and his final recognition of it both involve the building of his house and tower, a symbolic act that can be traced directly to Yeats.

By adopting this theme, Jeffers claims Yeats as well as himself as an ancestor, but the claim is just as willful as that which Yeats made with regard to the past owners of his tower. The boldness of the claim draws attention back to the self and fixes it there.

VI

PUBLIC SPEECH:
THE NINETEEN-THIRTIES

THE PROGRAM of modernization that Yeats announced in 1914 in *Responsibilities* reached its fulfillment in *The Tower*, published in 1928. The natural speech of the earlier volume lent reality to the speaker, but the revival of rhetoric in *The Tower* asserted the existence of a community whom the speaker addressed. Rhythm and diction were employed not merely to express but to persuade; the speaker attempted to speak for others as well as for himself, though those others might be no less an invention of the poet than was the image of himself that he created in his poems. As he explained in 1937, Yeats saw himself as going beyond Whitman because Yeats had set himself the task of creating a public (*EI* x). Although the attendant development of "public speech," as Archibald MacLeish termed it, can be traced through Yeats's volumes published between 1914 and 1928, many readers did not notice it until *The Tower*, partly because of a simple delayed reaction, but more especially because *The Tower* appeared at a time when world conditions seemed to demand that poets reassert the value of community. Exploring the ruins of community, in the manner of Eliot's early verse, would no longer serve, yet the community of religious faith to which Eliot had recently committed himself seemed further removed from contemporary reality than Yeats's Ireland. Ireland, moreover, was a community with which Yeats, as an individual, was often in conflict. This open dissent, lacking within the various orthodoxies of Eliot, Pound, and the leftist literati of the time, probably accounts for the wide influence of Yeats's type of public speech. Poems such as "Nineteen Hundred and Nineteen," "Meditations in Time of Civil War," and the title poem

of *The Tower* showed that it was possible to speak for others
without sacrificing the individual voice. As a result, these poems
won the attention of poets who stood at all points within,
and even outside, the political spectrum.[1]

VERSIONS OF PASTORAL:
TATE, RANSOM, AND WARREN

If Yeats's thought alone is considered, his position toward the
right of the political spectrum places him in the minority among
poets writing in English at the time, though that minority
included such notable figures as Pound and, less stridently,
Eliot. Pound's and Eliot's esteem for tradition, a distinguishing
trait of the political right, permanently alienated them from
the perpetual revolution in America, but there were areas in
America where tradition survived and where poets of the right
could thrive on native soil. Because the traditionalism of the
South especially marked that region as separate—or, as some
charged, backward—a group of Southern writers arose to
defend their region at a time when events such as the Scopes
evolution trial of 1925 and the increased impoverishment of
the Depression made it particularly vulnerable to criticism.
The group, whose most prominent poets were Allen Tate,
John Crowe Ransom, and Robert Penn Warren, came to call
themselves Agrarians because they defended the South as an
agricultural society against the industrial North. Yeats's re-
gionalism was an encouragement in this respect. As Robert
Penn Warren recalls, he and his friends "used to talk about
Yeats and Ireland vis-a-vis England as having a sort of parallel
to the writer in the South, in a retarded and depressed society
facing a big, booming, dominating society."[2]

The Agrarians found the "retarded" condition of the South
a useful standpoint from which to criticize the modern world,
but they adopted that standpoint only polemically, for they
recognized that they were modern themselves, whether they
liked it or not.[3] The question of Yeats's modernism was more
doubtful. In his early work Yeats seemed to be more a part
of his traditional world than the Agrarians were of theirs. At

first, during the early twenties, when the future Agrarians were working together on *The Fugitive* magazine in Nashville, Tennessee, Yeats was a poet to be envied but not imitated, because he was felt to have enjoyed advantages that were no longer available. The chief advantage seemed to be the presence of a myth that still functioned in society, thus providing the basis for a poetry that could assume public assent. Once the Nashville poets recognized that Yeats had made the failure of such assent one of his themes, they were ready to acknowledge Yeats as a modern poet from whom they had much to learn. But that recognition came late (*FR* 60, 179) and brought with it a conception of the poet that did not suit the Agrarian temperament.

Allen Tate, the member of the Nashville group who was always most eager to endorse "modern" trends in contemporary poetry, was the first of the group to appreciate Yeats's modernity. Even in Tate's case the recognition was delayed, though not entirely owing to failure on Tate's part. When Yeats came to Nashville during his 1920 tour of the United States, Tate went to hear his lecture on "My Own Poetry with Illustrative Readings," only to find the readings restricted to early poems such as "The Lake Isle of Innisfree," "The Fiddler of Dooney," "The Song of Wandering Aengus," "The Cap and Bells," and "He Wishes for the Cloths of Heaven," all written before 1900.[4] The distorted impression that Yeats thus encouraged was reinforced in 1922, when Tate began a friendship with Hart Crane, who delayed Tate's discovery of the later Yeats in two ways. Crane himself admired the early Yeats and would only have confirmed the popular notion that Yeats had written his major works in the previous century. On the other hand, Crane introduced Tate to the work of T. S. Eliot, which seemed so startlingly modern that it kept Tate from writing anything for some time.[5] Throughout the twenties, Eliot served Tate so completely as the touchstone of the modern that it would hardly have occurred to Tate to seek an additional touchstone in so unlikely an author as Yeats.

It was no wonder, then, that Tate first pictured Yeats as a

throwback to the time of William Blake, whose credulous mysticism was, in Tate's poem entitled "William Blake" (1922), the antithesis of Tate's modernist skepticism: "For William saw two angels on the point of a needle / As nobody since except W.B. Yeats" (*TCP* 192). Though Tate makes fun of such visionaries, he questions at the end of his poem whether modern men are truly superior or only blind. He is less disturbed by Blake's or Yeats's visions than by his own inability to see them. Failure of vision—more particularly, the vision of the early Yeats—is again the theme in "The Happy Poet Remembers Death" (1923), where the poet remembers also

> how I cursed a dissipated rime
> When despair laughed in fragrant mornings, only
> To rouse a cold Helen when the dawn distills
> Her forsaken beauty upon these quiet hills.[6]

Like the speaker in Yeats's "He Remembers Forgotten Beauty" (1899 version), Tate's poet looks to the past for consolation. Yeats's speaker finds that consolation in a palpable embrace, but Tate's speaker achieves only the vision of a phantom. Yeats, in the poems of *The Green Helmet* volume (1910), celebrates a Helen revived in flesh and blood; Tate's "cold Helen" confronts him with the ethereal indifference of Yeats's "Cold Heaven," from the second edition of *The Green Helmet* (1912).

The terrible alienation recorded in "The Cold Heaven" might have proved to Tate that Yeats, even at this stage, was more modern than he appeared, but Yeats's modernism seems to have crept into Tate's poetry before Tate was aware of it. As readers whose sense of the modern has been partly defined by Yeats, we hear in some of Tate's early poems a dialogue between two of Yeats's voices, modern and premodern. In "Advice to a Young Romanticist" (1924), later entitled "To a Romantic," Tate continues his attack on the supernaturalism with which, in "William Blake," he had linked Yeats explicitly:

         because your clamorous blood
     Beats an impermanent rest
     You think the dead arise
     Westward and fabulous.
                         (*TCP* 7)

In Tate's opinion, clearly, the dead in this poem have no more
chance of rising than did Helen in "The Happy Poet Remem-
bers Death." Yet Tate betrays a nostalgic yearning for the
romantic belief in the return of spirits. The poem's rhythm
mirrors the poet's ambivalence, the short, passionate bursts
seeming to defy traditional meter while in fact maintaining
an emphatic trimeter. The adoption of this meter complicates
the poem's relation to Yeats, for Yeats had made the meter
his own in a brilliant series of poems beginning with "Against
Unworthy Praise" (1910) and culminating in "Easter 1916"
(1916).[7] Yeats often combined this meter with a violent dic-
tion, to which Tate, in the passage quoted, owes particularly
the adjective "clamorous," applied by Yeats to the "clamorous
wings" of "The Wild Swans at Coole" (1917). Thus, against
a doctrine typical of the early Yeats, Tate deployed the tech-
niques of the later Yeats to defend his own position and thereby
certified those techniques at least as modern.

    Writing in 1968, Tate specified the two poems that opened
his eyes to Yeats's modernity: "I remember as if it were yester-
day the impact of 'The Second Coming' and 'In Memory of
Major Robert Gregory.' In retrospect it is difficult to define
or even describe that impact, or explain why I thought these
two poems . . . were entirely new, something that I had not
seen in poetry before. . . . the two poems by Yeats could not
have been written before 1914. I felt at once that here was a
poet with whom, by hard labor, I might make myself contem-
porary" (*EFD* 224-25). In these poems about the disintegra-
tion of the old order, Tate discovered that Yeats had survived
into modern disorder. The myth that underlies each poem
does not assume public assent; it is asserted for the poems as
metaphor more than myth. Under modern conditions, when
all public faiths have been shaken, public poetry must derive

authority from the poet's private assertion. These lessons provided the impact of "In Memory of Major Robert Gregory" and "The Second Coming," published in 1918 and 1920, respectively. Because of the distractions already noted, however, the impact did not register in Tate's work until a decade later.

In 1929 Tate transferred the opening image of "The Second Coming"—the falcon "Turning and turning in the widening gyre" until he cannot hear the falconer's call—to "The Eagle" in his poem of that title:

> Look! whirring on the rind
> Of aether a white eagle,
> Shot out of the mind,
> The windy apple, burning,
>
> Hears no more, past compass
> In his topless flight.
>
> (TCP 29)

In Tate's version the world itself, pictured as a rotting apple, is the center from which the eagle escapes. As the eagle of the mind, the bird charts man's attempt to escape the limitations of the natural world in the infinite spaces of the intellect. Such abstraction was the modern curse, it seemed to Tate, who found support for his analysis in Yeats's work. In his preface to *Reason in Madness* (1941), Tate described the problem through Yeats's phrase "the mad abstract dark," from "On a Picture of a Black Centaur by Edmund Dulac" (1922).[8] In "Fragment of a Meditation" (1935), Abstraction produces Tate's version of the "rough beast" of "The Second Coming":

> Perhaps at the age of thirty one shall see
> In the wide world the prodigies to come:
> The long-gestating Christ, the Agnulus
> Of time, got in the belly of Abstraction
> By Ambition, a bull of pious use.
>
> (TCP 79)

As with Yeats, Tate's Christ is derived not from tradition but
from personal vision, made all the more personal by Tate's
naming of his age, a practice sanctioned by Yeats in *Respon-
sibilities*. Yeats also supplied the pattern, in "Wisdom" (1928)
and "Tom at Cruachan" (1932), for Tate's tracing of alle-
gorical pedigree.

In other poems that bear the mark of "The Second Com-
ing," Tate represents the opposite of abstraction by the sea—
the caldron of raw experience whose destructive power is felt
in Yeats's lines: "The blood-dimmed tide is loosed, and every-
where / The ceremony of innocence is drowned." This power
is loosed in Tate's "Sonnets of the Blood" (1931) when man's
faculties are divided, and there is nothing to prevent the "un-
speaking fury" of the sea of time from fulfilling its impulse
"To drown out him who swears to rectify / Infinity, that has
nor ear nor eye" (*TCP* 53). If abstract man is drowned, how-
ever, perhaps the whole man can survive. This is the paradox
implied by the image of the sea in "Winter Mask" (1942),
which suggests the source of the image in its dedication, "To
the memory of W.B. Yeats," as well as in its final stanza:

> I asked the master Yeats
> Whose great style could not tell
> Why it is man hates
> His own salvation,
> Prefers the way to hell,
> And finds his last safety
> In the self-made curse that bore
> Him towards damnation:
> The drowned undrowned by the sea,
> The sea worth living for.
>
> (*TCP* 113)

A fellow Agrarian, Donald Davidson, objected that this
poem in its original version conceded too much to Yeats. Tate
changed "my master Yeats" to "the master Yeats" in response
to Davidson's objections, but he also pointed out to Davidson
that Yeats was not being treated uncritically. As Tate ex-
plained his intention, "I wanted to acknowledge Yeats as a

great poet, and at the same time ask a question which he never fairly faced (the question of the last stanza); so the 'my master Yeats' is partly ironic; as if to say, through the imitation of his style, 'You are a great stylist, and in that a master, but there's something you evaded.' "⁹ The question of the last stanza, "Why does man seek damnation?" is a restatement of the poem's initial question, "What does man have to live for?" Tate attempts to go beyond Yeats not only in asking the question but also in supplying an answer in the symbol of the sea. The symbol itself, however, is derived from "The Second Coming" and "Byzantium" (1933). It is the sea of experience that continually supplies, in the latter poem, "fresh images"; the "rough beast" of "The Second Coming" is at least a fresh image. If Yeats does not answer Tate's question for all men, he answers it for poets, which is as much as Tate can do. Experience is damnation, but without experience a poet cannot create. "What theme had Homer but original sin?" asks the Heart in Section VII of Yeats's "Vacillation" (1932).

When Tate referred to his imitation of Yeats's style in "Winter Mask," he was probably referring to the trimeter line he had used as early as "Advice to a Young Romanticist." By the time of "Winter Mask," which followed publication of the title poem of *The Tower*, it was even more deeply imbued with Yeatsian associations. But "Winter Mask" also owes important features of style to the second poem Tate named as a manifestation of Yeats's modernity, "In Memory of Major Robert Gregory." I have suggested that the ambivalence inherent in the trimeter line, which seems contemptuous of formal rules but in fact adheres to them quite strictly, expresses Tate's mixed emotions concerning the old order, which he dismisses to the past yet yearns to recapture in the present. The same ambivalence, on a larger scale, is implied in the structure of "In Memory of Major Robert Gregory," which Tate adopts in "Winter Mask." Both poems are elegies, to different degrees, and present appropriately formal façades, yet both poets defy that formality by taking us behind the façade and pointing out what they have not achieved. Tate's understanding of Yeats's method must have been aided by

John Crowe Ransom's discussion of another elegy, Milton's
"Lycidas," which defied formality at strategic points, accord-
ing to Ransom, in order to remind the reader of the man who
was writing the poem.[10]

Unlike Milton in "Lycidas," both Yeats and Tate refer di-
rectly to the writer by intruding the personal "I." In the final
stanza of "In Memory of Major Robert Gregory," Yeats con-
fesses that the plan of his poem has been thwarted by "a
thought / Of that late death":

> I had thought, seeing how bitter is that wind
> That shakes the shutter, to have brought to mind
> All those that manhood tried, or childhood loved
> Or boyish intellect approved,
> With some appropriate commentary on each.

Similarly, in the middle of "Winter Mask" Tate realizes that
his poem has not worked according to plan:

> I supposed two scenes of hell,
> Two human bestiaries,
> Might uncommonly well
> Convey the doom I thought.
>   (TCP 112)

The scenes of hell have not shocked sufficiently because dam-
nation is the normal condition in hell. Tate must go on to
reveal damnation even in the place where man has sought
salvation—in nature, which has been distorted by man's ex-
clusive rationalism. By drawing attention to their shifts in
subject, from the earlier dead to Robert Gregory, from hell
to nature, Yeats and Tate reveal that their real subject is the
writing of the poem or, more accurately, the mind of the poet
at the time of writing.

Having grasped this central subject, we can read the first
stanza of "Winter Mask" with the emphasis on "mind" that
the repetition of the word seems to demand:

> Towards nightfall when the wind
> Tries the eaves and casements
> (A winter wind of the mind

> Long gathering its will)
> I lay the mind's contents
> Bare, as upon a table,
> And ask, in a time of war,
> Whether there is still
> To a mind frivolously dull
> Anything worth living for.
>
> (*TCP* 111)

The baring of the mind, like the baring of the song in Yeats's "A Coat" (1914), promises a treatment of the self that will be specific, but not necessarily unmediated, because the self can be studied through its surroundings. Though the order of images in Tate's stanza might suggest that the stormy weather has produced the poet's mood, what Tate says about the images implies rather that his mood has been projected onto the weather. Nature, as Tate perceives it here, is a reflection of the mind, as it is for Yeats in the final stanza of "In Memory of Major Robert Gregory," in "A Prayer for My Daughter" (1919), and in "Coole Park and Ballylee, 1931" (1932), where "all the rant's a mirror of my mood." These examples from Yeats must have suggested to Tate the connection in his poem between setting and *persona*, between "winter" and "mask."

Tate's *persona* is also projected onto the political setting of his poem, the events of 1942, "a time of war." Through this projection, the individual *persona* is enlarged into a representative of contemporary man, whose collective state of mind makes war inevitable. "Winter Mask" is thus public poetry, but, like Yeats's Meditations "in Time of War" (1920) and "in Time of Civil War" (1923), it examines public issues within the privacy of the individual mind. This perspective is adopted not for convenience but out of necessity, for war is a time when the public world decays and the self is all that is left. As Yeats reports in "Meditations in Time of Civil War":

> We are closed in, and the key is turned
> On our uncertainty; somewhere
> A man is killed, or a house burned,
> Yet no clear fact to be discerned.

Tate's claim in "Winter Mask" that Yeats cannot provide an answer to his questions also reflects the decay of the public world, which includes literary as well as political traditions. What has been lost is lamented, yet, at the same time, there is a sense of satisfaction in declaring the bankruptcy of all that has its origin outside the self. Yeats ends "Meditations in Time of Civil War" by deliberately shutting himself in with his imagination, even though his imagination has just provided horrifying images. At the end of "Winter Mask," Tate finds man's "last safety" in a curse that is "self-made." Yeats's horror and Tate's curse are responses to worlds they have created, externalized, and thus demonized. The public poetry that results is truly poetry, according to Yeats's criterion, because it is made out of a quarrel not with others but with oneself.[11]

Despite Tate's claim to have surpassed Yeats in "Winter Mask," his acknowledgment of Yeats as a master suggests that his experience during the thirties profoundly changed his evaluation of Yeats's status. In an article written for the Yeats memorial issue of the *Southern Review*, published in the year before "Winter Mask," Tate confirms the change and does much to explain the reasons for it. "The profundity of Yeats's vision of the modern world and the depth of its perspective," Tate begins, "have kept me until this occasion from writing anything about the poetry of our time which I most admire" (*SRev* 591). This statement not only revalues Yeats but also implies a devaluation of Eliot, who had blocked Tate's appreciation of Yeats during the twenties. In fact, at the end of his article Tate explicitly compares his two masters, in Yeats's favor, when he asserts that Yeats's poetry is "nearer the center of our main traditions of sensibility and thought than the poetry of Eliot or of Pound" (*SRev* 599). The bulk of the article demonstrates Yeats's centrality but does not clearly explain why Eliot is less central. A later essay, "Poetry Modern and Unmodern" (1968), hints at an explanation: "Philosophically more restless and ambitious than his younger contemporaries, Pound and Eliot, he [Yeats] invented a 'system' that allowed him to speak in his own person and in that manner, also, to wear the disguise of a premodern poet" (*EFD* 235). Tate is pointing to the ambivalence—one foot in the past and one foot in the present—that he exploited in his adaptations of Yeats. The lack of ambivalence, the absolute modernism of Eliot's early poetry had attracted Tate as a young man but now seemed to offer the *persona* a temporal identity that was too limited. The religious assumptions of Eliot's later poetry, in contrast, seemed to reach beyond time, which is farther than Tate wanted to go (1936; *EFD* 550-51). Only within history could the poet speak "in his own person."

If Yeats's "system" allowed him to speak as a modern, that system had to be understood as something other than traditional myth, for possession of such myth was the distinguishing mark of the premodern poet. In his *Southern Review* article, Tate focuses on the key poems "In Memory of Major Robert Gregory" (*SRev* 597) and "The Second Coming" (*SRev* 599) to prove that Yeats's system is not an independent mythology from which, incidentally, poems can be created but is rather an "extended metaphor" (*SRev* 598) that has the creation of poems as its primary purpose. This priority is more obvious in the system of *A Vision*, which Yeats was developing during the twenties, than in the image of Ireland he had begun to fashion much earlier, but Tate now understood both "metaphors" in the same way. With a glance at William Empson, Tate described as "versions of pastoral" both the image of cultural perfection in Byzantium, as presented in *A Vision* (*SRev* 594), and the harmony of noble and peasant that Yeats projected onto Ireland (*SRev* 598). The phrase suggests why Tate changed his assessment of Yeats during the thirties, when the Agrarians were proposing another version of pastoral in their image of the South, with wealthy planter and yeoman farmer standing in for Yeats's noble and peasant. The South, in the Agrarian image, offered precisely that "concrete relation to life undiluted by calculation and abstraction" that Tate credited in the *Southern Review* to Yeats's pastoral (*SRev* 598).

Tate's broad definition of pastoral offers few clues to whatever specific contributions Yeats's pastoral may have made to the poems of Tate and his fellow Agrarians. However, comparison of those poems with traditional pastoral, which the Agrarians knew at firsthand thanks to their classical training at Vanderbilt University, helps to narrow the range of possible influences and to bring Yeats's example into focus. Tate has pointed out that when politics enters Yeats's poetry, "It's always elegiac, and back of it is the recurrent myth, the Golden Age, the Magnus Annus" (*FR* 196). Elegy and the notion of a golden age are the two elements frequent in traditional pastoral that constantly inform Tate's poems. Whether or not there is a dead companion to be lamented, the loss of the golden age itself is the chief cause of grief, as in the lines that Tate cites from "September 1913" (1913) to illustrate Yeats's "elegiac note": "Romantic Ireland's dead and gone, / It's with O'Leary in the grave." These lines represent also a divergence from the pastoral tradition, one specific enough to suggest that when Tate made a similar divergence, he was following Yeats. If "Romantic Ireland" is the golden age in "September 1913," it is, however idealized, located in history rather than myth. The same can be said of Byzantium, as Yeats treats it in *A Vision*, and the same can be said of the antebellum South as it is envisioned by Tate. The extent to which the golden age is historically located distinguishes Tate's generalized pastoral, as in "Idyl" (1926), "Pastoral" (1936), or "Cold Pastoral" (1936), from a series of specifically Southern poems, including "Idiot" (1927), "Ode to the Confederate Dead" (1927), "Emblems" (1931), and "To the Lacedemonians" (1932).

In "To the Lacedemonians," a Confederate Army veteran thinks back on his dead companions and further back to his childhood, where historical pastoral merges with the more traditional natural pastoral:

> Moved, an old dog by me, to field and stream
> In the speaking ease of the fall rain;
> When I was a boy the light on the hills
> Was there because I could see it, not because
> Some special gift of God had put it there.
>   (1936 version; *TCP* 86)

Although a right relation to nature was crucial to the Agrarian philosophy, we might expect Tate in this regard to look to masters other than Yeats, who seems in much of his poetry either to ignore nature or actually to defy it. Yeats is interested in the Irish peasant because he is in touch with the Sidhe, not just with the land, and Yeats's project of "Sailing to Byzantium" (1927) is intended to get him "out of nature." There is, however, a third pastoral locus for Yeats, the region centered on Lady Gregory's Coole Park, where nature takes on a special meaning. Coole is also a place in history, so Yeats's divergence from traditional pastoral applies here as well, but we can recover the course from which Yeats diverged by tracing Tate's favorite among the Coole poems, "In Memory of Major Robert Gregory," back to its predecessor by some months, "Shepherd and Goatherd," Yeats's only attempt at a formal eclogue. "In Memory of Major Robert Gregory" itself is thoroughly traditional in celebrating the dead companion's familiarity with the landscape:

> For all things the delighted eye now sees
> Were loved by him: the old storm-broken trees
> That cast their shadows upon road and bridge;
> The tower set on the stream's edge;
> The ford where drinking cattle make a stir
> Nightly, and startled by that sound
> The water-hen must change her ground.

The feeling for the landscape that made it part of the artist's "secret discipline" contributes to the Unity of Being that Gregory symbolizes for Yeats. For both Yeats and Tate, that Unity is the essence of pastoral, whether it be discovered in the countryside of Coole or in the city of Byzantium, where "religious, aesthetic, and practical life were one," according to a passage from *A Vision* that Tate quoted in the *Southern Review* (*SRev* 594).

Yeats's contribution to the Unity of Being represented in the Agrarian image of the South differed in emphasis depending on which Agrarian was reading him. When Tate read Yeats, the aesthetic life received most attention. The religious life, on the other hand, emerged prominently in Yeats as read by John Crowe Ransom. In 1930, the year when the Agrarian manifesto, *I'll Take My Stand*, was issued, Ransom published *God Without Thunder*, in which he used Yeats's "Down by the Salley Gardens" (1889) to illustrate man's decline from the pastoral golden age, or his fall from the religious Garden of Eden.[12] While still in the salley gardens Yeats's *persona* is advised, Ransom notes, to "take love easy." In the terms of Ransom's book, such love would seek only to enjoy its object, the approach "sanctioned by religion and honored in poetry," as opposed to love that seeks to use its object, which is love in the scientific mode, or lust.[13] Evidently, the lover in Yeats's poem was unable to control his desire, for at the end of the poem, Ransom points out, he is "full of tears." This ending establishes Yeats's poem as an elegy for a lost golden age rather than an escape to an imagined substitute. Escapist poetry, as Ransom later defined it, was romantic in the popular sense of the term, whereas elegiac poetry combined a modern sense of lost innocence with a premodern religious sense.[14] In 1939 Ransom argued that Yeats's achievement was comparable to Shakespeare's in keeping religion alive through unofficial poetry in an age when the official establishment had collapsed.[15]

Unofficial poetry is likely to foster unorthodox religion, as Ransom acknowledged when he assigned to *God Without Thunder* the subtitle, *An Unorthodox Defense of Orthodoxy*. God is no less distant from modern man than is the golden age, yet modern poets must measure that distance because they must somehow deal with God, "the most poetic of all terms possible," according to Ransom's introduction to his first collection of verse, *Poems About God* (1919; *PAG* vi). Chiefly indebted to Frost's quirky simplicity, that volume also demonstrates Ransom's acquaintance with Yeats's ironic allusions to God in his early poetry. Although Yeats seems to encourage retreat to a golden age landscape, the absence of human emotion makes "Into the Twilight" (1909 version) a decidedly cold pastoral, where "river and stream work out their will; / And God stands winding His lonely horn." "And God shone on in merry mood" (*PAG* 20) amid the dancing corn of Ransom's "Grace," even though the blazing sun causes the death of a man hired to harvest God's bounty. The recording of such paradoxical experience does not question the existence of God so much as it demonstrates the tragic significance that the idea of God can confer on poetry. As Ransom said of Yeats, "His gods are true gods rather than easy ones."[16] Because true gods do not make sense, they must be approached through an ironic defiance of sense that also defies orthodoxy. "God is sweetest of all / Discovered in a drinking hall," declares a man in Ransom's "Worship" (*PAG* 39), thus sharing the insight of the most blessed soul who "has seen in the redness of wine / The Incorruptible Rose" in Yeats's "The Blessed" (1897).

At an unorthodox extreme, Ransom places Yeats in the role of a god, with the justification that "the Unknown God has implanted in him that special degree of godhood which consists in the freedom of the aesthetic imagination." This image of Yeats emerged in the poem "Birthday of an Aging Seer" only after Ransom had fully recognized the relevance of Yeats's example to Agrarian ideals.[17] "Birthday of an Aging Seer" was prepared for the final edition of Ransom's *Selected Poems* (1969) as a revision of "Semi-Centennial," published in *The Fugitive* in 1925 to celebrate the fiftieth year of Vanderbilt University. In the revision the "old fugitive" who represented the university in the original marks his sixtieth birthday, as Yeats did, in 1925, and he is given a more individual identity, though he is still not named. Disinherited by the "proper gods," and thus initiated into the modern world, the seer has supplied what is lacking in that world by creating worlds of his own. He describes them in a new stanza that, even more than the agreement in age, confirms his identification with Yeats:

> My worlds are Irish, and it satisfies
> The Irish folk that I should exercise
> The ancestral arts of their theogony.
> I am their god, and they depend on me.

In his poems Yeats created images of Ireland not only for himself but also for the "Irish folk," who to an extraordinary extent remade themselves, Yeats liked to claim, according to his images. At times, as in "The Fisherman" (1916), Yeats presumes only to imagine an ideal audience, but in "The Man and the Echo" (1939) Yeats suggests that real Irishmen fought for independence because Yeats had created an image of their country on the stage. Ideally, the Agrarians wanted their work to have a similar social impact, but they lacked the presumption that allowed Yeats to claim he had created his audience and perhaps even to achieve the effect he claimed. As Ransom recognizes in "Birthday of an Aging Seer," Yeats wrote a very special sort of public poetry, as only the tradition of the self could produce it. To create as well as to describe the public world, a poet had to assume for himself the powers of a god. Ransom's refusal to assume those powers may lie behind his refusal to write poetry for a period of some thirty years, until he took up the revision of earlier poems that produced "Birthday of an Aging Seer."

Meanwhile, in his critical prose Ransom pondered the connection between the poet and the public world, taking Yeats as an important case for study. Ransom's contribution to the Yeats memorial issue of the *Southern Review* offered the generalization, "The enterprise which Yeats likes to follow in his poems is usually some one personal to himself, but the handling of it is public and ontological" (*SRev* 518). With his key term, "ontological," Ransom associates the terms "fundamental," "religious," and "magnificent" (*SRev* 517). Yeats's work is anomalous in being both magnificent and modern, Ransom argues, pointing out the ambivalence that had attracted Tate to Yeats and that characterizes the best work of the Agrarians. Modernity lies in the recognition that man has fallen from a state of idyllic, immediate contact with nature. Magnificence is achieved through the poet's ability to reestablish contact through a poetic leap of faith, the trope (*SRev* 539). This leap brings the poet out of the world of ideas, which we each contain separately in our heads, into the public world in the largest sense, the world of perception—"the world's body," in the phrase that became the title of the book in which Ransom explores these ideas most fully (1938).

The poem in which Ransom first recognized Yeats's ontological quality was "The Lake Isle of Innisfree" (1890). "I regarded the poem as a memorable document, perhaps equal to a fresh charter of poetic rights," Ransom wrote in the *Southern Review*, "because its poet had rediscovered the principle of the local and the particular" (*SRev* 528). He means "local" partly in the geographic sense. As in the case of Allen Tate, Ransom's use of the Southern landscape—for instance in "Conrad in Twilight" (1922), "Old Mansion" (1924), and "Antique Harvesters" (1925)—was encouraged by Yeats's success in writing about Irish places, such as Innisfree. Ransom's rereading of "Innisfree" after Yeats's death produced disappointment only in the observation that the poem was not consistently Irish. The "glories of rhetoric" (*SRev* 548) that Ransom had once admired now seemed out of place as literary importations. But he could still respect "the grim particularistic factuality in the second and third lines" (*SRev* 527), which read "And a small cabin build there, of clay and wattles made: / Nine bean rows will I have there, a hive for the honeybee." These particulars are not limited to Ireland any more than the natural description in poems by the Agrarians is limited to the South. At the most fundamental level, the locale that concerns the poet, in Ransom's view, is the ontological world of things rather than ideas. Yet the things that exist in a poem have an existence beyond themselves, as tropes. They function, as Ransom suggests in *The World's Body*, on a small scale or on a large scale.[18] On a small scale, "the linnet's wings" of "Innisfree" or "a wing's blue sheen" in Ransom's "The Sure Heart" (1922) function as synecdoche.[19] On a large scale, the things in Yeats's or Ransom's poems, by turning the reader back toward the lost ontological world as a whole, function as pastoral.

The fullest development of pastoral in the work of an Agrarian poet occurs in the verse of Robert Penn Warren. Warren emphasizes the momentary realization of the pastoral state in the imagination, whereas his colleagues emphasize the rare-ness of such moments and the difficulty of achieving them in history. This difference was recognized as early as 1924, when Tate addressed "To a Young Romanticist" to Warren. Even before that, Warren was nourishing his romanticism on Yeats's early poems, where he found a model for pastoral. Warren describes his first published poem, "Vision" (1922), as "pretty much an imitation of 'Innisfree' ":

> I shall build me a house where the larkspur blooms
> In a narrow glade in an alder wood,
> Where the sunset shadows make violet glooms
> And a whip-poor-will calls in eerie mood.[20]

Though at this stage the poet has clearly learned nothing from Yeats about diction, "Innisfree" is at least recognizable in Warren's project of building an isolated house in natural surroundings. That project is abandoned at the end of the poem, however, when the poet burns down his house and abruptly leaves the glade, apparently abandoning imitation of Yeats as well. But the melodramatic gesture is meant to underscore the implications of the title, and we are reminded that "Innisfree" also describes only a vision, dreamed in the streets of London. In his own way, each poet frames his vision within the limits of the modern condition.

Warren's later poetry locates the pastoral moment more frequently in the past than in the future, where it is placed in "Vision." The appeal of the Agrarian movement, Warren would agree with Tate, was that it tempered the simplicity of the golden age with the facts of history. As Warren explained, "your simpler world is something I think is always necessary— not a golden age, but the past imaginatively conceived and historically conceived in the strictest readings of the researchers. The past is always a rebuke to the present; it's bound to be, one way or another: it's your great rebuke. It's a better rebuke than any dream of the future" (FR 210). Warren captured the evolving Agrarian vision in a series of poems published together as "Kentucky Mountain Farm" (1935), where the rebuke of the past reveals its pastoral associations by coinciding with the rebuke of nature, the "Rebuke of the

Rocks" referred to in the title of the first poem (*WSP* 319). As in the work of other Agrarians, however, Warren's pastoral is not always explicitly Southern. In "Picnic Remembered" (1936) the speaker is rebuked to the point of regarding himself as dead after he recalls how nature, defined without regional detail, once appeared to him:

> That day, so innocent appeared
> The leaf, the hill, the sky, to us,
> Their structures so harmonious
> And pure, that all we had endured
> Seemed the quaint disaster of a child,
> Now cupboarded, and all the wild
> Grief cancelled; so with what we feared.
> (*WSP* 309-10)

Echoing stylistically the formal harmony of nature, the oratorical syntax and theatrical diction ("all" and "wild" make especially broad gestures) constitute Yeats's contribution to this picnic.

Because the pastoral experience in "Picnic Remembered" is located in the past, Warren can, and does, question the truth of the experience as he could not do in "Vision." To know that truth is to enter into another mode of pastoral—Ransom's ontological pastoral—the sense of the world as real, which both Ransom and Warren regard as a sense of blessedness. Concerning Warren's attempt to uncover the past in its reality, Cleanth Brooks, a friend of Warren's since Nashville days, has noted "resemblances to Yeats in Warren's almost obsessive concern to grasp the truth so that 'All is redeemed, / In knowledge.' "[21] As Ransom would have observed, there are resemblances in the religious nature of each man's concern with "redeeming" the past, the term employed in Brooks's quotation from Warren's *Brother to Dragons* (1953). There are further resemblances in the symbols each man uses to depict the mechanism by which the past is uncovered. "Time unwinds like a falling spool," writes Warren in "Arrogant Law" (1960; *WSP* 198), recalling the unwinding of "Hades' bobbin" in "Byzantium" (1932) and of "Plato's spindle," from which "Time is unwound" in "His Bargain" (1930). Finally, there are resemblances in each man's recognition that the poetry that seeks the truth about the past must seek that truth in the poet's own life. Brooks remarks further concerning Warren: "Again, as with Yeats, there is a tough-minded insistence upon the facts, including the realistic and ugly facts— a fierce refusal to shield one's eyes from what is there."[22] Such realism leads to confessionalism, a project to which Warren has fully committed himself from the mid-fifties in poems that define the poet through his ties to his parents, grandparents, daughter, and son.

Confession may be regarded as a further religious dimension to the work of Yeats and Warren, but Yeats assumes a fuller religious authority by redeeming the past through forgiveness as well as through knowledge. For a poet who accepts the conditions of modernism, forgiveness must be pronounced by the self, as Yeats pronounces it in the final stanza of "A Dialogue of Self and Soul" (1933):

> I am content to follow to its source
> Every event in action or in thought;
> Measure the lot; forgive myself the lot!

So in Warren's "The Mango on the Mango Tree" (1943), where God's separation of man and nature is condemned as the greatest of all sins, redemption of both man and God rests with man: "If I could only say *forgive*" (*WSP* 306). Forgiveness issues in a state of blessedness, of restored harmony between man and his world. The final stanza of "A Dialogue of Self and Soul" continues:

> When such as I cast out remorse
> So great a sweetness flows into the breast
> We must laugh and we must sing,
> We are blest by everything,
> Everything we look upon is blest.

Warren echoes this passage at the end of "The Mango on the Mango Tree," where the reunion of man and mango is conceived of in a pastoral vision:

> And I could leap and laugh and sing
> And it could leap, and everything
> Take hands with us and pace the music in a ring,
>
> And sway like the multitudinous wheat
> In a blessedness so long in forfeit—
> Blest in that blasphemy of love we cannot now repeat.
>
> (*WSP* 307)

But the conditional mood and the concluding negative frame this pastoral no less ironically, though more subtly, than the title and burning of the house do in the early "Vision." Although Warren's poetry records increasing success in grasping the reality of the world, he cannot recapture its innocence, or his own, because he cannot say "forgive." One of Warren's most recent poems, "Evening Hawk" (1975), adopts the viewpoint of a bird "under / Whose eye, unforgiving, the world, unforgiven, swings / Into shadow" (*WSP* 4).

According to Warren's treatment of the theme in his poetry, what hinders forgiveness, since that state is established by an act of speech, is what hinders the establishment of better relations between man and nature generally: the limitations of "the delirious illusion of language," as it is expressed in Warren's "Brotherhood in Pain" (1975; *WSP* 12). However, comparison of Warren with other Agrarian poets and with the Agrarians' image of Yeats makes it seem likely that limitation of the self is as much an obstacle to forgiveness as are the limitations of language. To concede the power of forgiveness to the self is to encroach on God's prerogative. Even in God's absence, neither Ransom nor Warren wished to be so presumptuous, though their interest in writing a public poetry and their interest in Yeats offered powerful temptations to move in that direction.

Both the temptation and the resistance were dramatically illustrated in 1956, when the former Agrarians and their earlier colleagues of *The Fugitive* met for a reunion. During a discussion of the role of the poet, William Yandell Elliott had to object, "Don't think he's God. This is an admiration of human beings which poets too frequently share" (*FR* 161).

Elliott was responding, first, to Allen Tate's comment that the poet's main task is not to communicate but "to create something real in language" and, second, to Andrew Lytle's suggestion, "doesn't he also create his reader, in a sense?" These are the accomplishments the Agrarians discovered in Yeats's example but found they could not take advantage of. By projecting himself, Yeats had created a world, and to people that world he had created an audience in his own image.

VISION OF SURVIVAL:
HORACE GREGORY

Agrarian literature stands at an opposite extreme from the proletarian literature of writers on the left, though the latter, too, embodies a pastoral vision, studied as such in William Empson's *Some Versions of Pastoral* (1935).[23] Just as the "simpler" world of the Southern past serves as a rebuke to the present, so the simplicity of the proletarian hero serves as a rebuke to the sophistication of middle-class intellectuals, who, for the most part, were the producers and consumers of proletarian literature. The curse of much leftist poetry during the thirties, however, was that it failed to maintain the double perspective that created it, becoming simple in itself instead of offering the sophisticated view of simplicity that creates the pastoral dialectic. An outstanding exception to this common failure was the work of Horace Gregory. Many of the characters in Gregory's first volume, *Chelsea Rooming House* (1930), suffer proletarian conditions in the Manhattan slum named in the title, yet the poems that present these characters betray the complex ironies of Eliot's Sweeney poems. Significantly, the dominant mood is that of isolation and despair, not revolutionary ardor. Although Gregory shares the doctrinaire leftists' hope for a future golden age—a further distinction from the backward-looking Agrarians—Gregory's characters are convincingly weighed down by the burden of the past. For Gregory himself, Yeats was part of that burden, to which he had to adjust before he could move on into the future.

Being distantly related to the Gregorys of Coole Park, Horace Gregory inherited Yeats's early poems as part of his boyhood reading, but he grew to dismiss them for the atmosphere of Celtic twilight that seemed foreign to his own concerns. Then he discovered the later Yeats in the poems that appeared in the *Little Review* from 1917 to 1919, and he went back to *Responsibilities* to trace the origins of Yeats's move toward modernity. As Gregory later explained in reference to one of the *Little Review* poems, " 'Solomon to Sheba' showed a new Yeats, livelier and fresher than the youngest of his contemporaries, the very latest poets."[24] Since the subject matter of "Solomon to Sheba" is hardly contemporary, Gregory must have been responding to the freshness of Yeats's style: the simplicity and directness of the diction, the informality of the trimeter rhythm that had attracted Allen Tate, and the earthiness of the imagery that allows Solomon to picture himself as "an old horse in a pound." Yeats was clearly very much alive, but it would take other poems to demonstrate that he was living in the same world as his readers.

Several poems in *The Tower*—most notably, for Gregory, "Meditations in Time of Civil War"—record the impact of contemporary public experience. Yet Gregory felt compelled to warn, in a review written for *Poetry* magazine, that Yeats "has been and still is a bad influence on modern poetry."[25] As "the most distinguished writer of English poetry on his side of the Atlantic," Yeats was bound to be influential. The influence was bad because Yeats was still producing "the old false magic" of such poems as "Two Songs from a Play." Gregory described Yeats's picture to account for the objectionable qualities of his verse: "You see the long hair, the tired eyes focused inward. You can almost hear the soft voice making syllables that are everlasting truths to him but are old lies and old deceptions to the rest of the world." With "eyes focused inward," Yeats could not possibly be open to contemporary experience. Instead, he dreamed of the past, offering magic, lies, and deceptions that were all *old*.

Five years later Gregory dismissed his doubts about Yeats and accepted *The Tower* as the beginning of Yeats's entry into the modern world. This revised opinion followed the publication of *The Winding Stair* (1933), which Gregory found to contain "the summation of experience in the modern world, an experience in which the individual is plunged against the mass to emerge at last as a symbol of all the separate units in that force which he recognizes as his enemy."[26] *The Winding Stair* seemed to convey this recognition most forcefully in the *Words for Music Perhaps* sequence, where Gregory found what he deemed to be the finest lyric in contemporary literature, "I Am of Ireland." There, one man with "stately head" stands apart from the crowd to reject an appeal to become involved in Ireland's disastrous attempts at harmony. Elsewhere in *The Winding Stair*, especially in "Swift's Epitaph," Gregory detected the presence of men who became involved in public affairs to their own undoing. The contentment expressed in "A Dialogue of Self and Soul" showed Gregory that, unlike Swift, Yeats had not been driven mad by his confrontation with the masses, but the two Irishmen shared a "savage indignation" that led Gregory to refer frequently to Swift in his later writing on Yeats.[27]

For Yeats, of course, the confrontation of the individual with the masses was not a new theme. Gregory's admission of Yeats into the modern world depended less on a new element in Yeats than on a new understanding on Gregory's part of what the modern experience involved. In 1933 Gregory found himself as an individual confronted with the mass in two threatening manifestations. Leftist literary critics were judging work by its conformity to political fashion rather than the integrity of its individual vision. Authors who deviated from the political standard were deliberately neglected, a punishment Gregory sought to mitigate by writing reviews of "untouchable" authors, including Yeats (*HJS* 210-11). Despite this rebellion, Gregory agreed with leftist criticism of society. The world that had been thoughtlessly patched together out of the pieces left from World War I was clearly disintegrating, and those who wished to survive into the new world would have to struggle to extract themselves from the chaos. In this conflict, history, the collective mistakes of past and present generations, was the mass in which the individual was plunged. In 1934 Gregory found the courage to face even this greater opponent during a trip into his family's past by way of England and Ireland. While in Ireland, Gregory had an opportunity to learn Yeats's view of the contemporary crisis at firsthand.

The story of Gregory's trip to Ireland is the climax of his book *The House on Jefferson Street: A Cycle of Memories* (1971). He recalls that after being invited to visit England by Bryher (Winifred Ellerman), his fascination with his grandfather Gregory tempted him to include Ireland in his itinerary as one of the few ways to come in touch with a man he had never known. The legend of Gregory's grandfather, who had emigrated from Ireland in his sixties and built the house on Jefferson Street in Milwaukee from which Gregory's memoir takes its title, presented an image of an eccentric, awesome Anglo-Irish patriarch similar to Yeats's image of William Pollexfen. While Gregory toured Dublin, where his grandfather had been an engineer, and while he visited the surrounding countryside, his grandfather was naturally brought to mind. So was Yeats, and the vision of the two Irishmen began to combine in Gregory's mind. The first evidence of that combination appears in the sequence of poems that emerged from Gregory's trip, *Chorus for Survival* (1935). So much of the material in that volume anticipates *The House on Jefferson Street* that *Chorus for Survival* may be considered a memoir in verse. It cannot be a coincidence that this "most frankly personal of Gregory's volumes," in Louis Untermeyer's opinion,[28] was produced at a time when Yeats's influence on Gregory was at its height.

Personal and literary influence prove to be inseparable in a comparison of Gregory's two memoirs. In Poem 19 of *Chorus for Survival* Gregory imagines his grandfather condemning the "Violent war behind each blinded eye" that was characteristic of the Irish (*CS* 120). Interpreting it as a legacy of the recent Irish Civil War, Gregory records this characteristic of Irish eyes in *The House on Jefferson Street*, where he associates it not with his grandfather but with Yeats. The characters of

Yeats's *Words for Music Perhaps* were like the people Gregory met in Ireland. "In them," Gregory wrote, "I heard much of the same discontent, the same slant-eyed distrust of one another" (*HJS* 251). The preoccupation with the eye, both in this passage and in *Chorus for Survival*, may be a reminiscence of the man in "I Am of Ireland" who "cocked a malicious eye."

In *The House on Jefferson Street* the spirit of Gregory's grandfather hovers over Yeats quite literally. Toward the end of his stay in Dublin, Gregory sent Yeats a note of admiration in which the American must have mentioned his grandfather. The next day, Mrs. Yeats contacted Gregory by phone to say that her husband had had a vision of Gregory's grandfather standing on the steps of Trinity College. The apparition had instructed Yeats to speak to Gregory before the latter left Ireland. When Yeats and Gregory met that afternoon at the Kildare Street Club, Yeats was full of ideas about the young social agitators from the "Garrets and Cellars." The phrase must have been in Yeats's mind from rereading the essay (1931) he was just issuing as the introduction to his new play, *The Words upon the Window-Pane* (1934). The play's subject, Jonathan Swift, would have interested Gregory, who was also delighted to have clarification from Yeats about the proper relation of the artist to politics. Gregory recalled in his memoir:

> In conversation, however wild some of his talk may have sounded, Yeats skillfully rode above the nonsense in which political directives were confused with the values of poetry. So much was clear. And he spoke with the authority of an elder poet who had been a Senator of the young Irish Free State, who knew the limitations and treacheries of political action, and who yet remained a poet of the first order. I was not merely impressed by what he said, but ready to be warned against deeper connection with Leftist causes and totalitarian beliefs. (*HJS* 254)

Thus Yeats's conversation further encouraged Gregory in the task of defining himself in opposition to literary-political fashion. Even more important was the encouragement Gregory received in his second task, that of defining himself in opposition to the past, which he accomplished, ironically, with the encouragement of the past itself. However modern his poetry might seem, Yeats was still a figure from the past, especially through his association with Gregory's grandfather. Through Yeats's words, Gregory's ancestry seemed to encourage the younger poet to strike off in a new direction. "It made me feel," Gregory wrote, "that a journey begun many years ago in those visits to my grandfather's house on Jefferson Street had completed its cycle, and that my own progress toward self-knowledge had begun" (*HJS* 254-55). Self-knowledge was the base from which Yeats securely defied literary fashion, from which he built his own tradition. In a review of Norman Jeffares's biography of Yeats (1949), Gregory insisted on reading Yeats's example in this light: "If one looks for moral character in Yeats—the search might well bewilder political and social moralists—the way of discovery lies along the channels of his highly personal devotion to his art. That devotion carried with it the disillusionments and responsibilities of a deeper self-knowledge than that possessed by any other poet of the time through which Yeats lived."[29]

In the context of this admiration for Yeats's self-knowledge, Gregory's earlier image of Yeats's "eyes focused inward" takes on a more favorable connotation, yet Gregory discovered new negative aspects of the inward gaze once he had acknowledged its necessity. In the 1949 review quoted above, Gregory uses Yeats's word "responsibility" to convey the burden of self-knowledge, but at the time of his meeting with Yeats, in the poems of *Chorus for Survival*, Gregory spoke of "bitterness":

> O bitter eyes
> Inward to see the dead,
>   those dead, our dead
> The bitter dying where the old world is dead.
>   (*CS* 124)

This vision could be an essential step in the discovery of a new world, but it could also become trapped in its own bit-

terness, the situation reflected in the "bitter eyes" that Gregory
noted in Yeats's poems and in his own observations in Ireland.
Poem 13 of *Chorus for Survival*, the poem most directly linked
to Gregory's trip to Ireland and one of four pivotal poems in
the sequence that Gregory prints in italics, grounds the im-
agery of bitterness and inwardness in an encounter in Wick-
low:

> I saw the naked, cowering man
> Shrink in the midnight of his eye,
> There, to eat bitterness within,
> And close the door and hide the sin
> That made his withering heart run dry.
>
> (CS 78)

A few lines later, "his eyelid closed the sky," and Gregory
returns from the image of the closed door to the dominant
image of the eye.

Although the theme of being closed within the self pervades
modern literature, Gregory's version can be traced back spe-
cifically to Yeats through the former's identification of the
theme with the eye imagery in *Words for Music Perhaps*. The
image itself, without Yeats's connotations, appears in Greg-
ory's work before Yeats's sequence is likely to have been avail-
able to Gregory. In *Chelsea Rooming House* the title motif
suggests the enclosure of doors rather than of eyelids, but
there are references to "eyelids closed" in "The Metaphysical
Head" and to "the iron-lidded, mysterious eye" in "Interior:
The Suburbs."[30] The retreat from the world represented in
such images is explicitly condemned in Gregory's next volume,
No Retreat (1933), which contains "New York, Cassandra."
In that poem the proletariat finds bitter satisfaction in the fall
of kings, including Macbeth, "sleep festering / under his eye-
lids," and Oedipus, who put out his eyes.[31] The poem con-
cludes, "We shall keep / our eyes though we learn nothing."
That eyes become associated with knowledge in *Chorus for
Survival* indicates the dramatic reevaluation that Yeats's in-
fluence set in motion in Gregory's work. Thereafter, having

gained a sure self-knowledge, Gregory is able to redirect his eyes outward. In "Fortune for Mirabell" (1940), "Spyglass" (1951), and "Boris MacCreary's Abyss" (1961) eyes appear "lidless" to symbolize a vision that connects the inner world with the outer and that shrinks from no truth, however terrible.[32] As a vehicle for that vision, the image derives from Yeats, specifically from "Upon a House Shaken by the Land Agitation" (1910), where the mark of the aristocrat is "the lidless eye that loves the sun." Yeats seems to have shown Gregory not only the way into the self but also the way out again.

The full scope of Yeats's lesson is encapsulated in Poem 13 of *Chorus for Survival*. Just before the Wicklow pauper's "eyelid closed the sky," Gregory mentions his *"venomous, dark unceasing eye,* / That turned on street and town and me" (Gregory's emphasis). The glance here is no doubt partly a reminiscence of the "malicious eye" of the man in Yeats's "I Am of Ireland," yet the action of Gregory's poem suggests another source in "Parnell's Funeral," first published in its entirety in the year Gregory visited Yeats in Ireland. "Come, fix upon me that accusing eye. / I thirst for accusation," Yeats writes. Similarly, Gregory seems to welcome the accusation implied in the eye of the Wicklow peasant, because in that accusation he discovers a bond that leaves both him and the other man less alone.

Although such a bond is not clearly implied in Yeats's poem, it is consistent with the note to the poem, also published in 1934, which Gregory quotes in *The House on Jefferson Street* (*HJS* 254) to represent his conversation with Yeats: "I am Blake's disciple, not Hegel's: 'Contraries are positive. A negation is not a contrary' " (*VPo* 835). Thus, contraries such as the Wicklow pauper and the American tourist form a single whole. When the other man closes his eyelid, Gregory is locked in with him. In that inner world he is able to examine both himself and the other, and he discovers a remarkable similarity:

O heart whose heart is like my own
And not to rest or sleep but climb
Wearily out of earth again
To feed again that venomous eye
That is the manhood of my time,
Whether at home or Wicklow town.

(CS 79)

From this local incident, Gregory constructs a symbol of the
condition of all men in this age, as he had watched Yeats do
before him. "*Words for Music Perhaps*," Gregory wrote in
his prose memoir, "had for its background an atmosphere not
unfamiliar to all men and women of a distracted twentieth
century" (*HJS* 251-52).

The atmosphere that best seemed to characterize the century
was one of death. "The old world is dead" (*CS* 124), Gregory
wrote in a passage already quoted, and those who were part
of that world linger on in a "bitter dying." *Chorus for Survival*
attempts to celebrate Gregory's newly discovered faith in his
ability to survive that figurative death and, perhaps, even the
literal death of the body, as the image of climbing out of the
earth in Poem 13 may suggest. Gregory was fascinated when
his study of Yeats led to his discovery of F.W.H. Myers's
Human Personality and Its Survival of Bodily Death (*HJS*
211). The survival emphasized in *Chorus for Survival*, how-
ever, does not depend on evidence of psychic phenomena but
may be related even more directly to Yeats. Following a path
he had already explored in "Poems for My Daughter," from
No Retreat, Gregory addresses the last poem of *Chorus for
Survival* to his son. "Only the young / shall outlive this dark
hour" (*CS* 127), but the old will live on in the young through
the ties of blood: "your portrait is my mirror." The message
of Yeats's poems to his son and daughter is very different
from Gregory's message, but Yeats was also writing about
himself in such poems, motivated by concerns that were shared
by Gregory, Robinson Jeffers, and, to a lesser extent, Robert
Penn Warren. For all of these men, writing about their children

was partly a means of acquiring self-knowledge. Gregory and
Jeffers also accepted Yeats's assumption that the images a
poet creates for his children are a natural extension of the
tradition of the self into the future.

In his desire to write a public poetry, Gregory transferred
so much value to the future that he severely limited the power
he could claim for himself. The symbolic implications of the
son in *Chorus for Survival* are expanded until Gregory can
address him in the final lines of the sequence as "brother, /
Comrade, son." As brother, he acquires a status equal to the
poet's, but as comrade, he grows even larger to become a
representative of the "millions" who will build the new world.
The explicit treatment of Emerson earlier in the sequence, in
Poem 14, reinforces the implication in Poem 19 that, by ad-
dressing his son, Gregory intends to address the Emersonian
Central Man. In American poets descended from Emerson,
Harold Bloom has found a typical desire to be influenced by
the Central Man, though that figure has yet to appear.[33] The
result of this desire in Gregory is that psychologically, if not
biologically, the father becomes the recipient, not the source,
of the son's energy, a complete reversal of the relationship
between parent and child that obtains in Yeats's work. Yeats
assumes the power to extend a blessing to his descendants
and even to withdraw that blessing if they go astray, as he
threatens in the fourth poem of "Meditations in Time of Civil
War." Yeats's dominance is the more easily maintained be-
cause his family never swells to the dimensions of an entire
society; it remains as a small group placed in opposition to
the larger public world. The poet attempts to speak for the
group, not for the world, and thus improves his chances of
success.

With regard to the past, if not the future, Gregory and Yeats
were in agreement. It was necessary to declare one's immediate
inheritance bankrupt and to strike out on one's own. Insofar
as Yeats was part of Gregory's inheritance, Gregory declared
independence in *Chorus for Survival*. There is little evidence
of Yeats on the surface of Gregory's later work, which con-
tinues to develop the ironic distance that Gregory had already

discovered in Eliot's dramatic monologues. Yeats helped
Gregory to develop not a style but an image of himself. We
can assume that that image forms the foundation even of the
impersonal later work and that the relationship Gregory es-
tablished with Yeats is responsible to some extent even for
the fact that Gregory produced later work at all. In his relation
to Yeats, Gregory could see himself as the son who belonged
to the future.

LANGUAGE OF BELIEF:
ARCHIBALD MACLEISH

Political identities during the nineteen-thirties were disturb-
ingly inconstant. In 1935, when the Marxist weekly *The New
Masses* virtually drummed Horace Gregory out of the Com-
munist movement for his insistence on separating art and
politics, the same paper was offering to pack the house for a
new play by Archibald MacLeish, even though it had previ-
ously condemned MacLeish as a fascist and even though
MacLeish himself considered the play, *Panic*, to be a critique
of economic determinism.[34] For the rest of the decade, the
American Communist party officially regarded MacLeish as
an ally in the Popular Front against fascism.

Meanwhile, Selden Rodman offered a more helpful iden-
tification of both MacLeish and Gregory when he designated
those poets as pioneers of "social symbolism."[35] Social con-
cern drew the poet outward toward the recognition of com-
rades, while, paradoxically, symbolist technique allowed him
to speak for his comrades only in a language that was his
alone, symbols being inevitably private in an age without a
commonly accepted myth. Despite the social disadvantages of
symbolism, Rodman was convinced that any poet who ig-
nored what that mode had achieved in modern poetry would
produce nothing but anachronism. Rodman accorded Yeats
conventional recognition as one of the founders of symbolism,
at least for poetry written in English, but Gregory and MacLeish
looked closer to discover also in Yeats the social concern their
synthesis required.

At first, both Gregory and MacLeish saw Yeats's early symbolism as a means of escape. The younger Gregory condemned such escape as a betrayal of the purpose of modern art, but MacLeish, who began publishing before modernism had established itself, was clearly tempted by Yeats's example. MacLeish built his own Axel's Castle in his first volume, *Tower of Ivory* (1917), which was intended, Lawrence Mason's foreword makes clear, as a refuge from the assaults of "brutal experience."[36] The symbolist retreats not in fear but in contempt of the temporal existence that obscures the truth of eternity. "Time, a taper guttering, / Drops in a slow decay," MacLeish writes in section II of "Realities," obviously echoing the first lines of Yeats's "The Moods" (1893): "Time drops in decay, / Like a candle burnt out."[37] In his second volume, *The Happy Marriage and Other Poems* (1924), MacLeish begins to show some willingness to approach the mundane, but he is so entangled in symbol that he cannot go very far in this new direction. An additional problem is that his symbols are not his own, as in the elegy for "Kenneth," which concludes with a nightmare pastiche of Yeats's Rose poems:

> O Rosa Mundi—in the rose that dies
> Something there is not mystical and far,
> But dear, familiar, sure
> As in a dream the happy voices are,
> Something that lives, that lives, that lives,
>   that does endure.[38]

Yeats's "The Rose of the World" was originally published with the Latin title "Rosa Mundi" (1892). The repetition in the last line of MacLeish's poem and the desire for the near and familiar trail lamely after "To the Rose upon the Rood of Time" (1892): "Come near, come near, come near—Ah, leave me still / A little space for the rose-breath to fill!"

In retrospect MacLeish has dated the emergence of Yeats as a poet of international stature to the time of *Responsibilities*, published the same year, 1914, that MacLeish met Yeats when the latter lectured at Yale.[39] *Responsibilities* proclaims Yeats's success in breaking out of the symbolist castle and finding a home for his symbols in the familiar world, an achievement MacLeish recognized by applying to Yeats's volume Louis MacNeice's observation that it uses the English language "as though it meant business."[40] But this recognition did not come to MacLeish, or to many others, until long after *Responsibilities* appeared. One of the first signs that MacLeish had understood and determined to follow Yeats's lead appears in "Invocation to the Social Muse" (1932). As Horace Gregory was to do shortly, MacLeish drew much criticism by proclaiming in this poem that the poet must remain apolitical:

> He that goes naked goes further at last than another.
> Wrap the bard in a flag or a school and they'll jimmy his
> Door down and be thick in his bed—for a month.
>
> (NCP 296)

Yeats had suggested in "A Coat," which appeared in *Responsibilities*, that "there's more enterprise / In walking naked," free of "old mythologies," open to experience. Though MacLeish was less enterprising than Yeats in borrowing rather than creating his nakedness, both men regarded nakedness as enterprise not only because it entailed a struggle against opposition, but also because it was no less a symbol, a product of craft, than the symbols it rejected.

The change that brought MacLeish the approval of leftists after mid-decade can be measured by comparing the treatment of nakedness in "Invocation to the Social Muse" with that in "Speech to Those Who Say Comrade," from the 1936 volume *Public Speech*. Here the goal is still openness to experience, but MacLeish diverges considerably from Yeats in denying the authenticity of any but shared experience:

> The unshared and single man must cover his
> Loneliness as a girl her shame for the way of
> Life is neither by one man nor by suffering.
>
> (NCP 304)

It would misrepresent MacLeish's divergence from Yeats simply to claim that Yeats speaks for the individual and MacLeish now chooses to speak for a group. Yeats often spoke for his nation or for his tradition, as in "Coole Park and Ballylee, 1931":

> We were the last romantics—chose for theme
> Traditional sanctity and loveliness;
> Whatever's written in what poets name
> The book of the people.

But the authority behind such a statement, already clearly established in earlier stanzas, is the poet's individual voice, the "one man" that MacLeish seems to be ashamed of in "Speech to Those Who Say Comrade." MacLeish defines his poem as a "speech" not with regard to the speaker but with regard to those whom it addresses, a formula sure to produce the rhetoric that Yeats condemned in Wordsworth. Vachel Lindsay had avoided Yeats's condemnation because his reliance on a tradition of popular oratory created a sense of a man behind the words, but MacLeish's oratory is curiously without personal conviction. He attempts to speak for the crowd by becoming the crowd, unaware that he cannot speak for anyone in general unless he speaks for someone in particular.

Some idea of what the particular voice might sound like in MacLeish is provided in *Public Speech* by the sequence entitled "The Woman on the Stair," which, as the history of a love affair, could hardly avoid a personal tone:

> I said your body was still yours
> And bore no bruise where he had been:
> Your mouth was still the mouth I knew,
> The hair was yours, the throat, the skin.
>   (*NCP* 318)

In this poem, the fourth of the sequence, the concentration on what is "said" draws attention, by its exclusion, to the contrasting sense of what is felt by the man behind the words. When MacLeish turns to less intimate subjects, as he does in most of the poems in *Public Speech*, he abandons the delicate irony that gives poetic statement an impression of privacy observed. The poet can assert that he is "Speaking alone for

myself," as he does in the final section of " 'Dover Beach'—
A Note to That Poem," but the imitation of Abbey Theatre
dialect in the lines that follow is enough to belie the assertion:

> it's the steep hill and the
> Toppling lift of the young men I am toward now,
> Waiting for that as the wave for the next wave,
> Let them go over us all I say with the thunder of
> What's to be next in the world. It's we will be
> under it!
>
> (NCP 313)

The lack of opposition here, the willingness with which the
speaker accepts the immersion of his own identity in the wave
of the next generation, is more reminiscent of Horace Greg-
ory's submission to the future than of Yeats's defiance in
"Coole Park and Ballylee."

The plays that MacLeish was writing at this time reveal
even more glaringly than the poems the weakness of his public
speech, because the creation of character is the primary func-
tion of the language of plays, though it may remain secondary
in poems. In *Panic*, for example, the absence of character in
the blind prophet's speech, among others, is especially dam-
aging:

> The violence works in the blood. The living inherit the
> Hard speech of the dead like the seed of a pestilence.
> They carry it close in their mouths and
>   their breath feeds it.
> You yourselves will feed it and will die.
> You yourselves in your own minds will make the
> Fate that murders you. The bursting seed of
> Death is rotting ripe beneath your tongues![41]

Yeats, too, writes of violence and blood to convey the distress
of the times, but fascination mingles with his fear of the "vio-
lence of horses" in "Nineteen Hundred and Nineteen" (1921),
and in "Blood and the Moon" (1928) he claims his share in
the "Odour of blood on the ancestral stair" even as he yearns
for the purity of the moon. Such ambivalence opens up a

dimension of personality that MacLeish's lines fail to uncover, because their meaning does not depend on the involvement of the man who speaks them. It may seem unfair to represent MacLeish with a speech that is intentionally disembodied, oracular, but the point is that such an effect is the logical outcome of the method MacLeish employed more generally. He ends up with the very language that his prophet condemns, the "speech of the dead," which finds its most appropriate expression in the play *The Fall of the City* (1937), where the oracle is a corpse.

An appreciation of the difference in public speech as practiced by Yeats and by MacLeish is necessary to offset the fact that, in theory, MacLeish intended to follow Yeats's example. In his 1938 article "Public Speech and Private Speech in Poetry," MacLeish argued that the task of modern poetry, and of Yeats most typically as "the best of modern poets," was to restore public speech after the perverse interlude of private speech during the nineteenth century, when poets had mistaken the quality of voice that characterizes all great work.[42] Recognizing the polemical value of MacLeish's terminology after reading this article in the *Yale Review*, Yeats reported to Dorothy Wellesley, "It commends me above other modern poets because my language is 'public.' That word, which I had not thought of myself, is a word I want" (*L* 908-09). Yet, along with his letter to Dorothy Wellesley, Yeats included the poem "Politics" as his reply to what he felt to be MacLeish's implication that public poetry must be political. The poem shows Yeats unable to pay attention to politics in the presence of a young girl. Public poetry, Yeats was saying, has its true source in private emotion.

The dichotomy of public and private in MacLeish's argument and the absence of the private voice in the poems he wrote at this time indicate that perhaps Selden Rodman was too hasty in attributing to MacLeish a synthesis of social concern and symbolism. Yeats had achieved such a synthesis by retaining the private speech of the eighteen-nineties and directing it to public, even political themes. He developed what might be called a private rhetoric. During the nineteen-thirties

Yeats finally acknowledged, in the introduction to his *Oxford Book of Modern Verse* (1936), that he and his fellow Rhymers had been wrong in objecting to rhetoric as a poetic vice: "When my generation denounced scientific humanitarian preoccupation, psychological curiosity, rhetoric, we had not found what ailed Victorian literature. The Elizabethans had all these things, especially rhetoric" (*OBMV* xxvi). At one time Yeats seemed to equate rhetoric with the abstraction that he claimed to have eliminated only at Pound's insistence. By 1936 Yeats associated rhetoric with an Elizabethan bravado he did not want eliminated; the key to retaining its vigor was to restrict its scope. The Globe Theatre had to shrink to Lady Cunard's drawing room, where Yeats could address a small circle of friends. If his audience was exclusive, the poet could afford to be inclusive and to strive for a speech that spoke for as well as to a group as intimately as if the poet spoke for himself.

Neither MacLeish nor Horace Gregory achieved a social symbolist synthesis such as Yeats's, and for the same reason: neither man was content to identify the individual with a limited group. Instead, they sought to speak for an entire generation, thus dispersing whatever personal force might have been theirs originally over too broad an area of identification. In his response to "Public Speech and Private Speech in Poetry" Yeats objected to MacLeish's contention that restricted scope, particularly the perspectives furnished by old age and the provincial setting of Ireland, had hindered Yeats in his advance toward public poetry. Again, "Politics," with its lament for the speaker's lost youth, suggests Yeats's answer. For him, Ireland and old age were particularizing agents, serving to ground his poetry in an individual voice that might still have resonance, as Gregory found, beyond its immediate context.

MacLeish eventually came to recognize this function during a rereading of Yeats in the nineteen-fifties, a decade that marks a crucial stage in his relationship to Yeats and in the development of his own poetry. Representing the proper treatment of "The Public World," the chapter on Yeats in MacLeish's *Poetry and Experience* (1960) notes approvingly that the circumstances that gave rise to Yeats's poem "September 1913" (1913) were felt by Yeats to be "tragic not for himself privately, or for mankind under the aspect of eternity, but precisely for the city of Dublin and the people of Ireland in the month of September and in the year 1913—that historical time and place."[43] The gaining of that tenable middle ground between the inaccessible private world and the illimitable public world is the synthesis implied in social symbolism.

The new direction that led MacLeish toward fuller appreciation of Yeats in the nineteen-fifties becomes apparent at the very end of the thirties in an article entitled "Poetry and the Public World," published in 1939.[44] Still remarking the limits of Yeats's achievement, MacLeish wishes to demonstrate how difficult it must be to create a public poetry under modern conditions by pointing out that even so great a poet as Yeats falls short of the goal. More important, however, is the distinction MacLeish draws between the goal of poets before World War I, such as Yeats, Eliot, and Pound, and the goal he recommends to contemporary poets. Before the war, poets responded to literary necessities, MacLeish argues, and their response was to destroy the old conventions. Now poets are confronted with "human and political necessities"—perhaps partly because their predecessors had done such a thorough cleaning of the literary shop—and the response must be to create a "language of acceptance and belief." Although MacLeish separates himself from Yeats in this distinction, he drew closer than ever to Yeats as his pursuit of a constructive "language of belief" led him to recognize Yeats's contribution both to the form and to the content of such a language.

In his search for a form that would serve the language of belief, MacLeish began to consider the symbol in a new light. During the thirties he had built his poems out of extensive sequences of images whose force lay in their concreteness rather than in their suggestion.[45] By the fifties he was experimenting with what might be more properly called symbols rather than images, since they were cultivated intensively rather than extensively, a single symbol often serving to organize a whole poem. The method recalls the symbolism, partly inspired by Yeats, of MacLeish's earliest work, except that his later symbols attempt a condensation of experience rather than a removal from it. If the cumulative images of the middle years evoke history, the later symbols evoke myth, although MacLeish preferred the more limited term "metaphor." "Invent the age! Invent the metaphor!" he exhorts his fellow poets at the end of "Hypocrite Auteur" (1952).[46] The type of symbol he was seeking could give order not only to a poem but also to an era.

"Hypocrite Auteur" demonstrates MacLeish's recognition of Yeats as a master of the mythic symbol as well as of the esoteric symbol, to which MacLeish had first been attracted. The third section of "Hypocrite Auteur" lists three metaphors, each central to its era: the journey of the Magi painted by Botticelli, the suffering of Oedipus in Sophocles' play, and the rape of Leda as depicted in a poem that is unidentified but is clearly meant to be Yeats's "Leda and the Swan" (1924):

> No woman living, when the girl and swan
> Embrace in verses, feels upon
> Her breast the awful thunder of that breast
> Where God, made beast, is by the blood confessed.
>   (NCP 416)

The third line refers to Yeats's description of the swan's embrace of Leda: "He holds her helpless breast upon his breast." But MacLeish ironically employs that image of power to measure the powerlessness of the image itself in its attempt to embrace the reader. Though MacLeish's admiration of Yeats's "awful thunder" shows his respect for Yeats as a mythmaker, "Hypocrite Auteur" insists that Yeats's myth belongs to a former age. Contemporary poets have been wrong to be content with a distant echo of Yeatsian thunder: "And we, like parasite crabs, put on the shell / And drag it at the sea's edge up and down" (NCP 416). MacLeish is repeating the argument of "Poetry and the Public World," that the forms of the prewar generation will not satisfy current need, but he is now willing to admit that the earlier generation, if Yeats is representative, was out to discover new organizing metaphors as well as to reject those of a still earlier time. The method, if not the metaphors it produced, was the same one MacLeish would recommend to his contemporaries.

In fact, the newness of the metaphors themselves might be questioned. If one is after myth, one can be satisfied with only the most elemental symbols; shells, rock, sea, birds are among those used repeatedly by MacLeish in his later work. These symbols have power because they have played a part in what MacLeish, in *Herakles* (1967), calls "the eternal tale, / the oldest story."[47] All that can be new about such symbols is their rediscovery by a new individual in a new set of circumstances. The particular context is so important that it, rather than the symbol itself, becomes the real substance of a poem that has as its ostensible purpose the presentation of the symbol. The drama is in the emergence of the symbol from its context, greeted by the poet's exultant cry, "Another emblem there!" as Yeats exclaims when he watches a swan take flight in "Coole Park and Ballylee, 1931." MacLeish feels a similar excitement in "The Rock in the Sea" (1952), when some "certainty hidden in our hearts before, / Found in the bird its metaphor."[48] Yet, although the symbol is virtually the same as Yeats's, the excitement is not identical because it belongs to "our hearts," not his. The type of symbol that MacLeish chose for his language of belief was inseparable from some suggestion of an individual speaker, a suggestion unfortunately lacking in much of his earlier work.

MacLeish's continuing work as a playwright reflects Yeats's role in the change that was taking place in MacLeish's poems, again perhaps even more clearly than the poems themselves show it. There were, after all, many modern poets in addition to Yeats who dealt in mythic symbols, but in poetic drama only two contemporaries had met with any marked success: Yeats and T. S. Eliot. MacLeish seems to have consciously made a choice between these two models in Yeats's favor. In the foreword to his play *This Music Crept by Me Upon the Waters* (1953), MacLeish considered that an American audience for poetic drama might be found either on Broadway, where Eliot had recently met with success, or in the little theater movement, to which Yeats had devoted himself in Ireland. The latter direction seemed more promising to MacLeish, whose play was produced at the Poet's Theatre in Cambridge, Massachusetts, which staged Yeats's *Purgatory* and *The Player Queen* on other occasions. The acceptance of the limited audience that MacLeish's choice entailed produced a result equivalent to the greater particularization of the speaker evident in MacLeish's poetry at this period. No longer addressing the potential mass audience of his earlier radio plays, *The Fall of the City* and *Air Raid* (1938), MacLeish could allow his characters to address each other in language that, for the most part, persuades the theater audience of the characters' reality.

Realism, in the usual sense of the term, was very far from MacLeish's intention, however. Here was a second issue in which MacLeish preferred Yeats's guidance to Eliot's. In a 1955 article entitled "The Poet as Playwright," MacLeish charged that Eliot's attention to naturalism was a subservience to appearances that obscured the underlying reality. Yeats had been bolder. "Yeats's *Purgatory*," MacLeish wrote, "has no prototype in actuality but it casts its shadow in the country where things *are*."[49] The emergence of this reality from the context of the theater's actuality is the equivalent in MacLeish's plays of what the poems display as the emergence of the symbol from its particular context. Both plays and poems at this period are directed toward reality rather than actuality, myth rather than history. In *This Music Crept by Me Upon the Waters*, reality is experienced in a sudden burst of euphoria such as that which overtakes Yeats in the conclusion, also echoed by Robert Penn Warren, of "A Dialogue of Self and Soul" and in the tea shop of "Vacillation": "It seemed, so great my happiness, / That I was blessed and could bless." Peter Bolt, in MacLeish's play, feels a similar influx of power during his moment of awareness: "such a surge of happiness went over me / Everything was possible" (*Music* 31).

Both Yeats and MacLeish stress the specialness of the symbolic moment by setting it in opposition to the context in which it occurs, though this opposition is at first less apparent in MacLeish. Yeats delights in discovering Love's mansion in the place of excrement, as in "Crazy Jane Talks with the Bishop" (1933), or blessedness in tea shops, as in "Vacillation." MacLeish, on the other hand, seems deliberately to avoid such ironic contrast in *This Music Crept by Me*. He carefully prepares for the advent of blessedness by placing his characters on an island in the Antilles and providing the occasion of a magnificent moonrise. A suggestion of irony enters through a reference to Yeats made by the Englishman, Oliver Oren, who refuses to believe that man can ever regain paradise: "Who was it said his whole life seemed / A preparation for what never happened?" (*Music* 5). Yeats made the remark at the close of *Reveries over Childhood and Youth* (1916; *Au* 106). Oren's view is associated with that of "the modern poet," "the sort for whom / No voyages ever come to shore." Although this generalization is based on Apollinaire, it includes Yeats, who is perpetually sailing to Byzantium even as it recedes from him (*Music* 6).

The outcome of *This Music Crept by Me* demonstrates that, according to Oren's criterion, MacLeish qualifies as a modern poet as well as Yeats and Apollinaire. Peter Bolt discovers his true affinity with Elizabeth Stone, who has also had a vision of reality at moonrise, but just as the two are preparing to go off together to establish their happiness permanently, they are called back to actuality by the disappearance of Peter's wife. Actuality now appears sordidly mundane in contrast to the symbolic revelation the play yielded earlier, but the play as a whole would have been both more plausible and more dramatic if, like Yeats, MacLeish had started out in a more ordinary actuality, where most of us start, after all.

The two principal plays that MacLeish wrote during this period, *This Music Crept by Me* and *J.B.* (1958), both use a tetrameter line that is related to the verse pattern to which T. S. Eliot called attention in Yeats's *Purgatory*, but the modification of Yeats's form did not help MacLeish to solve an old problem. Even in the intimate context of *This Music Crept by Me*, MacLeish could not prevent certain passages from detaching themselves from the characters who are supposed to be speaking, as Denis Donoghue has observed.[50] In *J.B.*, with a character representing the human condition and dialogue between God and Satan, the sepulchral tone of MacLeish's earlier public speech returns in full force. Appropriately, *J.B.* led MacLeish out of the privacy of the Poet's Theatre into public acclaim on Broadway.

This further shift in strategy did not mean that MacLeish had left Yeats's influence behind. The trend toward greater particularization of the speaker continued in MacLeish's poems, if not in the plays, and the content, if not the form, of Yeats's message left some impression on all of MacLeish's later work. That MacLeish had Yeats in mind when he was writing *J.B.* is indicated by the foreword to the actor's edition of the play. To MacLeish, the most intriguing aspect of the Book of Job, on which *J.B.* was based, seemed to be that, after all he had suffered, Job accepted God's gift of life all over again. This implied, MacLeish considered, that life itself was the only answer to man's search for the meaning of life, and he was reminded of Yeats's late pronouncement, "Man can embody truth but he cannot know it" (*L* 922). Both Yeats and Job are involved, then, when at the end of MacLeish's play J.B. concludes, "We can never *know*. . . . We are and that is all our answer."[51]

However limited, such a statement marks the farthest that MacLeish was ever able to go toward the "language of acceptance and belief" that he had urged upon young poets in 1939. Like Allen Tate, who also explored the question through a dialogue with Yeats, MacLeish concluded that the most that modern man could believe in was his own experience. MacLeish repeated Yeats's observation about the embodiment of knowledge in a lecture entitled "Yeats and the Belief in Life" (1957), in which he declared that the solution to the modern hunger for belief was not some dogma to be imposed on life but rather an acceptance of life on its own terms.[52] Again, at the end of his book *Poetry and Experience* MacLeish drew attention to lines from "Vacillation"—"What's the meaning of all song? / 'Let all things pass away' "—to argue that "To face the truth of the passing away of the world and make song of it, make beauty of it, is not to solve the riddle of our mortal lives but perhaps to accomplish something more."[53] The truth of the passing away of the world becomes a source of inspiration for MacLeish as he faces old age.

MacLeish's later poems celebrate life in a manner sometimes deliberately reminiscent of the poems of Yeats's old age. Grover Smith has suggested a relationship between the carnality of Yeats's Crazy Jane and that of Eve of MacLeish's *Songs for Eve* (1954), who sings "Adam, Adam, there are none / Enter flesh but flesh and bone," in "Adams's Jealousy: Eve's Answer."[54] Neither poet's *persona* denies the spirit; rather, each insists that spirit and flesh are not separate and that only the illusion of time makes that separation seem real. "All could be known or shown / If Time were but gone," sings Yeats's *persona* in "Crazy Jane on the Day of Judgment" (1932). MacLeish's "Eve in the Dawn" records the transcendence that Crazy Jane yearns for:

> Our bodies out of Eden leapt
>
> Together to a lifted place
> Past space of time and time of space.
>   (NCP 444)

That their bodies survive this transcendence marks an important difference from the decay of time described in MacLeish's early "Realities."

The carnality of MacLeish's next volume is directly attributable not to an imagined character but to the poet himself. By this time, MacLeish has discovered in himself the voice that he needed all along. "When you're beginning, you *think* you're after scope or direction," MacLeish has said in an interview. "You're really after a believable speaking voice."[55] MacLeish's voice is especially believable in poems that are explicitly confessional, but that voice is at the same time projected through a mask—ironically, the mask of the old man, which MacLeish had previously criticized as a hindrance to Yeats. The title of MacLeish's volume, *"The Wild Old Wicked Man"* (1968), is the same as that of Yeats's poem (1938). In addition, Yeats appears by name in "La Foce," where, stung by the renewal of spring toward the end of his life, MacLeish recalls that "All must run, / Yeats tells us, backward to be new begun" (*NCP* 477). The allusion is to "The Gyres" (1938), where Yeats looks forward to the time when "all things run / On that unfashionable gyre again." Lacking Yeats's belief in reincarnation, MacLeish must face up to the fact that a man's life is one thing that is not renewed, but to go on living with this recognition seems paradoxical. At the beginning of the title poem, MacLeish reflects on the paradox: "Too old for love and still to love!— / Yeats's predicament and mine—all men's" (*NCP* 492). An explanation of the predicament is found in the realization that man's quest for love, like Job's quest for justice, finds its end only in the never-ending stream of experience. The poem is effective because the quest is convincingly described not only as man's in general but as MacLeish's in particular. In that transition from the particular to the general, "Yeats's"–"mine"–"all men's," lies the clue to successful public speech.

VII

PRIVATE LIVES:
THE NINETEEN-FORTIES

THE VARIOUS PUBLIC FAITHS that inspired so much of the poetry of the nineteen-thirties could not survive the successive disillusionments of Stalinism, world war, and cold war, though even without these obstacles, it is doubtful whether poetry could have survived the strain of proclaiming public faith on its own initiative. In recent decades there has been a tendency to restrict the public scope of poetry, not to the point of abandoning public themes, but enough to make at least an equal contest of the conflict between public and private worlds. History is recorded as family history, whether the family consists of blood relatives or fellow artists. A similar restriction is imposed on the *persona*, which becomes more specifically identified with one man, the poet himself. These are the outstanding characteristics of confessional poetry, which has become identified with a group of poets who began to publish during the nineteen-forties, though, as I have already shown, older poets also produced confessional work in the postwar period.

The tradition of the self reaches its culmination in confessional poetry, but within that poetry there are signs of a radical departure from the tradition. As Yeats did, the confessional poet explicitly probes himself in his work. Unlike Yeats, however, the confessional poet often discovers the self to be incapable of filling the void left by the disintegration of the public world. The mere fact of difference may have inspired in the confessional poets the new boldness that characterizes their attitude toward Yeats, a boldness further encouraged by Yeats's death in 1939, whereupon "he became his admirers," as W. H. Auden announced.[1] But beneath the new boldness lies a deep despair, founded on the suspicion that the coherence that Yeats discovered in the self no longer resides there, or anywhere.

A FATHER'S AUTHORITY:
THEODORE ROETHKE

No poet has been bolder in openly challenging Yeats than Theodore Roethke, and no poet has demonstrated more clearly the ambivalence of that challenge. "I take this cadence from a man named Yeats," Roethke writes in the first poem (1953) of "Four for Sir John Davies," but then: "I take it, and I give it back again" (*RCP* 101). Why take it only to give it back? The initial gesture is of course intended to draw attention not to Yeats but to Roethke, the poet in the act of writing the poem and demonstrating his own strength by blithely claiming territory from his predecessor. The immediate return of that territory is probably intended as a further diminishment of Yeats, as if the territory was not worth the claiming, but the history of Roethke's relationship with Yeats suggests that the real motive is Roethke's fear of his own weakness. He calls on Yeats because he does not feel strong enough to rely on himself, and he rejects Yeats because he fears that the stronger presence might obliterate his identity altogether. This dynamic of simultaneous attraction and repulsion links Roethke's poetic treatment of Yeats with that of his father, which in turn links Roethke's poetry to a cardinal theme in the poetry of his generation.

Roethke's insecurity in his dealings with Yeats surfaced early in his career. In December 1937 Roethke wrote to Stanley Kunitz to ask for his judgment on a poem, which he enclosed. "What's troubling me is the 'influence' business," Roethke confessed. "It's so easy to say: 'Yeats: (1) three foot alternate rhymes (2) enumerations'" (*RL* 56). It is certainly easy to say "Yeats" when these criteria are applied to the poem that Ralph Mills, the editor of Roethke's letters, assumes was the one sent to Kunitz. "The Summons" enumerates the evils of the time:

> The human mired, the brute
> Raised up to eminence,
> The mimic following suit
> Until devoid of sense.
>
> (RL 54)

Yeats had used the same verse form to list his charges against his own period in "The Fisherman" (1916):

> The clever man who cries
> The catch-cries of the clown,
> The beating down of the wise
> And great Art beaten down.

In his letter to Kunitz, Roethke explained that he had written his poem as an attempt to turn away from hatred. "The hatred and the pride,— / These can be turned to love," Roethke wrote in "The Summons." The attempt must also be seen as an effort to turn away from Yeats, who derived much of his power from his hatred. In Yeats's "Ribh Considers Christian Love Insufficient" (1934), "Hatred of God may bring the soul to God." Delmore Schwartz recognized Roethke's effort to "answer" Yeats on this theme by suggesting that one of the ways in which Roethke is different from Yeats is that the former's verse is in general more affirmative.[2] The crucial question is whether the power of the poetry rests in the hatred or in the affirmation that transforms it. Does Roethke manage to transfer the power from Yeats's gesture to his own? Unfortunately, the answer in the case of "The Summons" and in much of Roethke's later poetry is a simple no. To deny is always easier than to affirm, of course, but affirmation is all the more difficult in the face of denial stated with Yeats's creative authority.

"The Summons" was not included in Roethke's first volume, *Open House* (1941), but several poems in that volume employ the Yeatsian trimeter or incorporate Yeatsian themes. The title poem does both in declaring Roethke's resolution, like Yeats's in "A Coat" (1914), to write the poetry of nakedness: "I'm naked to the bone, / With nakedness my shield"

(*RCP* 3). Roethke desires a nakedness that goes beyond the flesh "to the bone," because, like Archibald MacLeish, he shares Yeats's desire for a union of spirit and body beyond the temporal world. The mere mortal body seems to deserve the contempt that Yeats expressed when he flaunted beggar's rags to symbolize, as in "Sailing to Byzantium" (1927), the tatters of the mortal dress. So Roethke, in "Epidermal Macabre," wishes that he could dispense with "The rags of my anatomy" to become a "carnal ghost" (*RCP* 18). Further confirmation that Roethke inherited his rags from Yeats can be found in an epigram from the mid-fifties, in which Roethke refers to Yeats as "that Irishman / Who taught me how to wear a ragged sleeve" (*SF* 230).

The frustration involved in the desire for transcendence could arouse rage. Thus in "Nineteen Hundred and Nineteen" (1921), as Yeats observes a swan, symbol of the soul, leaping into the heavens, he comments, "That image can bring wildness, bring a rage / To end all things." Roethke felt a similar rage, which, like the Yeatsian hatred in "The Summons," he saw reason to restrain. The conclusion of "Open House" gives one reason: "Rage warps my clearest cry / To witless agony" (*RCP* 3). When Yeats, too, counseled the restraint of rage, Roethke was willing to express his agreement. There is very little difference between Roethke's "Reply to Censure" and Yeats's "To a Friend Whose Work Has Come to Nothing" (1913). Formally, both poems are written in trimeter with alternating rhyme. Even the number of lines is the same, though Roethke breaks up his poem into four-line stanzas. The message, as Yeats writes, is to "Be secret and exult" in the face of ignorant opposition. Roethke's final stanza also points to a secret contentment:

> The bold wear toughened skin
> That keeps sufficient store
> Of dignity within,
> And quiet at the core.
>   (*RCP* 19)

The poems considered so far involve Roethke's deliberate attempt to adopt or modify Yeats's poetic mask. Another poem from *Open House* presents a different problem. In "For an Amorous Lady" the poet tells the lady in question, "you, my dearest, have a soul / Encompassing fish, flesh, and fowl" (*RCP* 22). Since the poem has very little relation to "Sailing to Byzantium," it is difficult to decide whether the echo of Yeats's "Fish, flesh, or fowl" is of any significance, or whether in fact the phrase can be said to have come from Yeats at all. The problem could be ignored if it represented only an isolated instance, but phrases that could be attributed to Yeats abound in Roethke's verse at all periods. Often Roethke grounds the phrases in natural description, where Yeats's intention was more obviously symbolic. Thus Cuchulain's description of his soul as "a soft feathery shape" in *The Death of Cuchulain* (1939; *VPl* 1060) turns up in Roethke's notebook (1949-1950) as the "small feathery shape" of a seed floating in the wind (*SF* 59). In "The Tower" (1927) the "bird's sleepy cry" heralds the approach of death; "the sleepy cries of the towhee" in Roethke's "The Rose" (1964; *RCP* 196) are primarily a type of birdsong, though secondarily they carry connotations similar to those of Yeats's image.

Sometimes Roethke's Yeatsian phrases accompany his attempt to assume the bardic tone. In "The Changeling" (1952) Roethke writes, "I'll sing beyond the wind / Things of high wit and changes of the moon" (*RCP* 252), as if in answer to Owen Aherne's request, "Sing me the changes of the moon once more," in "The Phases of the Moon " (1919). The same visionary suggestion is intended by Roethke's "Before me / Floats a single star" in "All the Earth, All the Air" (1955; *RCP* 117) and by Yeats's "Before me floats an image, man or shade" in "Byzantium" (1932). On the other hand, two phrases occurring within two lines of each other in "A Walk in Late Summer" (1957) can be traced to Yeats but have merely a neutral function in Roethke. For Roethke a tree is "all out of shape" (*RCP* 144), like the younger generation Yeats describes in "Under Ben Bulben" (1939), and two wood thrush dwell "Beyond the ridge," like Mrs. French "Beyond that ridge" in "The Tower." The only reason we have for suspecting that these phrases derive from Yeats is that so many other phrases are subject to the same suspicion. They indicate

that Roethke was so thoroughly steeped in Yeats that the older
poet had colored even his most elementary diction.

Recognition of the danger that Yeats posed as an influence
from the start of Roethke's career enhances admiration for
the originality that Roethke achieved in *The Lost Son* (1948)
and *Praise to the End!* (1951), the two volumes that followed
Open House. Though Yeats's presence can be detected in
them, that presence is entirely contained within the structure
erected by Roethke. The poems that established Roethke's
reputation, involving his childhood among his father's green-
houses, appear in *The Lost Son*. In one of them, "Frau Bau-
man, Frau Schmidt, and Frau Schwartze," Louis Martz has
noted an echo of Yeats's "The Magi" (1914), but Yeats's
lines—"Now as at all times I can see in the mind's eye, / In
their stiff, painted clothes, the pale unsatisfied ones"—have
been transmuted to a degree unusual for Roethke. As a grown
man he recalls the figures of his childhood:

> Now, when I'm alone and cold in my bed,
> They still hover over me,
> These ancient leathery crones.[3]

As Martz argues, the symbolic dimension of "Frau Bau-
man" is not typical of the greenhouse series as a whole. A
poem such as "Flower Dump" is more representative in its
simple enumeration of the types of vegetation that make up
the dump. But Roethke, as he had told Stanley Kunitz, as-
sociated the technique of enumeration with Yeats, and a poem
from another section of *The Lost Son* demonstrates that
Roethke's image of the dump has a Yeatsian prototype. In
"The Return" Roethke incorporates himself in the dump:

> And I lay down with my life,
> With the rags and rotting clothes,
> With a stump of scraggy fang
> Bared for a hunter's boot.
>
>   (*RCP* 45)

Here again are Yeats's rags, in a setting that closely resembles
"the foul rag-and-bone shop" of "The Circus Animals' De-

sertion" (1939), a poem to which every confessional poet has
had to respond. The "Old kettles, old bottles, and a broken
can" of Yeats's poem are juxtaposed with the flower dump
in the title poem of Roethke's posthumous volume, *The Far
Field* (1964):

> Not too far away from the ever-changing flower-dump,
> Among the tin cans, tires, rusted pipes,
>   broken machinery,—
> One learned of the eternal.
>
> (RCP 193)

The Lost Son is Roethke's initial attempt to recover knowledge
of the eternal by sorting through the flower dump of his own
life. The volume has aptly been cited as a seminal work in the
development of confessional poetry.[4]

The combination of nursery rhyme and surrealist illogicality
in the poems of *Praise to the End!*, which followed *The Lost
Son*, allows little room for verbal echoes of Yeats, but these
poems continue Roethke's effort to come to terms with his
past and thus prepare the ground for his open acknowledg-
ment of Yeats as an ancestor. Roethke's progress can be meas-
ured by a comparison of the poem "Feud" in *Open House*,
which warns of "The menace of ancestral eyes" (RCP 4), with
the poem "Unfold! Unfold!" in *Praise to the End!*, which
concludes:

> In their harsh thickets
> The dead thrash.
> They help.
>
> (RCP 87)

Yeats had recorded a similar recognition in "Blood and the
Moon" (1928). Though there is menace in the "Odour of
blood on the ancestral stair," Yeats calls on his ancestors for
help, because "wisdom is the property of the dead."

In the year following the publication of *Praise to the End!*,
Roethke had an experience he later recounted as proof that
the dead can help. After a long period during which Roethke's
inspiration seemed to have deserted him, the poem "The Dance"

suddenly wrote itself within the space of one hour. This is the poem in which Roethke boasts, "I take this cadence from a man named Yeats" (*RCP* 101), and his account of the poem's creation explains why:

> I walked around, and I wept; and I knelt down—I always do after I've written what I know is a good piece. But at the same time I had, as God is my witness, the actual sense of a Presence—as if Yeats himself were *in* that room. The experience was in a way terrifying, for it lasted at least half an hour. That house, I repeat, was charged with a psychic presence: the very walls seemed to shimmer. I wept for joy. At last I was somebody again. He, they— the poets dead—were with me.   (*PC* 24)

In a notebook entry made around the time of his vision Roethke formulated Yeats's solution to the problem of loss of inspiration: "When he ran out of material, Yeats invented himself" (*SF* 201). When Roethke ran up against the same problem, he invented Yeats, thereby seriously impairing his chances of being himself.

Others besides Yeats contributed to the "Four for Sir John Davies" sequence that "The Dance" introduced in *The Waking* (1953). The debt Roethke acknowledged to Peter Viereck leads directly back to Yeats. In a review of the past year's poetry in the *Atlantic Monthly* for January 1952, Viereck had named Yeats's *Collected Poems* and Roethke's *Praise to the End!* as "the two most exciting poetry events of 1951."[5] That compliment was in Roethke's mind in 1953 when he sent Viereck a copy of the Davies sequence with an accompanying note: "I am certain my unconscious was stirred by your linking my name with Yeats' in *The Atlantic* review. Both consciously and unconsciously I set out to live up to your high praise" (*RL* 191). Consciously, Roethke had been moved to link himself with Yeats in the final stanza of "The Dance," perhaps thereby stimulating his unconscious to produce Yeats's ghost.

In the same letter to Viereck, Roethke commented on the style of his sequence: "As you'll see, it goes back to the very plain style of the 16th century—Ralegh and Davies, himself,

really not Willie Yeats." Although this attribution, made even
in the title of the sequence, seems plausible, it is difficult to
pin down precisely what Roethke learned from the sixteenth
century. In the twentieth century Roethke's style seems any-
thing but plain. It resembles rather a combination of the Yeats-
ian high style and the extravagant low style of Crazy Jane.
The two types can be isolated in two rhetorical questions,
another Yeatsian device, from the third poem, "The Wraith."
"What shape leaped forward at the sensual cry?" (*RCP* 103)
leads into reverie, and "Did each become the other in that
play?" (*RCP* 102) recalls "Crazy Jane Grown Old Looks at
the Dancers" (1930): "Did he die or did she die? / Seemed to
die or died they both?" Even if Roethke had not mentioned
Yeats by name, Yeats's signature in the Davies sequence could
be read in apparently purposeless echoes like those noted ear-
lier. The "body of his fate" from Poem 2, "The Partner" (*RCP*
102), is derived from the Body of Fate in Yeats's *A Vision*,
and "thought comes round again" in Poem 4, "The Vigil"
(*RCP* 103), echoes "prayer comes round again" in Yeats's "A
Prayer for Old Age" (1934).[6]
   If Roethke understands style to include meter and stanza
form, the resemblance between him and Davies extends no
farther than the fact that both wrote in pentameter. Davies's
Orchestra, with which Roethke evidently wishes his sequence
compared on grounds of sharing the dance as subject, was
written in a seven-line stanza. The stanza of Roethke's se-
quence consists of six lines rhyming in the *a b a b c c* pattern
employed by Yeats with varying meters in "The Scholars"
(1915), "At Algeciras—A Meditation upon Death" (1929),
"His Confidence" (1930), "His Bargain" (1930), and "The
Crazed Moon" (1932). The specific cadence for which Roethke
credits Yeats in "The Dance" is probably the concluding pen-
tameter couplet that Yeats developed in his adaptation of the
high style to *ottava rima*, admired as an innovation by W. H.
Auden.[7]
   Another candidate for recognition as the Muse of Roethke's
sequence is Beatrice O'Connell, the woman whom Roethke
married in January 1953. Her candidacy is supported on in-

ternal evidence by the fact that Roethke mentions Dante's
Beatrice in "The Vigil" and by the fact that the entire sequence
seems to be celebrating Roethke's discovery of a partner for
the dance, which is developed as a metaphor for sexual love.
But Mrs. Roethke has told Karl Malkoff that "The Vigil" was
written before she and Roethke were well acquainted.[8] More-
over, the theme of sexual love as it appears in the sequence
is itself a metaphor for Roethke's main interest, the union of
body and soul. In "The Dance" Roethke explicitly states that
he began by "dancing all alone" (RCP 101), and at the end
of "The Partner" he identifies the dancing couple with two
aspects of himself: "The body and the soul know how to play /
In that dark world where gods have lost their way" (RCP
102).

The principal partner that Roethke discovered is the body,
in its transcendent form, as an ally of the spirit. "The flesh
can make the spirit visible," Roethke writes (RCP 102), and
he demonstrates that thesis when the spirit emerges from the
dance as "The Wraith" of the poem of that title. Roethke's
treatment of these themes provides a further link to Yeats.
Not only did Yeats use the dance as a metaphor for sexual
love in poems such as "Crazy Jane Grown Old Looks at the
Dancers," but in "Among School Children" (1927) the dance
symbolizes a state of being in which "body is not bruised to
pleasure soul."[9] Normally, body and soul appear as antago-
nists, but in visionary moments, such as Yeats records at the
end of "Among School Children," the body unites with the
soul—serves, in fact, to make it visible. That vision is asso-
ciated with Yeats even in Roethke's earliest poetry. It is no
accident that when Roethke thought he had learned how to
make the spirit visible, Yeats's spirit became visible to him.

The recognition that the spirit requires flesh for its embod-
iment is one theme of Roethke's sequence "The Dying Man,"
which appeared in his next volume, Words for the Wind (1958).
Here there can be less dispute about the presiding spirit, for
the entire sequence is dedicated "In Memoriam: W. B. Yeats,"
yet Yeats becomes identified with Roethke's father and with
Roethke himself. The reconciliation of father and son is related

to the reconciliation of spirit and body. The dance, which symbolizes the latter reconciliation in the Davies sequence, links the living and the dead in "The Dying Man." Perhaps recalling that the titular hero of Yeats's "Tom O'Roughley" (1918) was prepared to dance on the grave of his dearest friend, Roethke declares, "All sensual love's but dancing on a grave" (*RCP* 148). Love and the dance both offer access to the spiritual state reached also through death. Thus the living, "Caught in the dying light," can be illuminated by death, an improvement over the condition of the young who are "Caught in that sensual music" in "Sailing to Byzantium."[10] But the dead in Roethke's poem require the bodily existence of the living: "A ghost comes out of the unconscious mind / To grope my sill: It moans to be reborn" (*RCP* 148).

Roethke is willing to entertain the dead because, like Yeats of "The Tower," he has a question for them. Yeats's "I would question all" is echoed by Roethke's "I dared to question all" (*RCP* 148), and the import of the questions is similar. The first question of "The Tower" is whether Yeats's predecessors "raged" as he does against their aging bodies, and Roethke implicitly wants to know if he must continue as "A spirit raging at the visible" (*RCP* 149). Is embodiment, through the dance, or disembodiment, through the grave, the preferable manifestation for the spirit? The desire of the dead to be reborn symbolizes Roethke's conclusion that he must love visible, embodied existence as they do. Paradoxically, Roethke reports that "I thought myself reborn" (*RCP* 148) after his glimpse through the eyes of the dying man. A similar impression was left when Yeats's ghost visited Roethke after he had written "The Dance": "I was somebody again."

After rebirth, however, the question that Roethke must always confront is whether he is truly himself again or simply a vehicle for the reborn spirits of the dead. In the first poem of "The Dying Man" Roethke effaces himself by supplying the father-figure of the poem with a speech set in quotation marks and couched in a trimeter beat in which Yeats would have felt comfortable. In the third poem Roethke admits, "I found my father when I did my work, / Only to lose myself in this small dark" (*RCP* 148). Yeats is referred to as one of Roethke's "fathers in eternity" in a notebook entry from the late fifties (*SF* 230), and the correlation of Yeats with Roethke's mortal father in "The Dying Man" is unmistakable. Both men represented the ultimate authority that brought order, to Yeats's verses or to Otto Roethke's greenhouses. In *The Lost Son* Theodore Roethke realized the benefit of appeal to that authority, but, despite frequent blustering, he seems to have assumed that he could never discover a similar authority in himself. His attitude toward the father-figure remains a mixture of attraction and fear, the latter a response to the threat of being lost in the father's shadow. A characteristic movement in Roethke's poems is an approach to the father's authority, followed by a wary retreat, as at the end of "The Dying Man": "The edges of the summit still appall / When we brood on the dead or the beloved" (*RCP* 150). Language characteristic of Yeats, who was "appalled" in "Vacillation" (1932) and who sought to "brood" no more in "Who Goes with Fergus?" (1892), confirms the persistence of Roethke's brooding on the dead.

Brooding on the beloved was the other obsession that brought Roethke closest to Yeats. *Words for the Wind* and *The Far Field* both contain a section of "Love Poems." The sequence in the later volume is evidently organized on the principles of the exchange between the young man and girl in *Words for Music Perhaps* (1932), as indicated by the Yeatsian titles "Her Words," "Her Reticence," "Her Longing," "Her Foreboding." Yeats's presence is felt more strongly in Roethke's earlier sequence, however. There, the characterization of the beloved is indebted to Yeats's portrayal of Maud Gonne's dual nature, "Half-lion, half-child," in "Against Unworthy Praise" (1910). Roethke's beloved is less human, "Half-bird, half-animal" in "Memory" (*RCP* 136), but her gestures are similar to other depictions of Maud. In "All the Earth, All the Air," "she shakes out her hair" (*RCP* 116) as the beloved is fond of doing in *The Wind Among the Reeds* (1899), and the hair becomes a trap, causing the lover in "The Swan" to cry out, "Must I stay tangled in that lively hair?" (*RCP* 135). His plight is that of the lover in "Brown Penny" (1910), who is "looped in the loops of her hair," but his cry takes its form from the last line of "He Thinks of His Past Greatness When a Part of the Constellations of Heaven" (1898): "Must I endure your amorous cries?"

Two of the love poems in *Words for the Wind* weave echoes of Yeats into the familiar theme of the transcendent union of body and spirit. The transcendence cannot be merely intellectual. Roethke implies this lesson in the second stanza of "The Pure Fury" (*RCP* 128) by juxtaposing Parmenides, Boehme, and Plato with the woman he loves, who confounds philosophic speculation merely by her physical appearance or the sound of her voice. Yeats also granted the body the last deflating word after a similar list of philosophers in the sixth stanza of "Among School Children."[11] Both poets agree, then, that the body must not be left behind in the transcendence they seek, but that they seek transcendence is confirmed by another passage, like that in "The Dying Man," which connects the alternative means of transcendence, love and death. In what is no doubt an unconscious recollection of the title of Yeats's "A Dream of Death" (1891), "The Pure Fury" associates a "Dream of a woman, and a dream of death" (*RCP* 129). Death, however, is assigned different objects by Yeats and Roethke in this case, which represents a signal disagreement between the two poets. Yeats dreams of the death of the beloved; Roethke, of the death of the self, for in his fury he is "out for his own blood" (*RCP* 128). The title poem of *Words for the Wind* clarifies the connection of such a death with love, for at the end of that poem Roethke rejoices at having lost himself in the beloved:

> And I dance round and round,
> A fond and foolish man,
> And see and suffer myself
> In another being at last.
>   (*RCP* 121)

The meter, the dance, and the mask of the "foolish, passionate man," as Yeats put it in "A Prayer for Old Age," suggest that, just as Roethke sought to become his beloved, he was also engaged in a project to become Yeats. His countless imitations argue a question not merely of technique but of identity.

The mystical experience of seeing oneself in another being would have to be difficult to present in prose, and Roethke usually decided not to try. Thus, when W. D. Snodgrass criticized the love poems in *Words for the Wind* for what he felt to be a tiresome recurrence of Yeats's voice, Roethke simply became annoyed. He was happy whenever his name appeared in a " 'not since Yeats' notey," but he naturally was not pleased to have resemblance to Yeats taken as a sign of failure.[12] In reacting to Snodgrass's review, Roethke denied that Yeats could be detected in the love poems; he was sure that in that genre, though not in the genre of "historical lyrics," he had surpassed Yeats.

The poem "In a Dark Time" (1961) provided another occasion on which Roethke denied the claims of critics who heard Yeats in his verse. Roethke participated with John Crowe Ransom, Babette Deutsch, and Stanley Kunitz in a symposium for which "In a Dark Time" served as text. Deutsch interpreted the heron mentioned in the poem in the light of the herons in Yeats's *Calvary* (1921) and *The Herne's Egg* (1938), and she glossed Roethke's "winding path" with that unwound by Hades's bobbin in "Byzantium." Roethke objected that the heron was a recollection of his father's game preserve and the winding path was both another recollection from childhood and an image "older than history."[13] No objections were made, however, when Stanley Kunitz alluded to Yeats's question at the end of "Among School Children," about the inseparability of the dancer and the dance, in connection with Roethke's question at the end of "In a Dark Time": "Which I is *I*?" (*RCP* 231). Roethke had claimed in his statement "On 'Identity' " (1963) that the quest for identity could be aided by the souls of the dead and by all living things, in all of which we can find echoes of the self (*PC* 24). During the symposium on "In a Dark Time" he explained that in the poem "I am calling to my aid, in addition to the animal world, a literary ancestor: Yeats." Specifically, Roethke was referring to his own lines,

"What's madness but nobility of soul / At odds with circum-
stance?" (*RCP* 231), which are modeled on Yeats's rhetorical
question in "Coole Park and Ballylee, 1931" (1932): "What's
water but the generated soul?" Roethke applied the formula
elsewhere, for instance in "All the Earth, All the Air," where
he asks, "What's hell but a cold heart?" (*RCP* 117).

We can feel justified in interpreting "In a Dark Time" in
the light of Yeats's work because Roethke has told us to do
so, but we cannot feel as secure in interpreting the echo in
"All the Earth, All the Air." The clear distinction in Roethke's
mind between what in his poetry is and what is not related
to Yeats is based solely on his intention. To hold with Babette
Deutsch that the heron and the winding path are images from
Yeats might tell us something about the source of the poem,
but it does not tell us about its purpose. At times Roethke's
echoes of Yeats are part of Roethke's purpose, but at other
times, apparently, they are only distractions.[14] Unfortunately,
Roethke was not able to keep Yeats out when he did not want
him, and as a result his poems are subject to misinterpretation
as well as censure for being derivative.

A number of theories have been proposed to explain what-
ever value Roethke may have intended for his allusions to
Yeats. Delmore Schwartz has suggested that imitation of Yeats
was the only way for Roethke to avoid self-imitation. Alter-
natively, Louis Martz has seen Roethke's project to be avoid-
ance of the formlessness of his second and third volumes.
Richard Wilbur describes the operation as a type of pump
priming; Roethke writes like Yeats for the mere sake of writing
until he can discover a way to write like himself.[15] All of these
theories assume Roethke's imitation to have been confined to
a specific period of his career, but in fact Yeats's idiom can
be detected in Roethke's poems at every period. We have
Roethke's own explanation for Yeats's presence in his poetry
during the fifties, when that presence was intentional. The
only explanation for Yeats's more pervasive presence is that
Yeats, like Roethke's father, had impressed Roethke indelibly
during his poetic infancy.

The fullest explanation of Roethke's dependence on Yeats

was made by W. D. Snodgrass when he suggested that the
forms Roethke took from Yeats and Eliot were intended as
poetic substitutes for the paternal strictures Roethke was un-
able to accept.[16] This theory needs to be qualified in two
respects. First of all, it is likely that Roethke was more suc-
cessful in assimilating the model of the *Four Quartets*—for
example, in "Meditations of an Old Woman" from *Words
for the Wind* and in the "North American Sequence" from
The Far Field—precisely because Eliot, unlike Yeats, did not
arouse Roethke's fear of the father. For the same reason,
however, Roethke's adaptation of Eliot could only be a half-
way measure in his poetic development; it did not confront
the central issue. Second, Snodgrass's assumption that Roethke
could not accept the model of his natural father must be
questioned. The mixture of acceptance and rejection is present
in that relationship as in Roethke's relationship with Yeats,
but the measure of acceptance seems greater in the former
instance. The difference explains why, when Roethke entered
his father's world in the greenhouse poems, he produced his
most successful work, whereas, when he attempted to enter
Yeats's world, he was always on the brink of failure.

Roethke was successful in the greenhouse world because he
entered it as a child and remained submissive to his father's
authority. It was not in his nature to assume that authority
for himself. This is what he attempted, however, in his con-
frontation with Yeats. "One dares to stand up to a grand
style, to compete with papa," Roethke explained with regard
to his attitude to Yeats (*PC* 70). Roethke's attempt to become
Yeats in his poetry was his attempt to usurp the role of a
natural father who was too awesome, but his choice of a poetic
father presented an obstacle equally insurmountable. That
self-defeating choice may have been dictated by the authority
of the father who, embedded in Roethke's psyche, sought to
punish Roethke for his rebellion. Roethke's poetry has many
strengths, one of which is its openness. One could not expect
such a poet to conceal his struggle with Yeats. Yet one cannot
help feeling that his work as a whole would have been even

stronger if he had been able to find in himself, rather than in Yeats, the authority he yearned for.

A Father's Fatality:
John Berryman

At first glance it is difficult to say why Yeats did not exercise on John Berryman the "disastrous" influence that Berryman felt Yeats had exercised on Roethke (*FP* 311). Berryman's relationship to Yeats, "whom I didn't so much wish to resemble as *to be*," he explained (*FP* 323), was no less a question of identity than it was for Roethke. As a young man, Berryman even had a vision of Yeats, though he recorded that experience in less detail than Roethke did (*FP* 99). More important to Berryman, if detailed recording can be taken as an index, was his meeting with Yeats in the flesh in 1938. Yeats, then seventy-two, impressed the twenty-three-year-old Berryman by his age, which set Yeats in marked opposition to another forerunner who haunted Berryman, his father. Berryman's father had deliberately cut his life short by committing suicide when his son was eleven years old. The contrast thus posed to the example of the durable Yeats is one of the factors that placed Yeats at a greater distance from Berryman than he was from Roethke, for whom the images of natural and poetic father combined into one irresistible force. Yeats and Berryman's father became part of a system of influences that pulled Berryman in opposite directions and supplied the tension of Berryman's most brilliant poetry. Yet, because Berryman's poetry was so intimately involved in his identity, when one side of the conflict finally prevailed, it meant the end of Berryman's life as well as his art.

Yeats first served Berryman as a useful counterweight to Pound and Eliot, whom he describes as "then-crushing influences" (*FP* 324), presumably referring to his senior year at Columbia University, 1935-1936, which he has specified as the period that sparked his interest in Yeats.[17] Having chosen Yeats as his first master (*FP* 323), however, Berryman sought out an alternative influence to make his discipleship less onerous. He found what he needed in the young English poet W. H. Auden. The two models worked well to keep each other in check but did not, at least at first, help Berryman in the more positive task of finding himself. As he explains in "Two Organs," from *Love and Fame* (1970):

> I didn't want my next poem to be *exactly* like Yeats
> or exactly like Auden
> since in that case where the hell was *I*?
>
> (*LF* 16)

Berryman frequently names Yeats and Auden in conjunction. At one stage of his career he succumbed to a violent hatred of Yeats, which he managed to subdue only under the influence of Auden and Rilke.[18] The system of counterbalancing influences could work to preserve as well as to limit the force of any one of its constituents.

Berryman was led toward a conscious recognition of the importance of limitation when he confronted Yeats with another counter-influence, R. P. Blackmur. At about the time he discovered Yeats, Berryman became so taken with Blackmur that he was almost persuaded to give up writing poetry and become a critic. The late poem "Olympus" describes how Berryman combined his two new enthusiasms:

> I wrote & printed an essay on Yeats's plays
> re-deploying all of Blackmur's key terms
> & even his sentence-structure wherever I could.
>
> (*LF* 19)

The essay, first printed in the 1936 commencement issue of the *Columbia Review*, acknowledged Yeats to be "probably the greatest living poet" (*FP* 246) but did not see him as a great dramatist. Berryman found Yeats's adaptations of Sophocles to be his most satisfactory plays, but he was more interested in analyzing the dance plays for their use of "ritual," which Berryman defined as "the formal character imposed on any experience as it is given objective existence by the imagination working in craft" (*FP* 248). "Craft," an important term for Berryman throughout his career, was very likely one

of the terms he picked up from Blackmur, who used it prom-
inently in the subtitle of *The Double Agent: Essays in Craft
and Elucidation* (1935). In Berryman's discussion of Yeats's
plays the term is associated with the deliberate acceptance of
"limitation," which Berryman saw as essential to the artist
and, by extension, to a creative life in general. In the *Dream
Songs* (1964, 1968) the problem of a wealthy friend is that
"he is *too* free, / he needs the limitations of Henry" (Song
346).

As a matter of personality rather than craft, the concept of
limitation is fundamental to confessional poetry. What the
poet confesses are his limitations, which ultimately reduce to
the fact of his humanity. Yet to be a poet requires a defiance
of personal limitations, and that defiance, in turn, singles the
poet out from the rest of humanity.[19] This paradox informs
Berryman's youthful admiration for Yeats, Eliot, Joyce, and
that "almost supernatural crafter" Ezra Pound, whom he lists
in "The Heroes" along with the following explanation:

> I had, from my beginning, to adore heroes
> & I elected that they witness to,
> show forth, transfigure: life-suffering & pure heart
> & hardly definable but central weaknesses
>
> for which they were to be enthroned & forgiven by me.
> They had to come on like revolutionaries,
> enemies throughout to accident & chance,
> relentless travellers long used to failure
>
> in tasks that but for them would sit like hanging judges
> on faithless & by no means up to it Man.
>
>   (LF 25)

The reference to revolutionaries recalls the Irish revolution-
aries about whom Yeats wrote and who, under Yeats's influ-
ence, were added to Berryman's list of heroes in other poems.
The *Dream Songs* refer several times (Songs 264, 309, 321)
to "Connolly and Pearse," as Yeats named the pair in "Easter
1916" (1916), and Song 340 quotes "The O'Rahilly" in the
same words employed by Yeats in his poem of that title (1938).

The heroic role in which Berryman remained most interested, of course, was that of the poet, who might on occasion assume the gestures of the revolutionary. Indeed, Yeats's youthful ideal, as expressed in "All Things Can Tempt Me" (1906), was the poet who wrote "with such airs / That one believed he had a sword upstairs." But the "craft of verse" was the weapon that lay more ready to hand for the poet. One of Yeats's most important contributions to confessional poetry has been his identification of the poet's heroic gesture with the writing of the poem itself, rather than with some vision that has occurred, so to speak, offstage, or that belongs to the imagined life of some *persona*. When the reader's attention is drawn to the poet in the act of writing, the distinction of a *persona* becomes virtually meaningless, for now, if ever, the poet himself has entered fully into his creation. The heroic dimension of this action is perhaps most obvious in the poem that records a testament, that asserts, through the act of writing, the poet's place in a tradition. Yeats's pride in this assertion is apparent in the final section of "The Tower"— "It is time that I wrote my will"—which echoes in the tone of Berryman's testament, left in his early poem, "A Point of Age" (1942):

> I make my testament. I bequeath my heart
> To the disappointed few who have wished me well;
> My vision I leave to one who has the will
> To master it, and the consuming art;
> What else—the sorrow, the disease, the hate—
> I scatter; and I am prepared to start.[20]

Both Yeats and Berryman employ the testament as a starting point rather than an ending. Having settled all external affairs, with heritage and inheritors, they are prepared to set out on a journey into the self.

At the time of his graduation from Columbia in 1936, Berryman was still coming to terms with his heritage. Like Pound thirty years earlier, he set "off to the strange Old World to pick their brains / & visit by hook or crook with W. B. Yeats," as Berryman explains in his poem "Recovery" (*LF* 31). Berryman continued his project of expounding his master, begun in his essay on the plays, by giving a talk on Yeats at Clare College, Cambridge, where Berryman was continuing his studies (see "Friendliness," *LF* 49). In the spring of 1938, at London's Athenaeum Club, Berryman achieved his goal of meeting Yeats, an event to which Berryman alluded five times in his poetry, from the sonnets of the nineteen-forties to the posthumous *Henry's Fate* (1977).[21]

Dylan Thomas, who did not share Berryman's reverence for elder poets, plotted to get Berryman drunk before sending him off to tea with Yeats, but drunk or not, Berryman managed to turn up. In Dream Song 88 Berryman recalls the aged poet:

> Yeats in the London spring half-spent,
> only the grand gift in his head
>
> going for him, a seated ruin of a man
> courteous to a junior.

The fullest treatment of the incident, Dream Song 215, adds little more about what took place at the meeting. Berryman lit Yeats's cigarette, the scones were hot, and Yeats "coughed with his sphincter, when it hurt / Henry, who now that fierceness imitates." Berryman's lasting impression was of Yeats's declining health and his own inability to match Yeats's grandeur: "Empires fall, arise semi-states."

This memory of Yeats became for Berryman an emblem of the inevitability of failure, the "central weakness" of the artist-hero that could be responded to in a variety of ways, some of which were suggested by Yeats's example. The mood of noble despair that Berryman found to characterize Yeats in person was also reflected in the poems in which Yeats dealt with the artist's defeat by time or circumstance. "In Memory of Major Robert Gregory" (1918) manages to turn defeat into a kind of victory while at the same time clearly conveying a sense of what has been lost in Gregory's death:

> We dreamed that a great painter had been born
> To cold Clare rock and Galway rock and thorn,
> To that stern colour and that delicate line
> That are our secret discipline.

Berryman transfers elements of this aesthetic to a different setting in "At Chinese Checkers" (1942), a poem that also owes to Yeats its willful elevation of a young artist, in this case a singer, to the status of hero:

> The shy head and the delicate throat conceal
> A voice that even undisciplined can stir
> The country blood over a Southern hill.[22]

The poem uses an eight-line stanza derived from the stanza form of Yeats's elegy for Gregory, a form to which Berryman devoted a lifelong study (*FP* 328). The lines just quoted begin a stanza that continues toward Yeatsian despair:

> Will Ingreet's voice bring her renown, bring her
> That spontaneous acclaim an artist needs
> Unless he works in the solitary dark?
> What prophecy, what hope can older heads
> Proclaim, beyond the exhaustion of the work?

The oratorical effect of this passage depends heavily on two of Yeats's favorite devices, rhetorical question and anaphora ("bring her . . . bring her"; "What prophecy, what hopes"), both prominent in "In Memory of Major Robert Gregory." Additionally, Berryman seems to be thinking specifically of Yeats's "The Choice" (1932), which consists of one eight-line stanza, where "perfection . . . of the work" can send the artist "raging in the dark."

For Yeats, rage was an alternative response to the circumstances that defeated the artist. In Berryman's work that alternative is especially noticeable in his volume *The Dispossessed* (1948), where Swift, a Yeatsian mask, "Began to document his rage" in "Cloud and Flame" (*HMB* 44). Like Roethke, however, Berryman distrusts rage, which usually appears in *The Dispossessed* as a subhuman violence of the kind Yeats both distrusted and admired. The difference between the two poets is illustrated when Berryman attempts to calm the "rough beast" of Yeats's "The Second Coming" (1920) with characteristic verbal eccentricity in "Rock-study with Wanderer," which compares the sound of the sea with "the rough of beast" (*HMB* 89). A number of other poems in *The Dispossessed* portray violence after a Yeatsian pattern. The anaphoristic "Violence upon the roads: violence of horses" of "Nineteen Hundred and Nineteen" becomes the "Violent touch, and violence in rooms" of "The Spinning Heart" (*HMB* 41). In Berryman's poem the violence responds "To the continual drum-beat of the blood," as in "Nineteen Hundred and Nineteen" the dance of history "Goes to the barbarous clangour of a gong." In "Byzantium" Yeats attributed a similar compulsive force to the blood in "The fury and the mire of human veins." Berryman echoes that poem in the "mire and violence" of his "Ancestor" (*HMB* 50).

The two versions of "The Animal Trainer," both included in *The Dispossessed*, reveal the full complexity of Berryman's dialogue with Yeats concerning the brutality of existence.[23] The poems are written in a dialogue form that recalls several of Yeats's poems, especially "The Folly of Being Comforted" (1902). As in that poem, Heart speaks as opponent in "The Animal Trainer," in this case in response to the trainer himself. The trainer proposes leaving his animals, which represent sex and the five senses, "to live like an artist in the sun," but Heart convinces him that he can live only "in the dark" among the animals (I, *HMB* 53). Berryman is "raging in the dark," as Yeats does in "The Choice," but Berryman also attempts to dissociate himself from Yeats by openly reversing the terms of "The Circus Animals' Desertion." There, the animals display the gaudiness of art, whereas for Berryman they suggest the sordidness of life as opposed to art. As for each poet's self-image, Yeats portrays himself as having fallen from the world of "pure mind"; Berryman yearns for that world as if he had never been there. In the end, however, the differences between Yeats and Berryman are resolved as the difference between art and life disappears. Each man declares his commitment to creating an art that will acknowledge, though perhaps also "train," the foulness that the artist finds in his life and in himself.

The second version of "The Animal Trainer" is more Yeatsian in detail, proving how close Berryman could be to Yeats

even when he was attempting to keep his distance. The trainer
in the second version cries out against his animals:

> —What soul-delighting tasks do they perform?
> They quarrel, snort, leap, lie down, their delight
> Merely a punctual meal and to be warm.
> Justify their existence in the night!

"Soul-delighting" appears to be a conflation of terms that
Yeats uses in a passage from "A Prayer for My Daughter"
(1919): "The soul recovers radical innocence / And learns at
last that it is self-delighting." The crowding of antithetical
verbs in response to the trainer's question recalls Yeats's prac-
tice in passages such as that in "Among School Children"
where the soul undergoing rebirth may variously "sleep, shriek,
struggle to escape." The trainer's exclamation resembles the
command to "Justify all those renowned generations" from
Yeats's "Three Songs to the Same Tune" (1934), though Yeats
counsels vindication where Berryman seeks explanation. In
both cases the motive derives from the central virtue of Yeats's
middle period, "responsibility," to which Heart explicitly ap-
peals in Berryman's poem.

Although Berryman produced variations on Yeatsian themes
throughout his career, he rarely used Yeats's language to the
extent that he does in the two versions of "The Animal Trainer."
As early as 1940, Berryman proved that he could defy Yeats
when he set his mind to it, for the tone of "extreme sobriety"
in "Winter Landscape" was produced as "a reaction, first,
against Yeats's gorgeous and seductive rhetoric" (FP 325).
Another poem published in the same year, "On the London
Train," shows Berryman suppressing Yeats's claim to the trim-
eter line through the counterbalancing influence of Auden.
One of the more Yeatsian passages in the poem speaks of the
embarrassment arising from the complexities of love:

> So it is and has been . .
> Summon an old lover's ghost,
> He'll swear no man has lied
> Who spoke of the painful and most
> Embarrassing ordeal this side
> Satisfaction.[24]

Bold enjambment and the strategic placement of multisyllabic
words, both techniques in which Auden excelled, shift the
weight away from the end of the last lines, until the rhymes
are barely heard and the meter, along with Yeats, is virtually
forgotten.

One form in which Yeats's expertise had a special attraction
for Berryman was the song, or, as Yeats would have said,
"Words for Music Perhaps." Yeats's association with this
form may have invited Berryman to indulge in violence with
less reluctance here than he does elsewhere. A Roman Crazy
Jane might be speaking in Berryman's "Song from 'Cleopa-
tra' " (1940):

> That Queen insulted Cicero.
> Lucan and Horace threw a jibe,
> But Antony and all his tribe
> Cut out the hearts that called her so.[25]

With equally deliberate indecorum, Helen is referred to as the
"first of all the tribe" in Yeats's "His Memories" (1926).
Yeats, as many critics have noted, made the refrain a distin-
guishing feature of his songs through his use of simple phrases
that subtly change their meaning with repetition. The refrain
of Berryman's "White Feather" (1948)—"The eye stared at
the feather"—is evidently intended to function in the same
fashion, though all subtlety is lost when the eye proves to be
made of glass.[26]

Berryman's interest in song culminates in his epic sequence,
the *Dream Songs*, whose disjunctive syntax is so peculiarly
Berryman's own that no question of Yeats's formal influence
seems to arise. If Berryman had not revealed the connection
himself, we would not know that Yeats provided the model
for the stanza form of the *Dream Songs*. "It goes 5-5-3-5-5-
3, 5-5-3-5-5-3, 5-5-3-5-5-3—that's the business," Berryman
explained, "and it's variously rhymed, and often it has no
rhyme at all, but it sounds as if it rhymed. That I got from
Yeats—three six-line stanzas. His songs don't really resemble
mine, but I did get that from him. It's rather like an extended,
three-part sonnet."[27] This revelation appears less surprising
when we recall Berryman's interest in the eight-line stanza of

"In Memory of Major Robert Gregory," which influenced the structure of his early poems, such as "At Chinese Checkers," and eventually, by Berryman's own admission (*FP* 328), helped to shape the stanza of *Homage to Mistress Bradstreet* (1953).

Berryman employed six-line stanzas as early as 1938, in "The Translation" and "Toward Statement," but he did not begin experimenting with the stanza in groups of three until "The Nervous Songs" from *The Dispossessed*.[28] It seems to be only in such grouping that Yeats served as model for the *Dream Songs*. Though Berryman uses rhyme schemes that Yeats used, Yeats did not vary the scheme from stanza to stanza as Berryman does, and Yeats rarely used pentameter lines in this type of stanza. The poem of Yeats's that comes nearest to incorporating all the aspects of Berryman's form is "To a Young Beauty" (1918), which consists of three six-line stanzas with the accentual pattern 4-4-3-4-4-3. However, more useful models for the *Dream Songs*, conceived of as a sequence, are the poems of Yeats's song sequences, *A Man Young and Old* (1928), *Words for Music Perhaps* (1932), and *A Woman Young and Old* (1933), many of which are limited to three six-line stanzas.[29] Viewed as extended sonnets, these poems represent what Berryman had early recognized as Yeats's devotion to craft.

In writing an epic of the self, Berryman inevitably invites comparison with Wordsworth, but the *Dream Songs* diverge from the Wordsworthian tradition of the poet's self as hero in two important respects. The first point of divergence is essentially Berryman's debt to Yeats, whose crucial contribution to the tradition was his claim that the poet creates the self, or chooses the mask, that he displays in his poems. Berryman espouses this principle in his prefatory note to the *Dream Songs* by insisting that his protagonist, Henry, is "an imaginary character (not the poet, not me)." Yeats would have understood Henry as a "phantasmagoria." Henry lives through the events of Berryman's life but, as with Yeats, the events of the poet's life acquire a symbolic closure in the poetry. This does not mean that what is true for Henry is not true for Berryman. Simply more is true for Berryman because, in the process of becoming art, Henry's life has been shaped into an orderly disorder, and certain elements have had to be eliminated. So long as this qualification is borne in mind, it is possible to read back from Henry's life to Berryman's in order to trace the further history of Berryman's interest in Yeats.

The second point at which Berryman diverges from his tradition in the *Dream Songs* separates him from Yeats as well as from Wordsworth. Although he was drastically revising the nature of the epic by making his hero himself, Wordsworth retained the classical conception of the epic hero as one who rises above, or passes through, obstacles that he meets in his path. Yeats retained Wordsworth's supreme confidence in the self, but, as in "The Circus Animals' Desertion," settled the self down among the obstacles, recognizing that some, including the capriciousness of the imagination, could not be overcome. That recognition made Yeats one of Berryman's flawed heroes, the flaw arising from the inevitability of some end to creativity—whether through death or final loss of inspiration—the heroism arising from a self-confidence that defies failure. Berryman was in awe of Yeats's ability to face up to some dreadful fact—say, the death of Robert Gregory—without looking through the fact to find some hidden consolation and yet continuing to write as if his own confidence had not been shaken. Berryman's Henry shares with Yeats a sense of the opacity of the human situation, but he lacks Yeats's faith that the inner light of the self can compensate for that opacity. On the other hand, Henry also lacks Roethke's faith that the extinction of the self will bring a spiritual gain. Stripped of all faiths, Henry is not merely a flawed hero; he is no hero at all.

Although Henry is obsessed throughout the *Dream Songs* with death as the ultimate end, the immediate end that confronts Berryman, who retains a good deal of heroic defiance, is the end of the Songs themselves. If the *Dream Songs* have a plot, it can be formulated in terms of a question: are the Songs going to be finished before their author disintegrates altogether? This problem commits a great deal of importance to the end, more so than would normally be expected in what is otherwise such a nonprogressive form. What we find at the end, roughly the last one hundred Songs, is an account of

Berryman's trip to Ireland in 1966-1967, during which time he in fact brought his epic to a virtual close. A number of motives are given within the Songs to explain Berryman's trip. First of all, he felt that he had to move somewhere: "Something's gotta give / either in edgy Henry or the environment" (Song 275). Survival was in question, as it had been for Horace Gregory during an earlier trip to Ireland, where, Berryman confirmed, even the past managed to live on: "The whole place is ghostly: no wonder Yeats believed in fairies / & personal survival" (Song 313). Moreover, Ireland was "the chief lion-breeding place" (Song 307). It had been a fountain of inspiration to "Synge, Joyce & Yeats" (Song 290), and Berryman hoped it would give him the continuing inspiration he needed to finish his Songs. Finally, Berryman explicitly states a major motive for his trip in the first lines of Song 312: "I have moved to Dublin to have it out with you, / majestic Shade." As he had done thirty years previously, Berryman crossed the Atlantic to meet with Yeats, whose authority had only been magnified by his death.

Dream Song 312 is Berryman's principal statement on Yeats. It moves from the open challenge of the first line to a concluding tone reminiscent of that which accompanied Berryman's description of his earlier meeting with Yeats in the flesh, a tone of humble self-disparagement:

> Your high figures float
> again across my mind and all your past
> fills my walled garden with your honey breath
> wherein I move, a mote.

In the body of the poem, Berryman recalls his youthful reading of Yeats and wonders if he correctly interpreted Yeats's "phases," which Yeats had outlined in *A Vision*. Then came the period of Berryman's disaffection:

> For years then I forgot you, I put you down,
> ingratitude is the necessary curse
> of making things new.

It is a compliment Pound might have appreciated better than Yeats, but the succeeding description of Berryman's prepa-

rations for his final attempt at interpretation clearly employs
Yeats's language in speaking of "remorse":

> I brought my family to see me through,
> I brought my homage & my soft remorse
> I brought a book or two
>
> only, including in the end your last
> strange poems made under the shadow of death.

Berryman himself was feeling that shadow encroaching. He
admired the equanimity with which Yeats confronted death
in such poems as "Cuchulain Comforted" in *Last Poems and
Two Plays* (1939), but Berryman's approximation of that mood
in Song 300, entitled "Henry Comforted," owes more to "three
gin-&-vermouths" than it owes to Yeats's example.

At times, when he considered the difficulty of achieving the
composure he thought Yeats had achieved, Berryman sensed
an immense gulf between himself and Yeats. Just as Yeats's
goal, as expressed in "Vacillation," was to "come / Proud,
open-eyed and laughing to the tomb," so Berryman also sought

> aplomb
> at the temps
> of the tomb.
> (Song 286)

But Berryman doubted his ability to follow through with
aplomb, and he contrasted his own doubts with Yeats's self-
assurance. The difference, Berryman recognized, was not merely
a matter of temperament but also involved a question of lit-
erary tradition, for Yeats's faith in the self linked him directly
to Wordsworth:

> Yeats knew nothing about life: it was all symbols
> & Wordsworthian egotism: Yeats on Cemetery Ridge
> would not have been scared, like you & me,
> he would have been, before   the bullet that was his,
> studying the movements of the birds,
> said disappointed & amazed Henry.
>
> (Song 334)

What especially amazed Henry was that Yeats managed to preserve his egotism even when he was not, like Wordsworth, lifted above the mundane. Yeats was not always like Forgael in *The Shadowy Waters* (1900), abstractedly studying the movements of the birds while his crew murmured about plunder and women. There were times when Yeats listened to the crew, when he heard "talk from . . . companions" (Song 331), though Berryman skeptically cuts the number of those times down to the bare minimum:

> Yeats listened once, he found it did him good,
> he died in full stride, a good way to go,
> making them wonder what's missing,
> a strangeness in the final notes, never to be resolved.
> (Song 331)

Yeats was at once removed from and involved in life. If Berryman could not imitate the removal, he could take the involvement even farther. Death in full stride was to be the solution to the plot of the *Dream Songs*, as of Berryman's life. The work ends on a dissonance that projects infinitely forward toward an impossible resolution. As a craftsman Berryman accepted the necessity of an end, yet he did not want the end to imply loss of vitality. Completion of the *Dream Songs* was not to indicate that their author had gone dry.

The closing dissonance is sounded by a juxtaposition of the last two poems, which present alternative attitudes toward death—rage and despair—the attitudes that distinguish the Yeatsian moments of Berryman's early poetry. Yeatsian "rage" informs the penultimate Song, in which Berryman imagines burrowing into his father's grave and punishing the corpse with an ax. Even in violent defiance of death, however, Berryman moves toward suicide, for through his imaginary action Berryman would be destroying his father's consequences, including himself, in keeping with the parricide's motive in Yeats's *Purgatory* (1939). As in his earlier work, Berryman prefers to subdue such violence, which he does here by giving the last word to the much gentler Song 385, which expresses Berryman's desire for his own death not in terms of "tragic joy"

but with a passive yearning. The immediate burden of life that
concerns Berryman here is the necessity of scolding his daugh-
ter, which would not be a necessity "If there were a mid-
dle   ground between things and the soul / or if the sky re-
sembled more the sea." Within this one poem, Berryman still
faces alternatives. His misery would be over if his soul could
somehow be insulated from, invulnerable to the world of other
people and things, as Yeats's soul seemed to be; but Berryman
could not maintain that separation for himself. The alternative
is to seek the end to all distinctions in death. Berryman faces
death at the end of the *Dream Songs* with a despair that lacks
the nobility that can be found in Yeats or, for instance, in his
own "At Chinese Checkers." There is now no hint that the
self remains paradoxically undefeated in the face of uncon-
querable circumstance. Henry must submit to slaughter along
with the Thanksgiving turkeys.

The vitality that Berryman hoped to ensure for the *Dream
Songs* by closing with two discordant poems served, ironically,
as a reminder of what Berryman could not do for himself.
"My house is made of wood and it's made well, / unlike us,"
Berryman observes in the last Song. What made Yeats's ex-
ample finally inaccessible to Berryman was Yeats's survival
not only in past creations but in continued creativity. Yeats
provided a model for the poet of longevity, which Berryman
attempted to weigh against the opposite model of the poet
dying young, represented by Keats:

> Keats glares at Yeats
> who full of honours died & being old sung
> his strongest. Henry appreciated that hate,
> but what now of Yeats'
>
> lucky of-Fanny-free feeling for Keats
> who doomed by Mistress Gonne proved barren years
> and saw his friends all leave,
> stale his rewards turn, & cut off then at his peak,
> promising in his seventies! all fears
> save that one failed to deceive.

>   (Song 190)

"That one" was the fear of losing inspiration, which finally proved unjustified for Yeats, who was silenced only by death. Like Yeats, Berryman saw the fulfillment of his fears of losing his friends and of his fame turning hollow. He made those fears principal themes of the *Dream Songs*. Wondering if even his final fear might prove valid if he lived too long, Berryman concluded that the sooner he died, the more certain he would be of dying in full stride. As he phrased it at the end of his comparison of Keats and Yeats, "best is the short day."

Berryman knew simply too many examples of the short life for him to be persuaded of the possibility of his emulating Yeats's long life. The only example he could think of on Yeats's side was William Carlos Williams,

> to whom was not denied
> the mysterious late excellence which is the crown
> of our trials & our last bride.
>
> (Song 324)

For examples of the short life, Berryman did not have to look to Keats, for among his own acquaintances there were Roethke, Randall Jarrell, and Delmore Schwartz. Schwartz was a particularly horrifying example because, even though he died young, Berryman saw that his later work had already lost the early strength (see Song 150). Looming behind all these figures was that of Berryman's father. In the end it was his example that Berryman chose to follow.

A FATHER'S NONENTITY: ROBERT LOWELL

Robert Lowell chose to follow neither the example of his father nor that of Yeats. On the one hand, he disdained his father's ineffectuality; on the other, he distrusted the potency of any literary influence. Yet, ultimately, one reason accounts for Lowell's rejection of both sorts of predecessor. Lowell's poetry is so obsessed with the past that it is easy to forget that his theme is not the past alone but its distance from the present. He might have said of all potential influences what he said of his "Grandparents" in his poem of that title: "They're altogether otherworldly now" (1959; *LS* 68). The acquiescent tone of this poem differentiates Lowell from Roethke and Berryman, who desperately conjured Yeats's ghost to prevent the other world from claiming him entirely, but their desperation betrays their tacit agreement with Lowell that whatever authority might reside in the past really lay beyond their reach. This sense of being without a tradition is the sense that, in Yeats, gave rise to the notion of the tradition of the self. Roethke, Berryman, and Lowell reject that notion by demonstrating the inability of a self that is "frizzled, stale and small," as Lowell describes it in "Home After Three Months Away" (1959; *LS* 84), to assume the proportions of a tradition. Lowell, however, carries his rejection even farther. For the self even to attempt to assume the role of tradition implies that there is value in that role, or, to use imagery more germane to confessional poetry, for the son to attempt to usurp the father, though it shows disrespect for the father as an individual, implies that the father has some authority to be usurped. Lowell brings even that assumption into question. Too painfully aware of his own failings to claim authority for himself, Lowell subjected others to the same unsparing scrutiny and made similar discoveries, which he was willing to lament but not overlook. At the end of "Grandparents" he reveals his urge for debunking by playfully defacing a picture of "the last Russian Czar" (*LS* 69), despite an evident nostalgia for the lost nineteenth-century world, including his grandparents, that the czar represents. In 1974 Yeats also had begun, in Lowell's view, to recede into the nineteenth century, a view that opened Yeats's work, like the picture of the czar, to possibilities of exploitation that Lowell did not live long enough to pursue.[30]

The first step in Lowell's rebellion against tradition was to separate himself from the tradition he inherited through his family and to choose a tradition that, because he had chosen it, he could call his own. He left Boston and Harvard College and headed South, where a different social tradition reigned, and where, more important, a new critical movement was revising the traditional canon of literature. Promulgated by the former Agrarians in accordance with the basic principles of modernism, the new canon, not surprisingly, awarded a prominent place to Yeats. Lowell later referred to this time as "the period of the famous book *Understanding Poetry*," the text published in 1939 by Cleanth Brooks and Robert Penn Warren, under whom Lowell studied at Louisiana State University in 1941-1942.[31] *Understanding Poetry* established the New Criticism in college classrooms throughout the country. It includes four poems by Yeats—compared, for instance, with two by Eliot—and the introduction refers to Yeats's essay "The Symbolism of Poetry" (1900) as authority for the essential New Critical doctrine of the organic relation between the parts of a poem.[32] During this same period, Lowell studied informally with Allen Tate, who reinforced the lesson of *Understanding Poetry* by insisting, according to Lowell, "that all the culture and tradition of the East, the South and Europe stood behind Eliot, Emily Dickinson, Yeats and Rimbaud."[33] Lowell built on Tate's list when he claimed to have been "explicitly influenced by Ransom, Tate, Williams, Jarrell, Eliot and Yeats."[34] Ransom, the dean of the New Criticism, was Lowell's mentor at Kenyon College from 1937 to 1940, the period when Lowell began keeping a commonplace book consisting of favorite poems. Among the poems he copied out are Yeats's "The Second Coming" and "All Souls' Night" (1921).[35]

Of the two qualities, "values and rhetoric," that Lowell recalled having admired in Yeats, the latter certainly helps to explain Lowell's selection of poems to copy.[36] "All Souls' Night" is an outstanding example of Yeats's faith in the power of rhetoric, for the poem is quite literally a conjurer's spell, intended to call up ghosts from the past: "And I call up MacGregor from the grave." Claiming such power seems to raise the speaker to a position above ordinary men. Hence, the statement is rhetorical in a sense that is often used disapprovingly, but Lowell was not afraid of disapproval when he seconded Yeats's claim in a poem entitled "A Prelude to Summer," published in the Kenyon College literary magazine, *Hika*, in 1939.[37] Though he calls on gods rather than ghosts, Lowell feels no less confident than Yeats: "I call on whom I

will." Evidently another model for Lowell is "In Memory of
Major Robert Gregory," which begins:

> Now that we're almost settled in our house
> I'll name the friends that cannot sup with us
> Beside a fire of turf in th' ancient tower.

Like the conjuring in "All Souls' Night," this passage reduces
the distance between author and *persona* by calling attention
to the act of writing (or speaking), a strategy for which Yeats
was admired by John Berryman as well as Lowell. In the first
lines of Lowell's poem the phrase "I speak" serves the function
of Yeats's "I'll name," and the act is given ceremonial im-
portance by the formality of its context:

> Now that the bushy shadows of warm trees
> Cast forth their idleness upon my nature
> Saved by the meanness of a country winter,
> A stamping ground of high-pitched energies
> I speak, quirites, with the biting ease
> Of Cato.

Yeats might be felt even more strongly in Lowell's poem were
it not for the young poet's delight in adjectives and for the
classical facade, a reminder that Lowell was both a classics
major at Kenyon and a student of Allen Tate.

Despite Lowell's avowed interest in Yeats's rhetoric, Yeats's
impact on Lowell's work in that regard was minor compared
with the impact of Tate. Yeats's first and enduring importance
for Lowell was in the area of private rather than public speech.
This is the distinction that John Berryman had in mind in a
1947 review when he listed among Lowell's debts in *Land of
Unlikeness* (1944) those to "Allen Tate as a Roman and po-
lemic writer, Yeats as a dynastic" (*FP* 287). Yeats's treatment
of the "dynastic theme," as Jon Stallworthy has called it,
accounts for Lowell's stated interest in Yeats for values as
well as rhetoric, for Yeats invoked his family tradition as a
standard by which to measure the value of his own achieve-
ment. Stallworthy argues that Yeats invented a new type of
poem by turning from the conventional cataloguing of the

hero's ancestors in poetic narrative to a mythic treatment of the poet's own ancestors.[38] In the tradition of the self, of course, the poet is his own hero, and his ancestors are the heroic extension of the self into the past.

The question of heroism suggests that another twist to the dynastic theme, one that cannot rightly be included within the tradition of the self, was created by Lowell. Jon Stallworthy points to a crucial difference when he observes that Yeats, in such poems as "Pardon, old fathers" (1914) and "Are You Content?" (1938), asks that his ancestors judge him, whereas Lowell takes it upon himself to judge his ancestors and finds them miserable rather than heroic.[39] Having demonstrated his independence of family tradition during his exile from New England, Lowell could look back at his family with a severely critical eye. The result was apparent in Lowell's poetry as early as 1939, when the *Kenyon Review* published "The Cities' Summer Death," a version of the first part of "In Memory of Arthur Winslow" (1944). Although the latter poem, which Lowell has linked to Yeats for both its ten-line stanza and its dynastic theme, gives a relatively sympathetic view of Lowell's maternal grandfather, the central sections submit damaging evidence of his spiritual and financial bankruptcy.[40] The family critique continues in such poems as "Mary Winslow" and "Rebellion," from *Lord Weary's Castle* (1946), and culminates in *Life Studies* (1959) with an unflinching dissection that treats the entire family but reserves the sharpest scalpel for Lowell's father.

Granted the more critical attitude adopted by Lowell toward his ancestors, he could still be included in the same tradition as Yeats if the difference went no further. Sitting in judgment on one's ancestors would seem only a natural consequence of the assumption that the self is the only true basis of authority, the only true hero. But in fact, Lowell also sits in judgment on himself, and, finding himself just as bankrupt as his ancestors, he progressively dismantles the superior stance that is common in his earliest work. "In Memory of Arthur Winslow" ends with a prayer "to Our Lady" that asks redemption for both Lowell's grandfather and for Lowell. Forgiveness can come only from the outside, through the intercession of the Virgin. Once Lowell abandons the framework of Catholicism, another base from which he defied family tradition, he can seek forgiveness only from sources that cannot offer it. In "Middle Age," from *For the Union Dead* (1964), Lowell makes a Yeatsian gesture in asking his father for forgiveness while in fact pronouncing it himself, but what he feels is not forgiveness but injury, committed both by himself and by his father:

> Father, forgive me
> my injuries,
> as I forgive
> those I
> have injured!
>
> You never climbed
> Mount Sion, yet left
> dinosaur
> death-steps on the crust,
> where I must walk.
>   (UD 7)

Lowell's last volume, *Day by Day* (1977), includes two poems, "Robert T. S. Lowell" and "To Mother," that show Lowell achieving a final acceptance of his parents, but he still cannot forgive them or himself. He tells his mother, "you are as human as I am . . . / if I am" (DD 79). Nagged by that doubt, Lowell was bound to find the absence of forgiveness harder to bear than did Robert Penn Warren.

As in Warren's case, an aid to Lowell's acceptance of his parents was his own experience of parenthood. The poems that arise from this experience take their place, along with poems by Warren and Berryman, in a long tradition of poems about the poet's children, but, like Robinson Jeffers and Horace Gregory, Lowell belongs to a special branch of that tradition created by a graft from Yeats's dynastic theme. Conceiving of the family as a dynasty confers a special public relevance on poems about family members, who are viewed not only as members of a larger society but as representatives of that society, whether real or ideal. The ideal society is the subject in Yeats's "A Prayer for My Daughter" and in Lowell's "Fourth of July in Maine" (1967), which Lowell acknowledged to be "heavily and consciously influenced by Yeats."[41]

Looking backward as well as forward in family history, "Fourth of July in Maine" invokes the blessing of Lowell's dead cousin, Harriet Winslow, on her namesake, Lowell's daughter:

> may your proportion strengthen her
> to live through the millennial year
> Two Thousand, and like you possess
> friends, independence, and a house,
> herself God's plenty, mistress of
> your tireless sedentary love.
>
> (NO 32)

The gifts that Lowell desires for his daughter compose a list of the values for which Lowell respected Yeats. All of them have analogues in "A Prayer for My Daughter": the ability to "find a friend"; the courage to be "self-delighting"; the "house / Where all's accustomed, ceremonious"; the Horn of Plenty. The house, especially important in Lowell's poem because he inherited a house from his cousin, serves as a leitmotiv for the dynastic theme throughout the work of both Lowell and Yeats.[42] Both men wrote elegies on houses, Yeats on Coole and Thoor Ballylee, Lowell on his grandfather's Dunbarton estate and on Milgate in England—each house a concrete symbol of tradition in decay. In "Fourth of July in Maine" Lowell's hopes for his daughter are qualified by the circumstances of the house, set against a run-down garden and a propped-up barn.

The house is representative of the type of symbol that Lowell could successfully take over from Yeats. I shall call it a circumstantial symbol because it is present among the circumstances in which the poet places himself; it becomes a symbol only by his selecting it for special notice. Another type of symbol, which Yeats inherited from the symbolist movement, exists only as a symbol, being called up in the poet's mind in association with some aspect of his circumstances. I shall call this type the associative symbol. Lowell's early work abounds in this type, often in the form of some traditional religious image, but as his career progressed, he relied more and more exclusively on the circumstantial symbol, the type that defines *Life Studies*. *Near the Ocean* (1967) makes a notable attempt to reintroduce the associative symbol, but Lowell never again felt entirely comfortable with that type. His discomfort is a measure of his distance from Yeats and of the new sensibility that has replaced the tradition of the self in contemporary poetry.

The first poem of *Near the Ocean*, "Waking Early Sunday Morning," traces in microcosm the move from associative to circumstantial symbol that characterizes Lowell's work as a whole. "O to break loose, like the chinook / salmon jumping and falling back," the poem begins.[43] The salmon is an associative symbol, an image present only in the poet's mind as he wakes up in bed. The association has been encouraged by Lowell's reading of Yeats's Byzantium poems, whose "salmon-falls" ("Sailing to Byzantium") and dolphins ("Byzantium")— the latter a prototype for the most prominent associative symbol in Lowell's later work—represent a principle of animal vitality that Lowell wishes to invoke here.[44] But the action of the salmon also represents its nature as an associative symbol: it breaks loose, free of circumstance, a condition Lowell envies in his reiterated desire to be "anywhere, but somewhere else!" (*NO* 18, 20). To his dismay, Lowell discovers that he cannot escape his circumstance, which gradually invades his consciousness to destroy the sense of freedom he felt at the moment of waking.

The salmon image, then, cannot be sustained because Lowell cannot release himself from the pressure of circumstance. His failure is stated explicitly in a stanza that Lowell cut after the poem's original publication in an effort to focus more clearly on public rather than private concerns. In the original version he wrote:

> Empty, irresolute, ashamed,
> when the sacred texts are named,
> I lie here on my bed apart,
> and when I look into my heart,
> I discover none of the great
> subjects: death, friendship, love and hate—
> only old china doorknobs, sad,
> slight useless things to calm the mad.[45]

This stanza makes it clear that "Waking Early Sunday Morning" is Lowell's version of that poem to which Roethke and Berryman also responded fruitfully, Yeats's "The Circus Animals' Desertion." Deserted by the great themes, Lowell is left with the heart's trivia; or, to return to my distinction of two sorts of symbols, Lowell is deserted by associative symbols— those he might have drawn from the sacred texts of the past, whether religious or literary—and left with symbols that are almost purely circumstantial. The china doorknobs are circumstantial because they appear in Lowell's heart only after being carried over from the woodshed that Lowell explores in the preceding stanza. But the woodshed is both a real place and Lowell's version of Yeats's "foul rag-and-bone shop," just as the shed's "dregs and dreck" consist of real objects that carry traces of associative meaning, only to point to the failure of such meaning:

> tools with no handle,
> ten candle-ends not worth a candle,
> old lumber banished from the Temple.
> (NO 19)

"The Circus Animals' Desertion" concedes that all of Yeats's ladders arise from the rag-and-bone shop, but it was unusual for Yeats to find himself down on the ground without any ladder to climb. That experience appears to have become normal for Lowell, who developed out of it not one poem but an entire aesthetic, which he defended in a series of "Circus Animals' Desertions." To aid in his defense, Lowell cited the precedent of W. H. Auden, who insisted that a responsible poem had to take into account the trivial facts of mundane existence. Lowell presents his view of Auden's position in the poem entitled "Truth" in *The Dolphin* (1973), where "the scouring voice of 1930 Oxford," based on inferences from Auden's published work and remarks made in conversation with Lowell, applies its standard of truthfulness particularly to Yeats.[46]

Not surprisingly, Yeats falls far short of the standard:

W. B. Yeats was not a gent,
he didn't tell the truth: *and for an hour,*
I've walked and prayed—who prays exactly an hour?
Yeats had bad eyes, saw nothing . . . not even peahens:
What has a bard to do with the poultry yard?
Dying, he dished his stilts, wrote one good poem,
small penance for all that grandeur of imperfection.

Although the last line sounds more like Yeats than Auden, the criticism in the preceding lines is typical of Auden's deliberately literal-minded objections to Yeats. In comments made on various occasions, Auden remarked that all dons are not bald and respectable (versus "The Scholars"), that a motorist is more likely to pass by than a horseman (versus "Under Ben Bulben"), and that Yeats did not really want to become a mechanical bird (versus "Sailing to Byzantium").[47] In "Truth" Lowell has Auden object to a line from "A Prayer for My Daughter"—elsewhere a model for Lowell—and to Yeats's response to a criticism of "The Indian to His Love" (1886). Characteristically, Yeats upheld the poetic tradition rather than the circumstantial evidence as the criterion for truth: "As to the poultry yards, with them I have no concern. The wild peahen dances or all Indian poets lie" (*L* 109). Yeats was less haughty in "The Circus Animals' Desertion," which records also the desertion of "stilted boys," to the approval of Lowell's Auden. In his judgment, concurring with the repeated approval of the real Auden, this is Yeats's "one good poem."[48] If Lowell's Auden interprets the poem as Yeats's resolution to confine himself to the truth, however, he needs to be reminded that Yeats only expresses his intention to lie down in his heart, not in the poultry yards.

In theory, Auden offered Lowell all he needed to justify his remaining among trivial circumstances once "the great subjects" had deserted him. To do so was to be truthful. Temperamentally, however, Lowell was incapable of dealing with ordinary things on Auden's friendly terms. As a result, he experienced a second desertion, this time not of Yeats's "beautiful lofty things," the title of a late poem (1938), but of "plain things," as Lowell called them in "Night Sweat" (1964): "Worktable, litter, books and standing lamp, / plain things, my stalled equipment, the old broom" (*UD* 68). This catalogue connects with neither subject nor predicate—fittingly, because these things have "stalled," leaving the poet momentarily alone with a self that has no connection to its circumstances other than that of simple perception. In this situation, very different from the freedom celebrated at the opening of "Waking Early Sunday Morning," the self is stalled like the things around it. In fact, things can seem quite active in their hindrance, as they are in the "Epilogue" to *Day by Day*. There, in yet another version of "The Circus Animals' Desertion," it is not the facts that have stalled but the poet's art, which seems "paralyzed by fact," thwarting the poet's desire "to make / something imagined, not recalled" (*DD* 127). A part of Lowell insisted that perhaps Yeats was right, that maybe truth really does reside in the imagination. "Yeats anxiously warned us not to lend a high / degree of reality to the Great War," Lowell writes, recalling a note that Yeats had made for *A Vision*, yet the continuation of Lowell's poem, "The Army of the Duc de Nemours," and the volume in which it appears, *History* (1973), are mired in the details of men's conflicts.[49] Suspecting with Yeats, in "A Meditation in Time of War" (1920), "that One is animate, / Mankind inanimate phantasy," Lowell, like Berryman, remains too human to extricate himself from mankind.

Ironically, Lowell's exploration of his humanity took him into experience that threatened to separate him from other men. The more Lowell wrote about himself and his personal circumstances, the more he risked making his verse too private, too limited in relevance. This would not have been the case had there been some set of public conventions, some tradition that could have provided an interpretive context for private experience, but all of the poets treated in this study agree that no such tradition exists. Since it is not given, tradition has to be created out of the self; the private has to be made public; the individual's humanity has to be enlarged to inhuman dimensions. Lowell was acutely aware of this necessity and consciously worked toward a more public poetry after producing the intensely personal *Life Studies*.[50] But he approached this task not as an opportunity, as Yeats did, but as a perverse self-mutilation that only further imperils an already wounded psyche. Lowell's poetry, as Gabriel Pearson has observed, "explores a condition in which public worlds have to be built and sustained out of the rubble of purely personal experience," through a process that Pearson calls "depersonalising."[51]

In "Truth" Lowell has Auden declare, "Nothing pushing the personal should be published."[52] For Auden, depersonalizing often meant simply excluding personal details from his poetry. His "unwritten poem," "Dichtung und Wahrheit" (1960), leads to the allegory of "Dame Kind" instead of a love poem.[53] "Dame Kind" is not as true to Auden's personal experience as a love poem would be, but neither is it false. It exists where "Dichtung und Wahrheit" says poetry should exist: in an impersonal realm in which judgments of truth and falsehood are irrelevant. What made Yeats's poetry subject to such judgments is that he could not keep personal detail out of his poetry, and in the course of including it he went through the process of arrangement and selection that converted his life into art—a process that distorted private truth into public lie, in Auden's view. Despite doubts arising from his sympathy with Auden's position, Lowell employed Yeats's method of depersonalizing. "What I have written was arranged to happen," he writes in *Notebook* (1970).[54]

The results of his arrangement continued to dissatisfy Lowell, because they measured up to neither of the standards

represented for him by Auden and Yeats. He seemed to have
arranged too much to meet Auden's requirements for factual
truth, too little to meet Yeats's requirements for imaginative
truth. His art was suspended between two conflicting tend-
encies, "heightened from life, / yet paralyzed by fact," to quote
once again from the "Epilogue" to *Day by Day* (*DD* 127).
A comparison drawn in that poem between the art of painting
and the technique of the posed snapshot suggests Lowell's
view of his own art as reasonably accurate but decidedly mi-
nor. The art is diminished to accord with its diminished sub-
ject, the self conceived not in the imagination, where the "self-
delighting" soul of "A Prayer for My Daughter" resides, but
in history, where "We are poor passing facts" (*DD* 127).
Lowell's difference from Yeats arises not because Lowell held
the latter view of the self and Yeats the former. Rather, Lowell
held one view; Yeats, both. The tradition of the self demands
a dualistic self, both object and subject, real and imagined,
man and mask, private and public, son and father. Lowell *felt*
that duality, but, unlike Yeats, he had no system that would
allow him to accept it intellectually, so his public world re-
duces to a private world, and fathers can be no more than
sons. The duality that Yeats understood in terms of Blake's
positive contraries, Lowell could only record, in his "Epi-
logue," as "misalliance," echoing Pound's despairing confes-
sion in the *Cantos*: "I cannot make it cohere" (*Cantos* 796).
That is the ultimate confession of confessional poetry, and it
is one that acknowledges the unraveling of the several threads
of the tradition of the self that had seemed such a sturdy fabric
in the hands of Yeats.

☒ VIII ☒

CONCLUSION:
THE END OF TRADITION

THE COHERENCE of the tradition that Yeats represented for American poets can be fully appreciated only if we keep in mind the prodigious variety comprised in Yeats's influence. Responses to a single poem could take any number of forms, some of which serve as reminders that influence, until our terminology is much refined, must be understood as a stimulus either to become like or to become unlike the influencing agent. Such an apparently simple poem as "The Lake Isle of Innisfree" became a subject for parody in Ezra Pound's "The Lake Isle," a text for deconstruction in Wallace Stevens's "Page from a Tale," a model for pastoral in Robert Penn Warren's "Vision," and "a fresh charter of poetic rights" in John Crowe Ransom's essay "The Irish, the Gaelic, the Byzantine."

Despite the common view of Yeats as a lyric poet, the works that have elicited response have not always been poems, as is shown by the attention Yeats's plays received from Frost, Stevens, Eliot, Jeffers, and MacLeish. Nor, when poems were concerned, were they always those we would expect, those that obviously bear on a poetry of the self, such as the intro-ductory poem to *Responsibilities*, "In Memory of Major Rob-ert Gregory," "A Prayer for My Daughter," "The Tower," and "The Circus Animals' Desertion." For many poets, in-cluding Pound, Frost, and Jeffers, it was not *Responsibilities* but *The Wind Among the Reeds* that first made Yeats a force to be reckoned with. Among the unexpected individual poems, "Innisfree" again serves as an example, for after the work of the confessional poets, it is difficult to see such a poem as representing the poet's self. Yet Yeats regarded the rhythm of "Innisfree" as an important step toward incorporating himself in his poetry. For the first time, he felt, he had been able to capture his "own music" (*Au* 153).

Considered from the standpoint of the poets who received the influence rather than the poet who produced it, the prospect is no less varied. It cannot be said, of American poetry at least, that there has been a School of Yeats in the sense that there is still a School of Pound or a School of Eliot. Radical and conservative, experimenter and traditionalist, patriot and expatriate—all have made use of Yeats's example in their different ways, though the meaning of that example has remained fundamentally the same in every case. To be a student of Pound or Eliot has meant, primarily, to write like Pound or Eliot. To be a student of Yeats has meant to "be Yeats," in Berryman's dark gloss, or to "be oneself," in Stevens's bright *scienza*. Of the poets considered in this study, only Stevens and Whitman were able to be themselves in their poems with an assurance that equals Yeats's.

This study has omitted many poets whose inclusion would have provided further evidence of the diversity of Yeats's influence. Marianne Moore and E. E. Cummings, for instance, seem to have been particularly interested in Yeats's prose.[1] However, my main purpose has been not to indicate the range of Yeats's influence but to depict the role of that influence within a limited, though dominant, poetic tradition, and the poets I have chosen have all furthered that tradition by producing a significant following. My main purpose has also determined the limit on poetic generations that I have observed. Although many younger poets have made evident use of Yeats, they have not done so within the context of the tradition of the self. As I have attempted to show in my discussion of Roethke, Berryman, and Lowell, the conception of the self on which that tradition was founded no longer seems tenable.

The poetry being written today may eventually amount to a demonstration that, along with a particular notion of the self, our poets have rejected not only a particular tradition but also the very idea of tradition. Now that Harold Bloom has explored the implications of viewing poetic influence in terms of the relationship between fathers and sons, we can make further use of those terms to define three stages in the evolution of the idea of tradition. First, there is the classical view of tradition, in which, ideally, the poet-son proudly emulates his father in the craft. Second, in the romantic view that Bloom's studies have defined, the son who comes late in tradition feels oppressed by the accumulated power of his many fathers, and, doubting his ability to confront that power directly, he attempts to put himself in the fathers' place by distorting or misreading their work. That we can derive from contemporary poetry some notion of a third stage in this evolution may mean that we are at last justified in speaking of a postromantic literature. In this stage, having placed himself in the role of the father, the son transfers to that role his own persistent self-doubt, so that the role itself loses the authority it once had. In a world in which the father is no better than the son—the sort of world reported in the poems of Robert Lowell—no tradition can be handed down, because, so to speak, no one is placed high enough to earn descendants.

If this schema is accurate, the poets to whom it applies, and whom the patriarchal imagery assumes to be male, will today find themselves in a position curiously similar to that which Sandra Gilbert and Susan Gubar describe as typical for the female poet who has been excluded from the patriarchal tradition: even before making particular claims of authorship, the poet must struggle to establish his or her right to be an author, to claim authority of the most basic sort.* Because it was tacitly understood, such a claim did not have to be explicitly established in the tradition of the self, which marks a transition between the second and third stages in the evolving relationship between literary fathers and sons. The romantic struggle with the father has been won. The son has fully replaced the father and assumed for himself the authority of tradition. Unlike the poet of the third stage, however, the poet of the tradition of the self has not yet lost faith in his ability to sustain the authority he has assumed. That faith underlies the audacity of Yeats's work and separates it from the work of poets who, like the Agrarians, are wary of equating the poet with God. In the view of contemporary poets, grounded, like Lowell's view, in the ethics if not the aesthetics of the late Auden, Yeats's audacity may appear as plain dishonesty. The concept of the self that has been rejected may have been simply a delusion. Our poets may have lost a certain grandeur, but gained in maturity, by acknowledging their own limitations and those of their fathers.

Yeats, of course, also recognized the limitations of the self. His poems frequently look behind the mask that they have created to reveal Yeats as "a comfortable kind of old scarecrow" ("Among School Children"), as "one that ruffled in a manly pose / For all his timid heart" ("Coole Park, 1929"), as "a coat upon a coat-hanger" ("The Apparitions"). Such insights could be reconciled with the visions of the Master of the Tower because Yeats conceived of the self as double. "I know now that revelation is from the self," Yeats explained in *The Trembling of the Veil*, "but from that age-long memoried self, that shapes the elaborate shell of the mollusc and the child in the womb, that teaches the birds to make their nest; and that genius is a crisis that joins that buried self for certain moments to our trivial daily mind" (*Au* 272). Because Yeats's conception of the self included that "trivial daily mind" to which recent poets have confined themselves, they may still benefit by attending to Yeats's example. And whatever view of the self they adopt, their poetry will surely benefit by responding to Yeats's admonition to seek revelation *from* the self, not merely revelation *of* the self. But to assume that poets can still learn from Yeats is to assume that tradition still operates, and the fact of that operation has been called into question.

Notes

I. Introduction

1. *Au* 463. Marjorie Perloff, " 'The Tradition of Myself': The Autobiographical Mode of Yeats," *Journal of Modern Literature,* 4 (February 1975), 529-73, applies Yeats's phrase to his poetry but gives little attention to the theoretical implications of such a tradition. Daniel O'Hara, "The Irony of Tradition and W. B. Yeats's *Autobiography*: An Essay in Dialectical Hermeneutics," *Boundary* 2, 5 (1977), 679-709, derives abundant theoretical speculation from Yeats's phrase but applies that speculation to Yeats's autobiographical prose rather than to his poetry.

2. Cf. Robert Langbaum on the importance of Yeats's external location of the unconscious in *The Mysteries of Identity: A Theme in Modern Literature* (New York: Oxford University Press, 1977), p. 159.

3. Cf. George T. Wright, *The Poet in the Poem: The Personae of Eliot, Yeats, and Pound* (Berkeley: University of California Press, 1960), pp. 89, 108.

4. Robert Langbaum, *The Poetry of Experience: The Dramatic Monologue in Modern Literary Tradition* (1957; rpt. New York: Norton, 1963).

5. See R.W.B. Lewis, *The American Adam: Innocence, Tragedy, and Tradition in the Nineteenth Century* (Chicago: University of Chicago Press, 1955); and Roy Harvey Pearce, *The Continuity of American Poetry* (1965; rpt. Princeton: Princeton University Press, 1977).

6. Cf. Quentin Anderson, *The Imperial Self: An Essay in American Literary and Cultural History* (New York: Knopf, 1971), p. 95.

7. M. L. Rosenthal, *The Modern Poets: A Critical Introduction* (1960; rpt. New York: Oxford University Press, 1975), p. 238. For other comments linking Yeats to confessional poetry, see Marjorie Perloff, "Yeats and the Occasional Poem: 'Easter 1916,'" *Papers on Language and Literature,* 4 (Summer 1968), 327; and Ralph J.

Mills, Jr., *Cry of the Human: Essays on Contemporary Poetry* (Urbana: University of Illinois Press, 1975), pp. 5, 24.

8. Cf. Steven K. Hoffmann, "Impersonal Personalism: The Making of a Confessional Poetic," *ELH*, 45 (Winter 1978), 688, 692.

9. Harold Bloom, *A Map of Misreading* (New York: Oxford University Press, 1975), p. 163.

10. René Wellek and Austin Warren, *Theory of Literature*, 3rd ed. (New York: Harcourt, Brace and World, 1956), p. 258.

II. AN AMERICAN TRADITION

1. Charles Johnston, "Emerson and Occultism," *Lucifer*, 1 (15 December 1887), 252-57. See William J. Sowder, *Emerson's Impact on the British Isles and Canada* (Charlottesville: University Press of Virginia, 1966), pp. 103, 120.

2. *The Book of the Poe Centenary*, ed. Charles William Hunt and John S. Patton (Charlottesville: University of Virginia, 1909), p. 207.

3. For reading *Walden*, *Au* 71; for "immortal," *Passages from the Letters of John Butler Yeats*, ed. Ezra Pound (Dundrum: The Cuala Press, 1917), p. 30. For an unconvincing attempt to locate Thoreau's influence in Yeats's late work, see Sidney Poger, "Yeats as Azad: A Possible Source in Thoreau," *Thoreau Journal Quarterly*, 5, no. 3 (1973), 13-15.

4. Henry D. Thoreau, *Walden*, ed. J. Lyndon Shanley (Princeton: Princeton University Press, 1971), pp. 66-67.

5. Yeats, "Friends of My Youth," in Robert O'Driscoll and Lorna Reynolds, eds., *Yeats and The Theatre* (Niagara Falls, N.Y.: Maclean-Hunter Press, 1975), p. 39. The journal version is retained in *Au* 469-70.

6. On Yeats's late expression of admiration for Wordsworth and Tennyson, see Joseph Hone, *W. B. Yeats 1865-1939* (New York: Macmillan, 1943), pp. 35-36; for Arnold, James V. Logan, *Wordsworthian Criticism* (Columbus: Ohio State University Press, 1961), pp. 50, 55-56; for D. G. Rossetti, *EI* 353; for J. B. Yeats, *J. B. Yeats: Letters to His Son W. B. Yeats and Others, 1869-1922*, ed. Joseph Hone (New York: Dutton, 1946), p. 47; for W. M. Rossetti, Harold Blodgett, *Walt Whitman in England* (Ithaca, N.Y.: Cornell University Press, 1934), p. 31; for Swinburne, ibid., p. 105; for Todhunter, ibid., p. 180. For a discussion of Whitman's reception in Ireland, see Herbert Howarth, "Whitman and the Irish Writers," *Comparative Literature: Proceedings of the Second Congress of the International*

Comparative Literature Association at the University of North Carolina, September 8-12, 1958, ed. Werner P. Friedrich, 2 vols. (Chapel Hill: University of North Carolina Press, 1959), II, 479-88.

7. "The Gospel According to Walt Whitman," in *The Artist as Critic: Critical Writings of Oscar Wilde*, ed. Richard Ellmann (New York: Random House, 1969), p. 125.

8. Quoted in an entry for 14 November 1925 in *Lady Gregory's Journals, 1916-1930*, ed. Lennox Robinson (New York: Macmillan, 1947), p. 263.

9. Blodgett, *Whitman in England*, pp. 47-48.

10. "Browning," in Yeats, *Letters to the New Island*, ed. Horace Reynolds (1934; rpt. Cambridge, Mass.: Harvard University Press, 1970), pp. 103-04. The same formula closed "Mr. William Wills" (1889), in *Letters to the New Island*, p. 76.

11. *L* 241. This and other major references by Yeats to Whitman are noticed in James E. Quinn, "Yeats and Whitman, 1887-1925," *Walt Whitman Review*, 20 (September 1974), 106-09.

12. Yeats, "The Poetry of Sir Samuel Ferguson," *Dublin University Review*, 2 (November 1886), 923-41, rpt. *UP* I, 87-104, with a note on order of composition, p. 81. Horace Traubel, *With Walt Whitman in Camden*, IV, ed. Sculley Bradley (Philadelphia: University of Pennsylvania Press, 1953), p. 347.

13. Traubel, *With Whitman in Camden*, p. 350.

14. Ibid., p. 349.

15. Yeats recalls Whitman's "Song of Myself"—"I, now thirty-seven years old in perfect health begin" (*LG* 29)—and Thoreau's chapter on "Higher Laws" in *Walden* (p. 219).

16. Quoted in Thomas McGreevy, "W. B. Yeats—A Generation Later," in E. H. Mikhail, ed., *W. B. Yeats: Interviews and Recollections*, 2 vols. (New York: Barnes and Noble, 1977), II, 413.

III. A LIVE TRADITION

1. For Pound's strongly ambivalent attitude to Whitman, see Herbert Bergman, "Ezra Pound and Walt Whitman," *American Literature*, 27 (March 1955), 56-61, and three articles by Charles B. Willard: "Ezra Pound's Appraisal of Walt Whitman," *Modern Language Notes*, 72 (January 1957), 19-26; "Ezra Pound and the Whitman 'Message,' " *Revue de Littérature Comparée*, 31 (January-March 1957), 94-98; "Ezra Pound's Debt to Walt Whitman," *Studies in Philology*, 54 (October 1957), 573-81. In "Ezra Pound's Appraisal

of Walt Whitman: Addendum," *Modern Language Notes*, 74 (January 1959), 23-28, Roy Harvey Pearce extends Willard's emphasis on the importance of Whitman for Pound's early writing by arguing that as late as the *Pisan Cantos* Pound's poetry is "in some basic aspects, quite Whitmanian" (p. 24).

2. Richard Ellmann, *Yeats: The Man and the Masks* (New York: Norton, 1979), p. 215, explains Pound's contribution as a transformation of genre. Curtis Bradford, *W. B. Yeats: The Making of "The Player Queen"* (DeKalb: Northern Illinois University Press, 1977), p. 6, without reference to Pound, speaks of the crucial change in the manuscripts in terms of tone rather than genre.

3. Richard Taylor, *The Drama of W. B. Yeats: Irish Myth and the Japanese No* (New Haven: Yale University Press, 1976), pp. 33, 100-01, confirms that the Noh offered traditional sanction for techniques Yeats had already developed.

4. Quoted in Noel Stock, *The Life of Ezra Pound* (London: Routledge and Kegan Paul, 1970), p. 130.

5. Ellen Williams, *Harriet Monroe and the Poetry Renaissance: The First Ten Years of "Poetry," 1912-22* (Urbana: University of Illinois Press, 1977), p. 54.

6. Richard Ellmann, *Eminent Domain: Yeats Among Wilde, Joyce, Pound, Eliot and Auden* (1967; rpt. New York: Oxford University Press, 1970), p. 64; see p. 78 for Pound's later editing of Yeats's "From the *Antigone*" (1929). "To a Child Dancing upon the Shore" appears in *The Collected Poems of W. B. Yeats* (New York: Macmillan, 1956) as "To a Child Dancing in the Wind."

7. For accounts that regard Pound's influence on Yeats as minimal, see Thomas Parkinson, "Yeats and Pound: The Illusion of Influence," *Comparative Literature*, 6 (Summer 1954), 256-64; Peter Faulkner, "Yeats, Ireland and Ezra Pound," *Threshold*, no. 18 (1963), 58-68; K. L. Goodwin, *The Influence of Ezra Pound* (London: Oxford University Press, 1966), pp. 75-105.

8. *CEP* 8. For Yeats and "La Fraisne," see Ellmann, *Eminent Domain*, p. 58.

9. *CEP* 35. For Yeats and "The Tree," see Ellmann, *Eminent Domain*, p. 58; Louis MacNeice, *The Poetry of W. B. Yeats* (1941; rpt. London: Faber, 1970), p. 98; N. Christoph de Nagy, *The Poetry of Ezra Pound: The Pre-Imagist Stage* (Bern: Francke Verlag, 1960), p. 103.

10. *CEP* 117-20. Thomas H. Jackson, *The Early Poetry of Ezra Pound* (Cambridge, Mass.: Harvard University Press, 1968), pp. 129,

193-94, refers to Yeats in his helpful discussion of this sequence. See also George Bornstein, *The Postromantic Consciousness of Ezra Pound*, ELS Monograph Series, no. 8 (Victoria, B.C.: University of Victoria, 1977), pp. 46-47.

11. Pound, "This Hulme Business" (1938), rpt. as Appendix I in Hugh Kenner, *The Poetry of Ezra Pound* (Norfolk, Conn.: New Directions, n.d.), p. 308.

12. Jackson, *Early Poetry of Pound*, pp. 134-36.

13. Pound, "Status Rerum," *Poetry*, 1 (January 1913), 125. Cf. Pound, "Le Prix Nobel" (1924), in *Pound/Joyce: The Letters of Ezra Pound to James Joyce*, ed. Forrest Read (New York: New Directions, 1967), p. 219.

14. For Confucius, see Virginia Moore, *The Unicorn: William Butler Yeats' Search for Reality* (New York: Macmillan, 1954), p. 465, n. 2; for Landor, see Stock, *Life of Pound*, pp. 189-90.

15. *Personae* 158. See K. K. Ruthven, *A Guide to Ezra Pound's "Personae" (1926)* (Berkeley: University of California Press, 1969), p. 243.

16. Pound, *Jefferson and/or Mussolini* (1935; rpt. New York: Liveright, 1970), p. 102; Pound, *Guide to Kulchur* (1952; rpt. New York: New Directions, 1970), p. 182.

17. Pound interviewed by Donald Hall, in *Writers at Work: The "Paris Review" Interviews*, 2nd ser. (New York: Viking, 1963), p. 47.

18. Pound, "Status Rerum," p. 125.

19. For image, see Pound, "Harold Monro" (1932), in *Polite Essays* (London: Faber, 1937), p. 9; for rhythm, see Pound, "On Music" (1912), *SP* 38.

20. *Vision B*, 67; see Ellmann, *Eminent Domain*, p. 60.

21. "Psychology and Troubadours," rpt. in *SR* 87-100; "Vorticism," rpt. in *GB* 81-94. Herbert N. Schneidau, "Pound and Yeats: The Question of Symbolism," *ELH*, 32 (June 1965), 220-37, refers to "Psychology and Troubadours" and stresses Pound's early attraction to spiritualism.

22. *Ex* 62. Cf. Pound, "Letters to William Butler Yeats," ed. C. F. Terrell, *Antaeus*, 21/22 (Spring/Summer 1976), 34.

23. Ezra Pound and Ernest Fenollosa, *The Classic Noh Theatre of Japan* (New York: New Directions, 1959), pp. 16, 12. The first edition of this book was entitled *Noh or Accomplishment*.

24. On Yeats's and Pound's contrasting views of Asia, see Parkinson, "Yeats and Pound," p. 262.

25. Yeats to Pound, 22 August 1920, Pound Papers, Beinecke Library, Yale University. Comparable to Yeats's comment on "Mauberley" is T. S. Eliot's remark on the "reticent autobiography" evident in the first appearance of the *Cantos*. See Ronald Bush, *The Genesis of Ezra Pound's "Cantos"* (Princeton: Princeton University Press, 1976), p. 5; Bush speculates, pp. 186-87, that Pound's depersonalizing of later drafts of the *Cantos* may have been undertaken in response to Eliot.

26. Charles Olson, *Charles Olson and Ezra Pound: An Encounter at St. Elizabeths*, ed. Catherine Seelye (New York: Grossman, 1975), p. 114.

27. Quoted in Richard Ellmann, *The Identity of Yeats* (1964; rpt. New York: Oxford University Press, 1968), p. 239.

28. Hugh Kenner, *The Pound Era* (Berkeley: University of California Press, 1971), p. 394.

29. Pound, *Guide to Kulchur*, p. 152.

30. Langbaum, *The Poetry of Experience: The Dramatic Monologue in Modern Literary Tradition* (1957; rpt. New York: Norton, 1963), p. 232.

IV. NATURAL SPEECH

1. Pound, "Status Rerum," *Poetry*, 1 (January 1913), 123.

2. Undated lecture notes in the Harriet Monroe Personal Papers, University of Chicago Library.

3. Edward Abood, "The Reception of the Abbey Theatre in America, 1911-1914" (Ph.D. diss., University of Chicago, 1962), p. 124, n. 1.

4. Padraic Colum, "Mr. Yeats' Selected Poems," *Dial*, 71 (October 1921), 465.

5. Lawrence Gilman, "The Last of the Poets," *North American Review*, 202 (October 1915), 595.

6. Bloom, *A Map of Misreading* (New York: Oxford University Press, 1975), p. 166.

7. "Mr. Lindsay on 'Primitive Singing,' " *Poetry*, 4 (July 1914), 161.

8. Vachel Lindsay, *A Handy Guide for Beggars* (New York: Macmillan, 1916), p. 12.

9. For Yeats and the poem, see Lindsay to Harriet Monroe, 14 March 1914, *Poetry* Papers, University of Chicago Library. The

entire pamphlet is reprinted in Lindsay, *Adventures, Rhymes and Designs* (New York: Eakins Press, 1968).

10. Lindsay to Harriet Monroe, 1 May 1914, *Poetry* Papers.

11. Quoted in Margaret Haley Carpenter, *Sara Teasdale: A Biography* (New York: Schulte, 1960), p. 190; see p. 71 for Teasdale's early admiration of Yeats.

12. Lindsay, *The Art of the Moving Picture* (New York: Macmillan, 1915), p. 276; see p. 235 for regional film companies.

13. For Yeats's influence on Lindsay's popularity in Britain, see Robert Nichols, "Introduction," in Lindsay, *General William Booth Enters Into Heaven and Other Poems* (London: Chatto and Windus, 1919), p. v.

14. Lindsay to Harriet Monroe, 3 February 1917, *Poetry* Papers.

15. Personal communication from Robert Fitzgerald, 1 July 1975.

16. Lindsay to Yeats, 6 October 1931, in Richard J. Finneran, George Mills Harper, and William M. Murphy, eds., *Letters to Yeats*, 2 vols. (New York: Columbia University Press, 1977), II, 521.

17. Reuben A. Brower, ". . . And of Recent Translations and Editions," pt. 1, *Yearbook of Comparative and General Literature*, 2, no. 7 (1952), 71; Brower is referring specifically to Dudley Fitts's and Robert Fitzgerald's translation of the *Antigone* (1939). In a personal communication to the author, 11 February 1975, Horace Gregory similarly connects Yeats and Fitzgerald.

18. A[lice]. C[orbin]. H[enderson]., " 'Too Far from Paris,' " *Poetry*, 4 (June 1914), 107-11.

19. For Yeats as Frost's favorite living poet, see Lawrance Thompson, *Robert Frost: The Early Years, 1874-1915* (New York: Holt, Rinehart and Winston, 1966), p. 412; for Pound, *PL* 7-8.

20. Frost quoted in Louis Mertins, *Robert Frost: Life and Talks-Walking* (Norman: University of Oklahoma Press, 1965), p. 301.

21. Thompson, *Frost: Early Years*, pp. 411-12.

22. Richard Ellmann, *Eminent Domain: Yeats Among Wilde, Joyce, Pound, Eliot and Auden* (1967; rpt. New York: Oxford University Press, 1970), p. 7, suggests this comparison.

23. *PRF* 8. Thompson, *Frost: Early Years*, p. 377, and Ellmann, *Eminent Domain*, p. 7, see Yeats in this poem.

24. Quoted in Thompson, *Frost: Early Years*, p. 362. The other plays produced were Marlowe's *Doctor Faustus*, Milton's *Comus*, and Sheridan's *The Rivals*.

25. "On Poetic Drama" (1925), in *Interviews with Robert Frost*,

ed. Edward Connery Lathem (New York: Holt, Rinehart and Winston, 1966), pp. 59-60.

26. Ellmann, *Eminent Domain*, p. 7.

27. Frost, "Remarks on the Occasion of the Tagore Centenary," *Poetry*, 99 (November 1961), 108.

28. Mertins, *Frost*, p. 112.

29. Thompson, *Frost: Early Years*, pp. 595-96.

30. Ibid., pp. 413-14. The internal debate Frost carried on about his own poses, particularly that of the farmer poet, is examined in detail in John C. Kemp, *Robert Frost and New England: The Poet as Regionalist* (Princeton: Princeton University Press, 1979).

31. *The Autobiography of William Carlos Williams* (New York: Random House, 1951), p. 114.

32. Ibid., p. 115.

33. "A Beginning on the Short Story (Notes)" (1950), in *Selected Essays of William Carlos Williams* (New York: New Directions, 1954), p. 308.

34. Williams, "Prologue to *Kora in Hell*," in *Selected Essays*, p. 21.

35. Williams, *Spring and All*, in *Imaginations*, ed. Webster Schott (New York: New Directions, 1970), pp. 102-03.

36. Quoted in John C. Thirwall, "William Carlos Williams' 'Paterson,' " *New Directions*, no. 17 (1961), 261.

37. Williams, *The Wedge* (Cummington, Mass.: The Cummington Press, 1944), p. 106.

38. *The Collected Later Poems of William Carlos Williams* (New York: New Directions, 1963), pp. 201-02.

39. Williams, "Measure," *Spectrum*, 3 (Fall 1959), 155.

40. Quoted in Vivienne Koch, *William Carlos Williams* (Norfolk, Conn.: New Directions, 1950), p. 148.

41. Williams, "Measure," pp. 137-38.

42. Gerard Manley Hopkins, "Author's Preface," in *The Poems of Gerard Manley Hopkins*, ed. W. H. Gardner and N. H. MacKenzie (London: Oxford University Press, 1967), p. 47.

43. Williams, *The Embodiment of Knowledge*, ed. Ron Loewinsohn (New York: New Directions, 1974), p. 34.

44. For the image of the dance in the symbolist tradition, see Frank Kermode, *Romantic Image* (London: Routledge and Kegan Paul, 1957), chap. IV. For Williams on Whitman, see Walter Sutton, "A Visit with William Carlos Williams" (1961), in Linda Welshimer

Wagner, ed., *Interviews with William Carlos Williams* (New York: New Directions, 1976), p. 42.

45. Steven Gould Axelrod, *Robert Lowell: Life and Art* (Princeton: Princeton University Press, 1978), p. 89.

46. Williams quoted in Sutton, "A Visit with Williams," p. 42.

V. ARTIFICIAL LIVES

1. [Harriet Monroe], "Mr. Yeats and the Poetic Drama," *Poetry*, 16 (April 1920), 34.

2. Denis Donoghue, *The Third Voice: Modern British and American Verse Drama* (1959; rpt. Princeton: Princeton University Press, 1966), p. 194.

3. For Yeats's age and his Old Man's fifty years, see Richard Ellmann, *Yeats: The Man and the Masks* (New York: Norton, 1979), pp. 218-19.

4. Quoted in A. Walton Litz, *Introspective Voyager: The Poetic Development of Wallace Stevens* (New York: Oxford University Press, 1972), p. 12.

5. Ibid., p. 12.

6. Stevens, *The Necessary Angel: Essays on Reality and the Imagination* (1951; rpt. New York: Vintage Books/Random House, n.d.), p. 141.

7. SCP 88. Litz, *Introspective Voyager*, p. 118, notes the similarity between this poem and Yeats's "To the Rose upon the Rood of Time."

8. Stevens, "About One of Marianne Moore's Poems" (1948), in Stevens, *Necessary Angel*, p. 101.

9. Edward Kessler, *Images of Wallace Stevens* (New Brunswick, N.J.: Rutgers University Press, 1972), p. 228, and Harold Bloom, *Wallace Stevens: The Poems of Our Climate* (Ithaca, N.Y.: Cornell University Press, 1977), p. 458, note the similarity between these poems.

10. OP 89. Bloom, *Wallace Stevens*, p. 370, refers to Yeats in connection with "Memorandum." However, for the approach to Yeats's Byzantium in Stevens's late work, see Alan D. Perlis, "Yeats' Byzantium and Stevens' Rome: A Comparison of Two Poems," *Wallace Stevens Journal*, 2 (Spring 1978), 18-25.

11. Frank Kermode, *Wallace Stevens* (Edinburgh: Oliver and Boyd, 1960), p. 10, compares these poems.

12. SCP 374. For Yeats in this poem, see Joseph N. Riddel, *The*

Clairvoyant Eye: The Poetry and Poetics of Wallace Stevens (Baton Rouge: Louisiana State University Press, 1965), p. 219; and Bloom, *Wallace Stevens*, p. 245.

13. For Eliot's early opinion of Yeats, see Eliot, "On a Recent Piece of Criticism," *Purpose*, 10 (April-June 1938), 91-92; "Yeats" (1940), *PP* 252; "Ezra Pound," pt. 1, *New English Weekly*, 30 (31 October 1946), 27; Donald Hall, interview with Eliot, in *Writers at Work: The "Paris Review" Interviews*, 2nd ser. (New York: Viking, 1963), p. 94.

14. Richard Ellmann, *Eminent Domain: Yeats Among Wilde, Joyce, Pound, Eliot and Auden* (1967; rpt. New York: Oxford University Press, 1970), p. 90.

15. "Shorter Notices," *Egoist*, 5 (June-July 1918), 87.

16. Eliot, "A Foreign Mind," *Athenaeum*, 4 July 1919, pp. 552-53.

17. Eliot, "The Three Provincialities," rpt. in *Essays in Criticism*, 1 (January 1951), 38.

18. Eliot, *After Strange Gods: A Primer of Modern Heresy* (London: Faber, 1934), p. 44.

19. Quoted in Richard Ellmann, *The Identity of Yeats* (1964; rpt. New York: Oxford University Press, 1968), p. 240.

20. Yeats, "Our Need for Religious Sincerity," *Criterion*, 4 (April 1926), 306-11. In the "Commentary" in this issue, p. 223, Eliot refers to Yeats's essay after noting Max Scheler's address to the Lessing-Akademie on the subject of freedom of speech. Eliot's "A Commentary," *Criterion*, 8 (December 1928), 185-86, refers to Yeats's "The Irish Censorship," *Spectator*, 29 September 1928, rpt. in *The Senate Speeches of W. B. Yeats*, ed. Donald R. Pearce (Bloomington: Indiana University Press, 1960), pp. 175-80.

21. Eliot, *After Strange Gods*, p. 46.

22. T. S. E[liot]., "A Commentary," *Criterion*, 14 (July 1935), 610-13.

23. Eliot, "The Aims of Poetic Drama," *Adam International Review*, 17 (November 1949), 10.

24. "Ezra Pound," pt. 1, p. 27. Cf. Ellmann, *Eminent Domain*, p. 90.

25. Carol H. Smith, *T. S. Eliot's Dramatic Theory and Practice* (Princeton: Princeton University Press, 1963), pp. 47-48.

26. Arnold Bennett's journal entry for 10 September 1924, quoted in David E. Jones, *The Plays of T. S. Eliot* (London: Routledge and Kegan Paul, 1960), p. 27.

27. The letter is quoted in Carol H. Smith, *Eliot's Dramatic Theory*, p. 62.

28. Margaret J. Lightfoot, *"Purgatory* and *The Family Reunion*: In Pursuit of Prosodic Description," *Modern Drama*, 7 (December 1964), 257.

29. E. Martin Browne, *The Making of T. S. Eliot's Plays* (Cambridge: Cambridge University Press, 1969), p. 96.

30. Lightfoot, *"Purgatory* and *The Family Reunion*," p. 265.

31. *Ah, Sweet Dancer: W. B. Yeats—Margot Ruddock, A Correspondence*, ed. Roger McHugh (London: Macmillan, 1970), p. 27.

32. See McGreevy, "Uileachán Dubh Ó," *Capuchin Annual* (1952), p. 228; and McGreevy, "W. B. Yeats—A Generation Later," in E. H. Mikhail, ed., *W. B. Yeats: Interviews and Recollections*, 2 vols. (New York: Barnes and Noble, 1977), p. 414. Yeats was commenting on McGreevy's monograph on Eliot (1931).

33. Eliot, "Ulysses, Order, and Myth," *Dial*, 75 (November 1923), 483.

34. See the letter from Eliot to Hallie Flanagan in 1933, quoted in Carol H. Smith, *Eliot's Dramatic Theory*, p. 62, and Smith's analysis of the ritual pattern.

35. For *At the Hawk's Well* in Eliot, see Kristian Smidt, "T. S. Eliot and W. B. Yeats," *Revue des Langues Vivantes*, 31 (November-December 1965), 564. For "Three Things" in Eliot, see Grover Smith, Jr., *T. S. Eliot's Poetry and Plays* (Chicago: University of Chicago Press, 1956), p. 275. For Yeats on bones in Eliot, see *OBMV* xix. A more questionable connection to Yeats in *East Coker* is discussed in Christopher Brown, "Eliot on Yeats: 'East Coker, II,' " *T. S. Eliot Review*, 3, nos. 1-2 (1976), 22-24.

36. Eliot to John Hayward, 1941, quoted in Helen Gardner, *The Composition of "Four Quartets"* (New York: Oxford University Press, 1978), p. 67.

37. Maurice Johnson, "The Ghost of Swift in *Four Quartets*," *Modern Language Notes*, 64 (April 1949), 273; Smidt, "Eliot and Yeats," p. 555; letter from Eliot to John Hayward, 1942, quoted in Gardner, *Composition of "Four Quartets,"* pp. 64-65.

38. Information concerning the drafts is drawn from Gardner, *Composition of "Four Quartets,"* pp. 66, 187.

39. Eliot to John Hayward, 1941, quoted in ibid., pp. 64-65.

40. Grover Smith, *Eliot's Poetry and Plays*, p. 284; Smidt, "Eliot and Yeats," p. 555; Hayward, in Gardner, *Composition of "Four Quartets,"* p. 193.

41. Gardner, *Composition of "Four Quartets,"* p. 68, follows Ellmann and Smidt in making this connection.

42. Ellmann, *Eminent Domain*, p. 95, quotes these lines in connection with the passage from *Little Gidding*.

43. *Fauna*, in Jeffers, *Roan Stallion, Tamar and Other Poems* (New York: Boni and Liveright, 1925), p. 216; originally in the volume *Tamar*.

44. *The Selected Letters of Robinson Jeffers, 1897-1962*, ed. Ann N. Ridgway (Baltimore: Johns Hopkins University Press, 1968), pp. 200-01.

45. Melba Berry Bennett, *The Stone Mason of Tor House* (Los Angeles: Ward Ritchie Press, 1966), p. 40.

46. Ibid., pp. 101, 98.

47. Jeffers, "Introduction," in *Visits to Ireland: Travel-Diaries of Una Jeffers* (Los Angeles: Ward Ritchie Press, 1954), p. 6.

48. For Una Jeffers, see Bennett, *Stone Mason of Tor House*, p. 195. For the "wild swan," cf. Jeffers, *Medea* (New York: Random House, 1946), p. 42; "Love the Wild Swan," (1935), "Flight of Swans" (1935), "Shiva" (1938), in *SPRJ* 573, 577, 611.

49. Jeffers, "Preface to 'Judas,' " *New York Times*, 5 October 1947, sec. 2, p. 3.

50. Cf. Jeffers, *Selected Letters*, p. 369, and a letter to Sydney S. Alberts, quoted in Bennett, *Stone Mason of Tor House*, p. 132.

51. Jeffers, *Selected Letters*, p. 146.

52. Jeffers, *The Women at Point Sur* (New York: Boni and Liveright, 1927), p. 9.

53. For Jeffers's declared intention, see Bennett, *Stone Mason of Tor House*, p. 132.

54. Quoted in ibid., p. 206.

55. Jeffers, *The Beginning and the End* (New York: Random House, 1963), p. 60.

56. Ibid., p. 64.

VI. Public Speech

1. For the impact of *The Tower*, see Cleanth Brooks, *Modern Poetry and the Tradition* (1939; rpt. Chapel Hill: University of North Carolina Press, 1967), p. 173; and Stephen Spender, "The Influence of Yeats on Later English Poets," *Tri-Quarterly*, no. 4 (Fall 1965), pp. 83-85. For the reaction against Eliot, see Louis MacNeice, *The Poetry of W. B. Yeats* (1941; rpt. London: Faber, 1970), p. 191.

2. Personal communication from Robert Penn Warren, 2 May 1974. For a detailed consideration of the parallels between Yeats's Ireland and the American South as literary environments, see Cleanth Brooks, "Faulkner and W. B. Yeats," in Brooks, *William Faulkner: Toward Yoknapatawpha and Beyond* (New Haven: Yale University Press, 1978), pp. 329-44.

3. See Louis D. Rubin, Jr., *The Wary Fugitives: Four Poets and the South* (Baton Rouge: Louisiana State University Press, 1978), p. 96.

4. Personal communication from Allen Tate, 4 January 1974. For the readings, see Joseph Hone, *W. B. Yeats 1865-1939* (New York: Macmillan, 1943), p. 343.

5. For early Yeats, see Crane's use of "He Bids His Beloved Be at Peace" (1896) and "The Wanderings of Oisin" (1896) in "Voyages II" (1926), *The Complete Poems and Selected Letters and Prose of Hart Crane*, ed. Brom Weber (Garden City, N.Y.: Doubleday, 1966), p. 36. For Eliot, see Tate, "Poetry Modern and Unmodern" (1968), *EFD* 225-26.

6. *Fugitive*, 2, no. 6 (1923), 54. Tate has rewritten this poem as "Reflections in an Old House," *TCP* 198-99.

7. For comments associating Yeats with Tate's use of this meter, see John M. Bradbury, *The Fugitives: A Critical Account* (Chapel Hill: University of North Carolina Press, 1958), p. 164; Monroe K. Spears, *Dionysus and the City: Modernism in Twentieth-Century Poetry* (New York: Oxford University Press, 1970), p. 173; Radcliffe Squires, *Allen Tate: A Literary Biography* (New York: Pegasus/Bobbs-Merrill, 1971), p. 166.

8. Spears, *Dionysus and the City*, p. 167.

9. Tate to Davidson, 1943, in *The Literary Correspondence of Donald Davidson and Allen Tate*, ed. John Tyree Fain and Thomas Daniel Young (Athens: University of Georgia Press, 1974), p. 337.

10. On such informality as a special feature of "In Memory of Major Robert Gregory," see David Young, " 'The Living World for Text': Life and Art in *The Wild Swans at Coole*," in Louis L. Martz and Aubrey Williams, eds., *The Author in His Work: Essays on a Problem in Criticism* (New Haven: Yale University Press, 1978), pp. 145-46, 149; for Ransom's view of "Lycidas," see Ransom, *The World's Body* (New York: Scribner, 1938), p. 26.

11. See Yeats, *Mythologies* (New York: Macmillan, 1959), p. 331.

12. Ransom, *God Without Thunder: An Unorthodox Defense of Orthodoxy* (New York: Harcourt, Brace, 1930), p. 126.

13. Ibid., p. 137.

14. Ransom, *The World's Body*, pp. ix-xi.

15. Ransom in James Hall and Martin Steinmann, eds., *The Permanence of Yeats: Selected Criticism* (New York: Macmillan, 1950), p. 97; essay originally entitled "Yeats and His Symbols."

16. Ibid., p. 107.

17. Ransom, *Selected Poems* (New York: Knopf, 1969), p. 139. For the poem, see *Selected Poems*, pp. 136-39, where two versions are printed with a commentary. In a parenthetical note to the title Ransom mistakes the date of Yeats's birth as 24 June, rather than 13 June, 1865.

18. Ransom, *The World's Body*, p. 135.

19. *Fugitive*, I, no. 2 (1922), 54; the poem appears under Ransom's pseudonym, Roger Prim.

20. "Vision," *American Poetry Magazine*, 5 (December 1922), 23; on "Innisfree," personal communication from Warren to the author, 2 May 1974.

21. Cleanth Brooks, *The Hidden God: Studies in Hemingway, Faulkner, Yeats, Eliot, and Warren* (New Haven; Yale University Press, 1963), p. 98.

22. Ibid. Spears, *Dionysus and the City*, p. 186-95, gives a concise overview of Warren's "confessional poetry."

23. Empson, *Some Versions of Pastoral* (1935; rpt. New York: New Directions, 1968), chap. I.

24. Horace Gregory, "Like a Chambered Nautilus," *New York Times Book Review*, 22 December 1957, p. 5; a review of Yeats's *Variorum Poems*. Gregory comments on the move from the *Little Review* to *Responsibilities* in a personal communication to the author, 11 February 1975.

25. Gregory, "After a Half-Century," *Poetry*, 33 (October 1928), 42.

26. Gregory, "Yeats: Envoy of Two Worlds," *New Republic*, 77 (13 December 1933), 135.

27. Cf. Gregory, "Yeats: Last Spokesman," *New Republic*, 84 (18 September 1935), 164; "W. B. Yeats and the Mask of Jonathan Swift," *SRev*, 492-504; "Yeats as Dublin Saw Him," *Yale Review*, 32 (March 1943), 601.

28. Louis Untermeyer, ed., *Modern American Poetry / Modern British Poetry*, combined ed. (New York: Harcourt, Brace, 1942), p. 599 (in *Modern American Poetry*).

29. Gregory, "Yeats: A Self-Made Poet," *New York Times Book Review*, 25 December 1949, p. 14.

30. Gregory, *Selected Poems* (New York: Viking, 1951), pp. 15, 24.

31. Gregory, "New York, Cassandra," in Jack Salzman, ed., *Years of Protest: A Collection of American Writings of the 1930's* (Indianapolis: Pegasus/Bobbs-Merrill,1970), pp. 363-65.

32. Gregory, *Selected Poems*, pp. 70, 112, and Gregory, *Medusa in Gramercy Park* (New York: Macmillan, 1961), p. 6.

33. Bloom, *A Map of Misreading* (New York: Oxford University Press, 1975), p. 166.

34. Daniel Aaron, *Writers on the Left: Episodes in American Literary Communism* (New York: Harcourt, Brace and World, 1961), pp. 278-79, 429; Ellen Perley Frank, "MacLeish Relives an Early Stage Work," *New York Times*, 6 July 1980, sec. 2, p. 16.

35. Selden Rodman, "The Social Symbolists," a letter, *New Republic*, 96 (28 September 1938), 216.

36. Lawrence Mason, foreword to Archibald MacLeish, *Tower of Ivory* (New Haven: Yale University Press, 1917), p. viii.

37. MacLeish, *Tower of Ivory*, p. 69. Yeats reprinted "The Moods" in the text of *Per Amica Silentia Lunae* (1917); see Yeats, *Mythologies*, p. 357.

38. MacLeish, *The Happy Marriage and Other Poems* (Boston: Houghton Mifflin, 1924), pp. 73-74.

39. Donald Hall, "Visiting the MacLeishes," *New York Times Book Review*, 9 July 1978, p. 30.

40. Cf. MacLeish, *Poetry and Experience* (Boston: Houghton Mifflin, 1960), p. 123; and MacNeice, *Poetry of Yeats*, p. 94.

41. MacLeish, *Panic* (Boston: Houghton Mifflin, 1935), p. 33.

42. MacLeish, "Public Speech and Private Speech in Poetry," *Yale Review*, 27 (March 1938), 544.

43. MacLeish, *Poetry and Experience*, p. 124.

44. MacLeish, "Poetry and the Public World," rpt. in *A Time to Speak* (Boston: Houghton Mifflin, 1941), pp. 89-96.

45. On this technique as employed by MacLeish, see Brooks, *Modern Poetry and the Tradition*, pp. 118-19.

46. *NCP* 417. Grover Smith, *Archibald MacLeish*, University of Minnesota Pamphlets on American Writers, no. 99 (Minneapolis: University of Minnesota Press, 1971), p. 39, remarks on Yeats's influence in "Hypocrite Auteur."

47. MacLeish, *Herakles* (Boston: Houghton Mifflin, 1967), p. 19.

48. MacLeish, *Collected Poems 1917-1952* (Boston: Houghton Mifflin, 1952), p. 154.

49. MacLeish, "The Poet as Playwright," *Atlantic Monthly*, 195 (February 1955), 51.

50. Denis Donoghue, *The Third Voice: Modern British and American Verse Drama* (1959; rpt. Princeton: Princeton University Press, 1966), pp. 197-99.

51. MacLeish, *J.B.* (New York: Samuel French, 1959), p. 110; MacLeish discusses Yeats on p. 10 of the foreword.

52. MacLeish, "Yeats and the Belief in Life," in MacLeish, *A Continuing Journey* (Boston: Houghton Mifflin, 1968), p. 20.

53. MacLeish, *Poetry and Experience*, p. 199.

54. NCP 445, and Grover Smith, *Archibald MacLeish*, p. 39.

55. Quoted in Hall, "Visiting the MacLeishes," p. 28.

VII. Private Lives

1. W. H. Auden, "In Memory of W. B. Yeats" (1939), *Selected Poems*, ed. Edward Mendelson (New York: Vintage Books/Random House, 1979), p. 81.

2. Delmore Schwartz, "The Cunning of the Craft of the Unconscious and the Preconscious" (1959), in *Selected Essays of Delmore Schwartz*, ed. Donald A. Dike and David H. Zucker (Chicago: University of Chicago Press, 1970), p. 199; review of Roethke's *Words for the Wind*.

3. RCP 42. See Louis L. Martz, "A Greenhouse Eden," in Arnold Stein, ed., *Theodore Roethke: Essays on the Poetry* (Seattle: University of Washington Press, 1965), pp. 28-29; and Jenijoy LaBelle, *The Echoing Wood of Theodore Roethke* (Princeton: Princeton University Press, 1976), pp. 142-44.

4. Robert Phillips, *The Confessional Poets* (Carbondale: Southern Illinois University Press, 1973), p. xiv.

5. Peter Viereck, "Technique and Inspiration: A Year of Poetry," *Atlantic Monthly*, 189 (January 1952), 81.

6. Karl Malkoff, *Theodore Roethke: An Introduction to the Poetry* (New York: Columbia University Press, 1966), p. 117, notes the relevance of *A Vision* to "body of his fate."

7. Auden, "Don Juan" (1962), in Auden, *The Dyer's Hand and Other Essays* (New York: Random House, 1962), pp. 397-98.

8. Malkoff, *Theodore Roethke*, p. 120n.

9. Ralph J. Mills, Jr., *Theodore Roethke*, University of Minnesota

Pamphlets on American Writers, no. 30 (Minneapolis: University of Minnesota Press, 1963), p. 32, sees Yeats's influence in Roethke's treatment of sex as a dance.

10. *RCP* 148. Malkoff, *Theodore Roethke*, p. 153, compares these phrases.

11. This similarity is noted by Malkoff, *Theodore Roethke*, p. 144; and William Meredith, "A Steady Storm of Correspondences: Theodore Roethke's Long Journey Out of the Self," in Stein, ed., *Theodore Roethke*, p. 52.

12. For "not since Yeats," *RL* 208; for W. D. Snodgrass, "Spring Verse Chronicle," *Hudson Review*, 12 (Spring 1959), 116; for Roethke's annoyance, *RL* 231.

13. "On Theodore Roethke's 'In a Dark Time,'" in Anthony Ostroff, ed., *The Contemporary Poet as Artist and Critic* (Boston: Little, Brown, 1964), pp. 50-51.

14. Cf. William Heyen, "The Yeats Influence: Roethke's Formal Lyrics of the Fifties," *John Berryman Studies*, 3 (1977), 33-34.

15. Schwartz, "The Cunning of the Craft," p. 198; Martz, "A Greenhouse Eden," p. 28; Richard Wilbur, "Poetry's Debt to Poetry," *Hudson Review*, 26 (Summer 1973), 279.

16. Snodgrass, "'That Anguish of Concreteness'—Theodore Roethke's Career," in Stein, ed., *Theodore Roethke*, p. 91.

17. John Berryman, "Three and a Half Years at Columbia," in Wesley First, ed., *University on the Heights* (New York: Doubleday, 1969), p. 59.

18. BBC Television interview with Berryman, produced by Gavin Millar, 1967.

19. George T. Wright, *The Poet in the Poem: The Personae of Eliot, Yeats, and Pound* (Berkeley: University of California Press, 1960), p. 108, discusses the combination of fallibility and heroism in Yeats's *persona*.

20. Berryman, *Poems* (Norfolk, Conn.: [New Directions], 1942), p. 19; rpt. in Berryman, *Short Poems* (New York: Farrar, Straus and Giroux, 1967), p. 10.

21. Sonnet 5, in *Berryman's Sonnets* (New York: Farrar, Straus and Giroux, 1967); Dream Songs 88 and 215; "In Memoriam (1914-1953)," in *Delusions, Etc.* (New York: Farrar, Straus and Giroux, 1972), p. 29; "Roots," in *Henry's Fate and Other Poems, 1967-1972* (New York: Farrar, Straus and Giroux, 1977), p. 58.

22. Berryman, *Poems*, p. 10; rpt. in Berryman, *Short Poems*, pp. 38-39. Cf. J. M. Linebarger, *John Berryman* (New York: Twayne,

1974), p. 30; and Joel Conarroe, *John Berryman: An Introduction to the Poetry* (New York: Columbia University Press, 1977), pp. 30-31.

23. Yeats's relevance to Berryman's "Animal Trainer" poems has been noted by Richard Ellmann, *Eminent Domain: Yeats Among Wilde, Joyce, Pound, Eliot and Auden* (1967; rpt. New York: Oxford University Press, 1970), p. 8; Linebarger, *John Berryman*, p. 30; Conarroe, *Berryman: An Introduction*, p. 40.

24. Berryman, "Twenty Poems," in *Five Young American Poets* (Norfolk, Conn.: New Directions, 1940), p. 52; rpt. in Berryman, *Short Poems*, p. 19. For Berryman's combination of Yeats and Auden in this poem, see Jerome Mazzaro, "The Yeatsian Mask: John Berryman," in Mazzaro, *Postmodern American Poetry* (Urbana: University of Illinois Press, 1980), pp. 115-16.

25. Berryman, "Twenty Poems," p. 54.

26. Berryman, *Short Poems*, p. 54.

27. "An Interview with John Berryman," *Harvard Advocate*, 103 (Spring 1969), 8.

28. "The Translation," in *New Directions in Prose and Poetry 1938* (Norfolk, Conn.: New Directions, 1938), n. pag.; "Toward Statement," *Southern Review*, 4 (Summer 1938), 172.

29. "First Love," "His Memories," "The Secrets of the Old," from *A Man Young and Old*; "Crazy Jane and Jack the Journeyman," "Crazy Jane Talks with the Bishop," "Young Man's Song," "Three Things," "Lullaby," "Mad As the Mist and Snow," "Tom the Lunatic," from *Words for Music Perhaps*; "A First Confession," "Meeting," from *A Woman Young and Old*.

30. Interview (13 November 1974) and personal communication (21 November 1974) from Lowell to the author.

31. Lowell quoted in Philip Cooper, *The Autobiographical Myth of Robert Lowell* (Chapel Hill: University of North Carolina Press, 1970), p. 36.

32. Cleanth Brooks and Robert Penn Warren, *Understanding Poetry: An Anthology for College Students* (New York: Holt, 1939), pp. 19-20; cf. *El* 155-56.

33. Lowell, "Visiting the Tates," *Sewanee Review*, 67 (Autumn 1959), 558.

34. Steven Gould Axelrod, *Robert Lowell: Life and Art* (Princeton: Princeton University Press, 1978), p. 19.

35. Ibid., Appendix A, p. 246.

36. Personal communication from Lowell to the author, 21 November 1974.

37. *Hika*, June 1939, p. 15.

38. Jon Stallworthy, "The Dynastic Theme," in Stallworthy, *Vision and Revision in Yeats's "Last Poems"* (Oxford: Oxford University Press, 1969), p. 6.

39. Ibid., p. 15.

40. On Yeats, interview with Lowell, 13 November 1974; "In Memory of Arthur Winslow," *Poems 1938-1949* (1950; rpt. London: Faber, 1960), pp. 29-32; "The Cities' Summer Death," *Kenyon Review*, 1 (Winter 1939), 32.

41. Lowell to the author, 21 November 1974. For "Fourth of July in Maine" and "A Prayer for My Daughter," see Cooper, *Autobiographical Myth*, p. 133; Alan Williamson, *Pity the Monsters: The Political Vision of Robert Lowell* (New Haven: Yale University Press, 1974), p. 132; Axelrod, *Robert Lowell*, p. 189.

42. See Herbert Leibowitz, "Robert Lowell: Ancestral Voices," in Michael London and Robert Boyers, eds., *Robert Lowell: A Portrait of the Artist in His Time* (New York: David Lewis, 1970), p. 211; and John Peck, "Reflections on Lowell's 'Domesday Book,' " *Salmagundi*, no. 37 (Spring 1977), 33-34.

43. *NO* 15. For Yeats's influence in this poem, see Cooper, *Autobiographical Myth*, pp. 121, 123; Patrick Cosgrave, *The Public Poetry of Robert Lowell* (New York: Taplinger, 1972), pp. 11, 198-201; Stephen Yenser, *Circle to Circle: The Poetry of Robert Lowell* (Berkeley: University of California Press, 1975), pp. 251, 253.

44. Interview with Lowell, 13 November 1974; Lowell acknowledged the relevance of Yeats's salmon to his own.

45. *New York Review of Books*, 5 August 1965, p. 3.

46. Lowell, "Leaving America for England," Poem 3: "Truth," in *The Dolphin* (New York: Farrar, Straus and Giroux, 1973), p. 67. Lowell discussed the sources of this poem in his interview with the author, 13 November 1974.

47. Auden, *The Dyer's Hand*: "Making, Knowing and Judging" (1956), p. 43; "Robert Frost" (1962), p. 353; "D. H. Lawrence" (1962), p. 281.

48. "Circus Animals' Desertion" identified in interview with Lowell, 13 November 1974. Auden refers to the poem in *Secondary Worlds* (London: Faber, 1968), p. 135, and in his introduction to *The Complete Poems of Cavafy* (1961), rpt. in Auden, *Forewords*

and Afterwords, ed. Edward Mendelson (New York: Vintage Books/ Random House, 1974), p. 336.

49. Lowell, *History* (New York: Farrar, Straus and Giroux, 1973), p. 56. A different version, also alluding to Yeats, appears in the two editions of *Notebook*. Yeats's note is quoted in Richard Ellmann, *Yeats: The Man and the Masks* (New York: Norton, 1979), p. 282.

50. Lowell, "A Conversation with Ian Hamilton," *American Poetry Review*, 7 (September-October 1978), 24.

51. Gabriel Pearson, "Robert Lowell," *The Review*, no. 20 (March 1969), 5. Pearson's sensitive analysis provides a corrective to the tone-deaf interpretation of Karl Malkoff in *Escape from the Self: A Study in Contemporary American Poetry and Poetics* (New York: Columbia University Press, 1977), which reads signs of the self's disintegration as evidence of a desirable "escape."

52. Lowell, *Dolphin*, p. 67.

53. Auden, *Homage to Clio* (New York: Random House, 1960), pp. 35-49.

54. "A Second Plunge, A Dream," in Lowell, *Notebook* (New York: Farrar, Straus and Giroux, 1970), p. 182.

VIII. CONCLUSION

1. See Moore, "The *Dial*: A Retrospect," in *Predilections* (New York: Viking, 1955), pp. 104-06; note in *Observations*, 1st ed. (New York: Dial Press, 1924), pp. 30-31; "To William Butler Yeats on Tagore" and "Poetry," in *Poems* (London: The Egoist Press, 1921), pp. 8, 22. For Cummings, see *Selected Letters of E. E. Cummings*, ed. F. W. Dupee and George Stade (New York: Harcourt, Brace and World, 1969), pp. 188, 255.

2. Sandra M. Gilbert and Susan Gubar, *The Madwoman in the Attic: The Woman Writer and the Nineteenth-Century Literary Imagination* (New Haven: Yale University Press, 1979), pp. 47-49.

INDEX

(Page numbers in italics indicate principal discussions.)

Abbey Theatre, 44, 60, 64, 77, 81, 106, 112, 170. *See also* Irish National Theatre
Adam, 7, 179
Adelphi Club (London), 77
AE, *see* Russell, George
Aeschylus, *The Eumenides*, 113
Agrarians, 135, 136, 140, 145, 146, 147, 148, 150, 151, 152, 153, 155, 156, 214, 227
Allingham, William, 12
America, United States of, 63, 64, 67, 76, 77; Boston, Mass., 70, 213; California, 124; Carmel, Calif., 122; Chicago, 60, 61; Eastern, 60, 214; Ernest Rhys in, 24; idiom of, 33, 81; image of, in literature, 22, 29, 81, 85, 98, 101; Irish literature received in, 22-23, 35, 59-61, 69, 225-26; literary climate in, 4, 11, 31, 59-61, 65-66, 88, 129, 135, 175; literary tradition of, 4-5, 7-8, 11-12, 14, 18, 21-23, 30, 31-32, 33, 59-61, 65-66, 103, 165, 226; Midwestern, 60, 65; Milwaukee, Wis., 159; Nashville, Tenn., 136, 153; New England, 69, 216; New Hampshire, 75; New York City, 75, 88, 156; Northern, 135; Oscar Wilde in, 21; Paterson, N.J., 85; Southern, 135, 145, 146, 147, 151, 153, 156, 202, 213, 214; Springfield, Ill.,

65; Vermont, 75; W. B. Yeats in, 11, 61, 88, 136, 167
American Prefaces, 79
Anticosti Island (Canada), 79
Antilles Islands, 177
Antony, Mark, 205
Apollinaire, Guillaume, 177
Aristotle, *Poetics*, 76
Arnold, Matthew, 20, 103; "Dover Beach," 170
Athenaeum Club (London), 201
Atlantic Monthly, 188
Auden, W. H., 181, 189, 198, 204-05, 220-24, 228; "Dame Kind," 223; "Dichtung und Wahrheit," 223
Axelrod, Steven Gould, 86

Ballet Russe, of Diaghilev, 117
Berryman, John, 56, 57, 58, 197-212, 215, 217, 220, 222, 226; "Ancestor," 203; "The Animal Trainer," I and II, 203-04; "At Chinese Checkers," 202, 206, 211; *Berryman's Sonnets*, 201; "Cloud and Flame," 202; *The Dispossessed*, 202-03, 206; *Dream Songs*, 199, 205-12; *The Freedom of the Poet*, 56, 57, 197, 202, 204, 206; "Friendliness," 201; "Henry Comforted," 209; *Henry's Fate*, 201; "The Heroes," 199, 201; *Homage to Mistress Bradstreet*, 206; *Love*

Berryman, John (*cont.*)
  and Fame, 198; "The Nervous
    Songs," 206; "Olympus," 198;
    "On the London Train," 204-05;
    "A Point of Age," 200; "Recov-
    ery," 200; "The Ritual of W. B.
    Yeats" (*Columbia Review*), 198-
    99; "Rock-study with Wan-
    derer," 202-03; "Song from
    'Cleopatra,' " 205; "The Spin-
    ning Heart," 203; "Toward
    Statement," 206; "The Transla-
    tion," 206; "Two Organs," 198;
    "White Feather," 205; "Winter
    Landscape," 204. *See also* Smith,
    John
Blackmur, R. P., 198-99; *The Dou-
    ble Agent*, 199
Blake, William, 5, 21, 105, 137,
    163, 224; *The Four Zoas*, 5
Blast, 34
Blavatsky, H. P., 13
Bloom, Harold, 9, 62, 165, 226-27
Boehme, Jacob, 13, 193
Boston Pilot, 22
Botticelli, Sandro, 174
Brawne, Fanny, 211
Bridges, Robert, 83
Brooks, Cleanth, 153, 214; *Under-
    standing Poetry* (with Robert
    Penn Warren), 214
Browne, E. Martin, 108
Browne, Maurice, 60
Browning, Robert, 35, 41, 63, 76;
    "Love Among the Ruins," 63
Brunetto Latini, 116
Bryher (Winifred Ellerman), 159
Byron, George Gordon, Lord, 19
Byzantium, 72, 73, 93, 98, 146,
    147, 177

Cable, George Washington, 22
Cambridge University, *see* Clare
    College
Catholicism, 217
Cato, 215

Catullus, 44-45
Cavalcanti, Guido, 52-56
Chaucer, Geoffrey, 82
China, 51
Cicero, 205
Clare College, Cambridge, 201
Cleopatra, 205
Coleridge, Samuel Taylor, 94
Colum, Padraic, 60-61
Columbia Review, 198
Columbia University, 197-200
Communist Party, U.S.A., 166
Confessional poetry, 8-9, 50-51,
    56, 86, 130, 154, 181, 187, 199,
    200, 213, 224, 225
Confucius, 44, 49-50
Connolly, James, 199
Coole Park, 147, 157, 218. *See
    also* Gregory, Isabella Augusta,
    Lady; Yeats, W. B.
Cornford, F. M., *The Origin of At-
    tic Comedy*, 112
Cox, Sidney, 69, 71, 72, 74
Crane, Hart, 136
Criterion, 104, 105, 110
Cummings, E. E., 226
Cunard, Maude, Lady, 172

Dante, 33, 112, 116, 190; *Inferno*,
    116
Davidson, Donald, 140
Davies, Sir John, 188, 189; *Orches-
    tra*, 189
Decadents, 14, 19
Depression, the Great, 135
DeQuincey, Thomas, 76
Dermot Mac Murrough (Diar-
    muid), 112
Dervorgilla, 112
Deutsch, Babette, 194, 195
Dial, 52, 60
Diarmuid, *see* Dermot Mac Mur-
    rough
Dickinson, Emily, 214
Donne, John, 103
Donoghue, Denis, 89, 178

Dowden, Edward, 21
Dowson, Ernest, 4, 41, 77; "Non sum qualis eram bonae sub regno Cynarae," 77
Dublin University Review, 24
Dunbarton, 218

Easter Rebellion (Ireland, 1916), 112, 150, 199
Eberhart, Richard, 80-81
Egyptian sculpture, 52
Eliot, George, 23
Eliot, T. S., 3, 77, 78-79, 87, 91, *101-18*, 119, 134, 135, 136, 144-45, 156, 166, 173, 175-76, 177, 196, 197, 199, 214, 225, 226; *After Strange Gods*, 103, 104; "The Aims of Poetic Drama," 105; "Andrew Marvell," 103; *Ash Wednesday*, 111; "The Beating of a Drum," 106-07; *Burnt Norton*, 114-15; *The Cocktail Party*, 109-10, 113; "Commentary" (*Criterion*), 104-05; *The Confidential Clerk*, 113; *The Dry Salvages*, 115; *East Coker*, 115; *The Elder Statesman*, 113; *The Family Reunion*, 107-09, 113; "A Foreign Mind," 102-03; "Four Elizabethan Dramatists," 117-18; *Four Quartets*, 114-15, 196, 235; "The Hollow Men," 111; *Little Gidding*, 113, *115-18*; *Murder in the Cathedral*, 112-13; "The Music of Poetry," 105; "Philip Massinger," 114; "Poetry and Drama," 105, 107-08, 109; *The Rock*, 112; "Shorter Notices," 102; *Sweeney Agonistes*, 107, 112; "The Three Provincialities," 103; "The Three Voices of Poetry," 114; "Tradition and the Individual Talent," 3, 101-02, 113-14; "Ulysses, Order, and Myth," 111; *The Waste Land*, 112;

"Yeats," 91, 106, 107, 110, 111-12, 113, 114, 117
Ellerman, Winifred, *see* Bryher
Elliott, William Yandell, 155-56
Ellis, Edwin, *Fate in Arcadia*, 18
Ellmann, Richard, 71, 102
Emerson, Ralph Waldo, 5, 9, *11-14*, 15, 16, 17, 21, 23, 26-27, 62, 165; "Saadi," 12; "Shakespeare; or, The Poet," 12-13, 26; "Swedenborg; or, The Mystic," 26-27
Emery, Florence Farr, *see* Farr, Florence
Empedocles, 47
Empson, William, *Some Versions of Pastoral*, 145, 156
Euripides: *Alcestis*, 113; *Ion*, 113; *Medea*, 124
Europe, 4, 23, 31, 60, 77, 101, 157, 200, 214
Evans, Mary Ann, *see* Eliot, George
Eve, 179
Exile, The, 44

Farr, Florence, 46
Fascism, 56, 166
Fenollosa, Ernest, 32; *Noh or Accomplishment* (with Ezra Pound), 49, 107
Ferguson, Sir Samuel, 24-26
Fitzgerald, Robert, 65
Flanagan, Hallie, 107
Ford, Ford Madox (Hueffer), 45-46, 50
France, 99, 116; Paris, 51, 66
Francesca da Rimini, 112
Frederick II (the Great), King, 128
Freud, Sigmund, 48
Frost, Elinor, 67, 74
Frost, Robert, 59, 66-76, 84, 124, 148, 225; "After Apple Picking," 70-71; *A Boy's Will*, 67-68, 70, 71, 75; "Come In," 72; "The Death of the Hired Man," 71; "In a Vale," 68; "In Neglect,"

Frost, Robert (*cont.*)
67; "Into My Own," 72; "A Late Walk," 68; "A Line-Storm Song," 68; "Love and a Question," 68; "A Masque of Mercy," 73-74; "The Mountain," 71; "My November Guest," 68; "New Hampshire," 75; *North of Boston*, 70; "Remarks on the Occasion of the Tagore Centenary," 71; "Rose Pogonias," 70; *Selected Letters*, 67, 68-69, 71, 72, 74-75; "The Self-Seeker," 70; "Stopping by Woods on a Snowy Evening," 72, 75
Fugitive, The, 136, 149, 155
Fugitives' Reunion, 136, 146, 152, 155-56

Gaudier-Brzeska, Henri, 46, 51, 57
Georgian poetry, 69
Gibson, W. W., 69
Gilbert, Sandra, 227
Gilman, Lawrence, 61
Globe Theatre, 172
God, 148-49, 154, 155, 178, 183, 228
Gonne, Maud, 192, 211
Gosse, Sir Edmund, 77
Gourmont, Rémy de, 51
Great Britain, 51, 112, 198; American literature received in, 13, 20-21, 23, 64; American poets in, 33, 37, 59, 67, 69, 76-77, 102, 159; idiom of, 105, 115; image of, in literature, 16-17, 135; Irish literature received in, 23, 103, 105; literary climate in, 51, 103; literary tradition of, 4-5, 7-8, 16-17, 18-20, 21-22, 30, 33-34, 59, 61, 69, 76, 103, 106, 115; London, 17, 21, 33, 37, 49, 51, 59, 67, 76, 77, 110, 115, 152, 201; Sussex, 49
Greece, 36, 45, 51, 53, 54, 63, 65, 74

Gregory, Horace, *156-66*, 167, 168, 170, 172, 208, 217; "After a Half-Century," 157; "Boris MacCreary's Abyss," 163; *Chelsea Rooming House*, 156-162; *Chorus for Survival*, 159-60, 161-62, *163-65*; "Fortune for Mirabell," 163; *The House on Jefferson Street*, 158, 159-61, 163-64; "Interior: The Suburbs," 162; "Like a Chambered Nautilus," 157; "The Metaphysical Head," 162; "New York, Cassandra," 162; *No Retreat*, 162, 164; "Poems for My Daughter," 164; "Spyglass," 163; "Yeats: Envoy of Two Worlds," 158; "Yeats: A Self-Made Poet," 161
Gregory, Isabella Augusta, Lady, 33, 147. *See also* Coole Park
Gregory, John, 159-61
Gregory, Robert, 142, 147, 201-02, 207
Gubar, Susan, 227

Hamsa, Bhagwan Shri, 14
Hardy, Thomas, 103
Harte, Bret, 22
Harvard College, 213
Hawthorne, Nathaniel, 66
Hayward, John, 116
Hegel, G.W.F., 163
Helen, 121, 137, 205
Henderson, Alice Corbin, " 'Too Far from Paris,' " 65-66
Heuffer, Ford Hermann, *see* Ford, Ford Madox (Hueffer)
Hika (Kenyon College), 214
Hitler, Adolf, 128
Hofmannsthal, Hugo von, 105
Homer, 27, 31, 49, 141; *Odyssey*, 111
Hone, Joseph, 110
Hopkins, Gerard Manley, 81, 83, 84
Horace, 54, 205
Houseman, A. E., 41

I'll Take My Stand (Agrarian manifesto), 148
Imagist aesthetic, 38-39, 45-46
Indian philosophy, 13-14, 26, 50
Ireland, 71, 77, 99, 104, 105, 112, 115, 122, 158, 160; American poets in, 74, 123, 159-60, 163, 208; Aran Islands, 49; Ballyshannon, 12; Clare, 201; Dublin, 14, 159, 160, 173, 208; Galway, 201; idiom of, 81, 105, 116; image of, in literature, 22, 66, 98, 134, 135, 146-47, 149-50, 151, 160, 172-73, 208; literary climate in, 3-5, 13, 22, 66, 104, 129, 172-73; literary tradition of, 3-5, 12, 14, 21-22, 25, 30, 69, 81, 103, 105, 175-76; Wicklow, 162, 163-64
Irish Civil War, 143, 159
Irish National Theatre, 5, 22-23, 60. *See also* Abbey Theatre
Italy, 36, 52-53; Pisa, 56; Rapallo, 51, 52, 53; Venice, 35

Jackson, Thomas H., 40
James, Henry, 51
Janus of Basel, 35
Jarrell, Randall, 212, 214
Jeffares, Norman, 161
Jeffers, Robinson, 9, 87, *118-33*, 164, 217, 225; "Apology for Bad Dreams," 131; *At the Birth of an Age*, 121, 124; *At the Fall of an Age*, 121; "Battle (May 28, 1940)," 129; *Be Angry at the Sun*, 128-30; *The Beginning and the End*, 131; *The Bowl of Blood*, 127-28; "But I Am Growing Old and Indolent," 131-32; *Californians*, 124; *Cawdor*, 126, 131; *The Cretan Woman*, 124; *Dear Judas*, 125-27, 128; "The Deer Lay Down Their Bones," 131; *The Double Axe*, 130; "Drunken Charlie," 129; "Epilogue" to *Flagons and*

Apples, 118-19, 123, 130; *Fauna*, 120, 126; *Flagons and Apples*, 118-22, 124, 129, 132; "Granddaughter," 131; "Great Men," 130; "Hungerfield" (poem), 130; *Hungerfield* (volume), 130-31, 132; Introduction to *Visits to Ireland*, 123; "I Shall Laugh Purely," 129-30; "Mara," 129; "Margrave," 123-24, 130; *Medea*, 124-25; "The Old Stonemason," 132; "Post Mortem," 126; "Preface to 'Judas,' " 125; *Roan Stallion*, 127; *Selected Letters*, 122, 125; "Something Remembered," 120-21; *Tamar* (poem), 121, 131, 132; *Tamar* (volume), 120; "Thurso's Landing," 121, 131; "To Helen About Her Hair," 119-20, 121; "To the House," 123, 132, 157; *The Tower Beyond Tragedy*, 124; *The Women at Point Sur*, 126; "The World's Wonders," 130
Jeffers, Una, 122, 123, 124, 130, 131
Jesus, 73-74, 125-27, 139-40
Job, 178, 180
Johnson, Lionel, 4
Johnston, Charles, "Emerson and Occultism," 13
Joyce, James, 111, 199, 208; *Ulysses*, 111, 112
Judas, 125, 126

Keats, John, 76, 211, 212
Kenner, Hugh, 52
Kenyon College, 214, 215
Kenyon Review, 216
Kildare Street Club (Dublin), 160
Kunitz, Stanley, 182, 183, 186, 194

Landor, W. S., 44
Langbaum, Robert, 6, 55
Lazarus, 125
Lewis, Wyndham, 57

Lightfoot, Margaret, 108, 109
Lindsay, Vachel, 61-66, 88, 124, 169; *The Art of the Moving Picture*, 64; "The Black Hawk War of the Artists," 64; "The Congo," 61, 62, 63, 66; "The Firemen's Ball," 64; "General William Booth Enters into Heaven" (poem), 61, 63; *General William Booth Enters into Heaven* (volume), 61; "Mr. Lindsay on 'Primitive Singing,' " 62-63; "The Perilous Road," 63, 65; "Poems to Be Chanted," 64; *Rhymes to Be Traded for Bread*, 63; "The Santa Fé Trail," 63-64
Little Review, 157
Little Theater (Chicago), 60
Litz, A. Walton, 93
Longfellow, Henry Wadsworth, 23
Longinus, *On the Sublime*, 76
Louisiana State University, 214
Lowell, James Russell, 11, 16
Lowell, Robert, 3, 9, 86, 212-24, 226, 228; "The Army Of the Duc de Nemours," 222; "The Cities' Summer Death," 216; *Day by Day*, 217, 224; *The Dolphin*, 221; "Epilogue" to *Day by Day*, 222, 224; *For the Union Dead*, 217; "Fourth of July in Maine," 218; "Grandparents," 213; *History*, 222; "Home After Three Months Away," 213; "In Memory of Arthur Winslow," 216-17; *Land of Unlikeness*, 215; *Life Studies*, 216, 219, 223; *Lord Weary's Castle*, 216; "Mary Winslow," 216; "Middle Age," 217; *Near the Ocean*, 219; "Night Sweat," 222; *Notebook*, 223; "A Prelude to Summer," 214-15; "Rebellion," 216; "Robert T. S. Lowell," 217; "A Second Plunge, A Dream," 223; "Those Before Us," 3; "To Mother," 217; "Truth," 221-22,

223; "Visiting the Tates," 214; "Waking Early Sunday Morning," 219-20, 222
Lowell, Robert (Senior), 212, 216, 217
Lucan, 205
Lucifer, 13
Lytle, Andrew, 156

McAlmon, Robert, 80
McGreevy, Thomas, 111
MacLeish, Archibald, 9, 134, 166-80, 184, 225; "Adam's Jealousy: Eve's Answer," 179; *Air Raid*, 176; " 'Dover Beach'—A Note to That Poem," 169-70; "Eve in the Dawn," 179; *The Fall of the City*, 171, 176; "La Foce," 180; *The Happy Marriage and Other Poems*, 167; *Herakles*, 175; "Hypocrite Auteur," 174; "Invocation to the Social Muse," 168; *J.B.*, 177-78; "Kenneth," 167; *Panic*, 166, 170-71; "The Poet as Playwright," 176; *Poetry and Experience*, 168, 172-73, 178-79; "Poetry and the Public World," 173, 174, 178; *Public Speech*, 168-70; "Public Speech and Private Speech in Poetry," 171, 172; "Realities," 167, 179; "The Rock in the Sea," 175; *Songs for Eve*, 179; "Speech to Those Who Say Comrade," 168-69; *This Music Crept by Me Upon the Waters*, 175, 176-78; *Tower of Ivory*, 167; "The Wild Old Wicked Man" (poem), 180; *"The Wild Old Wicked Man"* (volume), 179; "The Woman on the Stair," 169; "Yeats and the Belief in Life," 178
MacNeice, Louis, 168
Malkoff, Karl, 190
Mallarmé, Stéphane, "Le Tombeau d'Edgar Poe," 116
Mangan, James Clarence, 14

Martz, Louis, 186, 195
Marvell, Andrew, 103
Mary, 125, 216-17
Masefield, John, 61, 69
Mason, Lawrence, 167
Masques, Jacobean, 73
Massinger, Philip, 114
Masters, Edgar Lee, 61, 88
Mathers, MacGregor, 214
Mercury Theatre (London), 110
Mertins, Louis, 74
Milgate, 218
Mills, Ralph J., 182
Milton, John, 122, 142; "Lycidas," 142
Modernism, 3, 11, 111, 115, 135-38, 139, 141, 149, 150, 154, 158, 166, 167, 177, 178; distinguished from post-modernism, 3, 227; distinguished from romanticism, 3, 6, 148; Eliot's place in, 3, 110, 111, 115, 136, 145; Yeats's place in, 3, 110, 115, 135-38, 161, 214
Monroe, Harriet, 60, 61, 63, 64, 81, 88; "Mr. Yeats and the Poetic Drama," 88. See also Poetry magazine
Moore, Marianne, 226
Mosher, Thomas B., 67
Myerberg, Michael, 125
Myers, F.W.H., Human Personality and Its Survival of Bodily Death, 164

Napoleon, 128
New Criticism, 214
New Life, Society of the, 21
New Masses, The, 166
New York Times, 125
Nicholas II, Czar, 213
Noh drama, 33, 49, 87, 88, 107, 125, 127

Olson, Charles, 52
O'Rahilly, Michael Joseph, 199
Ossian, 21

Ovid, 53, 55
Oxford University, 221

Paolo Malatesta, 112
Parmenides, 193
Pearse, Patrick, 199
Pearson, Gabriel, 223
Pennsylvania, University of, 76
Philoponus, John, 49
Pinkerton Academy (New Hampshire), 69
Pirandello, Luigi, 111
Plato, 74, 193
Plutarch, 19
Poe, Edgar Allan, 12, 14-16, 17, 19, 20, 23, 66, 116; "The Philosophy of Composition," 15; "The Pit and the Pendulum," 15; "The Poetic Principle," 15; "The Raven," 15; Works, 15, 16, 19
Poetry magazine (Chicago), 32, 33, 59-63, 64, 65, 66, 67, 82, 88, 157. See also Monroe, Harriet
Poet's Theatre (Cambridge, Mass.), 176, 178
Pollexfen, William, 159
Porphyry, 49
Post-modernism, 3, 227
Pound, Ezra, 7, 31-58, 59-60, 61, 62, 66-68, 70, 76, 77-78, 80, 81, 84, 85, 87, 102, 103, 106, 120, 125, 134, 135, 144, 172, 173, 197, 199, 200, 208, 224, 225, 226; "The Age Demanded," 50; A Lume Spento, 35-37, 39, 45, 46; "Amities," 43; "Au Jardin," 42; Cantos, 40, 45, 46, 48, 51, 54-58, 224; Canzoni, 41; "Cavalcanti," 52-54, 55-56, 87; "Cino," 36; Collected Early Poems, 35, 41, 46, 48, 60; "E. P. Ode pour l'election de son sepulchre," 50, 56; Exultations, 37, 55, 44; "'Fair Helena' by Rockham," 37; "The Fault of It," 42; "The Flame," 42; "La Fraisne," 35, 36, 47, 48, 56;

Pound, Ezra (*cont.*)
   Guide to Kulchur, 45, 53; "The
   Hard and Soft in French Poetry,"
   50; "Harold Monro," 46;
   "Hugh Selwyn Mauberley," 50-
   51, 53, 55, 56-57; "In Exitum
   Cuiusdam," 43; " 'It is a
   Shame,' " 43; *Jefferson and/or
   Mussolini*, 44; "The Lake Isle,"
   43, 225; "Laudantes Decem Pul-
   chritudinis Johannae Templi,"
   37-39, 41, 45, 68; *Letters*, 48,
   49, 51, 60, 76, 78; *Literary Es-
   says*, 35, 38-39, 44, 45, 46, 59;
   Noh or Accomplishment (with
   Ernest Fenollosa), 49, 107; "On
   Music," 46; "Patria Mia," 33;
   Personae (1909), 40; *Pisan Can-
   tos*, 54-57, 87; "Plotinus," 46;
   "Psychology and Troubadours,"
   47-49, 53, 55; "The Return,"
   52; "Revolt Against the Crepus-
   cular Spirit in Modern Poetry,"
   40-41; "Salutation the Third,"
   34, 35; *Selected Prose*, 31, 33,
   34, 57; "Sestina for Ysolt," 37;
   "Song of the Bowmen of Shu,"
   78; *Spirit of Romance*, 78; "Sta-
   tus Rerum," 41, 45, 60; "This
   Hulme Business," 39;
   "Threnos," 36; "The Tree," 36-
   37, 39, 47, 55; "Und Drang,"
   41-42; "Villanelle: The Psycho-
   logical Hour," 44; "Vorticism,"
   47-48; " 'What I feel about Walt
   Whitman,' " 31, 33
Pre-Raphaelites, 106, 113. *See also*
   Rossetti, Dante Gabriel
Propertius, 45

Quest, The, 47

Raleigh, Sir Walter, 188
Ransom, John Crowe, 135, 142,
   148-51, 153, 155, 194, 214,
   225; "Antique Harvesters," 151;

"Birthday of an Aging Seer"
   ("Semi-Centennial"), 149-50;
   "Conrad in Twilight," 151; *God
   Without Thunder*, 148; "Grace,"
   148-49; "The Irish, the Gaelic,
   the Byzantine" (*Southern Re-
   view*), 151, 225; "Old Man-
   sion," 151; *Poems About God*,
   148-49; *Selected Poems*, 149;
   "Semi-Centennial," *see* "Birthday
   of an Aging Seer"; "The Sure
   Heart," 151; *The World's Body*,
   142, 150-51; "Worship," 149;
   "Yeats and His Symbols," 148,
   149
Read, Forrest, 61
Realism, 45, 93, 176
Rhymers' Club, 61, 77, 172
Rhys, Ernest, 21, 24
Rilke, Rainer Maria, 198
Rimbaud, Jean Arthur, 214
Rodman, Selden, 166, 171
Roethke, Beatrice, 189-90
Roethke, Otto, 182, 186, 190, 192,
   196
Roethke, Theodore, 182-97, 202,
   207, 213, 220, 226; "All the
   Earth, All the Air," 185, 192,
   195; "The Changeling," 185;
   "The Dance," 182, 187-88, 189,
   190, 191; "The Dying Man,"
   190-92, 193; "Epidermal Ma-
   cabre," 184; "The Far Field"
   (poem), 187; *The Far Field* (vol-
   ume), 187, 192, 196; "Feud,"
   187; "Flower Dump," 186; "For
   an Amorous Lady," 185; "Four
   for Sir John Davies," 182, 188-
   90, 191; "Frau Bauman, Frau
   Schmidt, and Frau Schwartze,"
   186; "Her Foreboding," 192;
   "Her Longing," 192; "Her Reti-
   cence," 192; "Her Words," 192;
   "In a Dark Time," 194-95; *The
   Lost Son*, 186-87, 192; "Medita-
   tions of an Old Woman," 196;

"Memory," 192; "North American Sequence," 196; "On 'Identity,' " 188, 191, 194; *On the Poet and His Craft*, 196; "Open House" (poem), 183-84; *Open House* (volume), 183-85, 186, 187; "The Partner," 189, 190; *Praise to the End*, 186, 187, 188; "The Pure Fury," 193; "Reply to Censure," 184; "The Return," 186; "The Rose," 185; *Selected Letters*, 182-83, 188, 194; *Straw For the Fire*, 184, 185, 188, 192; "The Summons," 182-83, 184; "The Swan," 192-93; "Unfold! Unfold!" 187; "The Vigil," 189, 190; *The Waking*, 188; "A Walk in Late Summer," 185; "Words for the Wind" (poem), 193-94; *Words for the Wind* (volume), 190, 192-94, 196; "The Wraith," 189, 190

Rolleston, T. W., 24

Romanticism, 3, 4, 5-7, 8, 45, 54, 66, 93, 146, 148, 152, 169, 227

Rome, 205, 215

Rosenthal, M. L., 8-9

Rossetti, Dante Gabriel, 20, 36, 41, 76. *See also* Pre-Raphaelites

Rossetti, William Michael, 20

Ruskin, John, 23

Russell, George (AE), 14

Sandburg, Carl, 88

Sappho, 84

Schwartz, Delmore, 183, 195, 212

Schwob, Marcel, 31

Scopes Trial, 135

Shakespeare, William, 12-13, 70, 106, 113, 114, 148; *Macbeth*, 162

Shelley, P. B., 5, 19, 21, 30, 122; *Alastor*, 5

Smidt, Kristian, 116

Smith, Grover, 116, 179

Smith, John (father of John Berryman), 197, 210, 212

Snodgrass, W. D., 194, 196

Solomon, 157

Sophocles, 65, 124, 174; *Oedipus at Colonus*, 113; *Oedipus the King*, 162, 174. *See also* Yeats, W. B.

Southern Review, 144, 145, 147, 150, 151

Spectator, 104

Spenser, Edmund, 12

Spiritualism, 13, 46-49, 52-53

Stalinism, 181

Stallworthy, Jon, 215-16

Stevens, Elsie, 93

Stevens, Wallace, 87, 88-101, 118-19, 131, 225, 226; "About One of Marianne Moore's Poems," 97; "As You Leave the Room," 99, 131-32; *Bowl, Cat and Broomstick*, 90, 91, 98, 101; *Carlos Among the Candles*, 89; "The Comedian as the Letter C," 94, 101; "Credences of Summer," 99-101, 118; "Examination of the Hero in a Time of War," 99; "Frogs Eat Butterflies . . . ," 94, 101; "Home Again," 93-94; "Hymn from a Watermelon Pavilion," 94-95, 101; "Imagination as Value," 95-96; *Letters*, 93, 98, 99; "The Man on the Dump," 88, 97-98; "Memorandum," 98; "Le Monocle de Mon Oncle," 90-92, 94, 95, 99, 100, 101; *Opus Posthumous*, 99; "Page from a Tale," 95, 96, 100, 225; "A Quiet Normal Life," 89; "Someone Puts a Pineapple Together," 99; *Three Travellers Watch a Sunrise*, 88-89; "To the One of Fictive Music," 96-97, 100, 101; "The Well-Dressed Man with a Beard," 99

Swedenborg, Emanuel, 13, 20, 26, 49, 52
Swift, Jonathan, 116, 158, 160, 202
Swinburne, A. C., 21, 76
Symbolist aesthetic, 14, 85, 87, 89-90, 166-67, 171-73, 219
Synge, John, 14, 60, 208

Tate, Allen, 135, 136-47, 150, 151, 152, 156, 157, 178, 214, 215; "Advice to a Young Romanticist" ("To a Romantic"), 137-38, 141, 152; "Cold Pastoral," 146; "The Eagle," 139; "Emblems," 146; Essays of Four Decades, 145; "Fragment of a Meditation," 139-40; "The Happy Poet Remembers Death," 137, 138; "Idiot," 146; "Idyl," 146; "Ode to the Confederate Dead," 146; "Pastoral," 146; "Poetry Modern and Unmodern," 138, 144-45; Reason in Madness, 139; "Sonnets of the Blood," 140; "To a Romantic," see "Advice to a Young Romanticist"; "To the Lacedemonians," 146; "William Blake," 137; "Winter Mask," 140-44; "Yeats' Romanticism" (Southern Review), 144-46, 147
Teasdale, Sara, 63
Tennyson, Alfred, Lord, 18, 19-20, 122; In Memoriam, 20
Theocritus, 31
Theosophists, 13. See also Spiritualism
Thomas, Dylan, 201
Thompson, Francis, 76
Thompson, Lawrance, 75
Thoor Ballylee, 100, 122-23, 133, 147, 218, 228. See also Yeats, W. B.
Thoreau, Henry David, 11, 12, 16-17, 21, 22, 27; Walden, 16-17, 27
Todhunter, John, 21

Tradition of the self, 5, 6-7, 9, 10, 18, 23, 35, 48, 57, 75, 87, 91, 104, 122, 132, 150, 216, 223, 225-28; American and European traditions combined in, 7, 101; corollaries of, defined, 7-8, 29, 31; distinguished from confessional poetry, 9, 58, 181, 213, 216, 219, 223, 224, 226-28; distinguished from romanticism, 5-6, 7, 8, 227; paradox of influence in, 9, 31, 66, 86, 98-99, 101
Transcendentalism, 16, 21, 27
Traubel, Horace, 24, 26
Trinity College, Dublin, 21, 160
Troubadours, 33, 36, 45, 48, 52-53

United Ireland, 23
United States of America, see America, United States of
Untermeyer, Louis, 75, 159
Upanishads, 14, 104

Vanderbilt University, 146, 149
Vassar College, 107
Verlaine, Paul, 19
Viereck, Peter, 188
Vorticism, 46-47, 56

Warren, Austin, 10
Warren, Robert Penn, 135, 151-56, 164, 176, 214, 217, 225; "Arrogant Law," 153; "Brotherhood in Pain," 155; Brother to Dragons, 153; "Evening Hawk," 155; "Kentucky Mountain Farm," 152; "The Mango on the Mango Tree," 154-55; "Picnic Remembered," 153; "Rebuke of the Rocks," 152-53; Understanding Poetry (with Cleanth Brooks), 214; "Vision," 152, 153, 155, 225
Weekes, Charles, Reflections and Refractions, 18
Wellek, René, 10

Wellesley, Lady Gerald (Dorothy), 83, 171

Werfel, Franz, *Goat Song*, 125

Whitman, Walt, 4, 5, 7, 9, 11, 12, 14, 17-30, 31, 32, 33, 34, 55, 60, 66, 81, 85-86, 129, 134, 226; *Leaves of Grass*, 17, 22, 26; "Song of Myself," 4, 5, 27, 28; "A Song of the Rolling Earth," 20

Whittemore, Reed, 79

Wilbur, Richard, 195

Wilde, Oscar, 19, 20, 21, 28, 30, 33; *Salome*, 33

Williams, Florence, 86

Williams, William Carlos, 9, 51, 59, 76-86, 93, 124, 212, 214; "Asphodel, That Greeny Flower," 86; *Autobiography*, 77; "A Beginning on the Short Story (Notes)," 77; "Cuchulain," 80; *Detail and Parody*, 79; *The Embodiment of Knowledge*, 85; "The Gentle Negress" ("Lillian"), 79-80; *Kora in Hell*, 77, 80; "Lillian," *see* "The Gentle Negress"; "Measure," 81, 82; *Paterson*, 78-79, 84, 85; *Poems*, 76; *Selected Letters*, 76, 80, 81, 82, 83; *A September Afternoon*, 81; *Spring and All*, 78; "To Daphne and Virginia," 86; *The Wedge*, 79

Winslow, Harriet, 218

Wordsworth, William, 5, 18, 19, 20, 21, 22, 27, 122, 169, 206, 207, 209-10; "Tintern Abbey," 5

World War I, 4, 51, 56, 158, 173, 174, 222

World War II, 9, 56, 115, 128, 129, 130, 143, 181

Yale Review, 171

Yale University, 167

Yeats, Georgie, 160

Yeats, J. B. (father of W. B. Yeats), 16, 20

Yeats, William Butler: "Against Unworthy Praise," 138, 192; "All Souls' Night," 214; "All Things Can Tempt Me," 44, 130, 200; "America and the Arts," 11-12, 16; "Among School Children," 85, 117, 190, 193, 194, 204, 228; "The Apparitions," 228; "An Appointment," 44; "Are You Content?" 216; "At Algeciras—A Meditation upon Death," 189; *At the Hawk's Well*, 89, 90-93, 100, 106-07, 114-15; *Autobiographies*, 4, 5, 14, 16, 71, 119, 226, 228; "The Autumn of the Body," 15; "Beautiful Lofty Things," 222; "The Blessed," 63, 149; "Blood and the Moon," 44-45, 170, 187; "Browning," 22; "Brown Penny," 193; "Byzantium," 72, 117, 141, 153, 185, 194, 203, 219; *Calvary*, 111, 125-27, 194; "The Cap and Bells," 42, 43, 136; *Cathleen ni Houlihan*, 69, 71; *The Celtic Twilight*, 35, 56; "Certain Noble Plays of Japan," 125; "The Choice," 202-203; "The Circus Animals' Desertion," 98, 99, 131, 186-87, 203, 207, 220-22, 225; "A Coat," 143, 168, 183; "The Cold Heaven," 137; *Collected Poems*, 188; *Collected Works*, 32; "Coole Park, 1929," 228; "Coole Park and Ballylee, 1931," 3, 143, 169, 170, 175, 195; *The Countess Cathleen and Various Legends and Lyrics*, 37-38; *The Countess Kathleen* (play), 70; "The Crazed Moon," 189; "Crazy Jane Grown Old Looks at the Dancers," 189, 211; "Crazy Jane on the Day of Judgment," 179; "Crazy Jane on the Mountain," 129; "Crazy Jane Talks with the Bishop,"

Yeats, William Butler (*cont.*)
177; "Cuchulain Comforted,"
209; *The Cutting of an Agate*,
102; "The Dawn," 44; *The
Death of Cuchulain*, 185;
Deirdre, 32-33; "A Dialogue of
Self and Soul," 154, 158, 176;
Discoveries, 17; "Down by the
Salley Gardens," 79-80, 148;
The Dreaming of the Bones,
111-12, 125; "A Dream of
Death," 193; "Easter 1916,"
138, 199; *Essays and Introduc-
tions*, 12, 14, 20, 29, 83-84, 97,
99, 134; "The Everlasting
Voices," 38; *Explorations*, 14,
16, 23, 49, 104; "Fallen Maj-
esty," 34; "The Fascination of
What's Difficult," 125; "The Fid-
dler of Dooney," 136; "The
Fisherman," 150, 183; "The
Folly of Being Comforted," 120-
21, 203; *Four Plays for Dancers*,
8, 32, 87, 89, 107, 111, 125,
127, 198; "Friends of My
Youth," 19; *The Green Helmet*
(play), 90; *The Green Helmet*
(volume), 8, 43-44, 59, 89, 121-
22, 137; "The Gyres," 180; "He
Bids His Beloved Be at Peace,"
37; "He Remembers Forgotten
Beauty," 39-40, 137; "He Re-
proves the Curlew," 37; *The
Herne's Egg*, 83, 194; "He
Thinks of His Past Greatness
When a Part of the Constella-
tions of Heaven," 36-37, 39,
193; "He Thinks of Those Who
Have Spoken Evil of His Be-
loved," 53; "He Wishes for the
Cloths of Heaven," 40, 65, 120,
136; "He Wishes His Beloved
Were Dead," 120; "His Bar-
gain," 153-54, 189; "His Confi-
dence," 189; "His Memories,"
205; "His Phoenix," 121; "The

Host of the Air," 123; "I Am of
Ireland," 158, 160, 163; "The
Indian to His Love," 221; "In
Memory of Major Robert Greg-
ory," 138-39, 141-43, 145, 147,
201-02, 205-06, 215, 225; *In the
Seven Woods*, 120-21; "Into the
Twilight," 42, 148; "John Eglin-
ton and Spiritual Art," 15; "The
Lake Isle of Innisfree," 16-17,
43, 93-95, 100, 136, 151, 152,
225-26; *The Land of Heart's De-
sire*, 64, 68-70, 71; "Lapis La-
zuli," 115; *Last Poems and Two
Plays*, 209; "Leda and the
Swan," 85, 174; *Letters*, 14, 15,
21, 23, 24, 33, 34, 46, 50, 62,
83, 85, 110, 171, 178, 221;
"Lines Written in Dejection," 44;
"The Lover Mourns for the Loss
of Love," 37; "The Lover Pleads
with His Friend for Old
Friends," 42-43; "The Madness
of King Goll," 35, 68; "The
Magi," 186; "Magic," 47; "The
Man and the Echo," 150; "Man-
dookya Upanishad," 104; "The
Man Who Dreamed of Fairy-
land," 36; *A Man Young and
Old*, 206; "A Meditation in
Time of War," 143, 222; "Medi-
tations in Time of Civil War,"
134, 143-44, 157, 165; *Memoirs*,
15, 19, 22, 27-28, 32; "Meru,"
97; "The Moods" (essay), 48;
"The Moods" (poem), 68, 167;
"The Mountain Tomb," 34, 82,
84; "My Own Poetry with Illus-
trative Readings," 136; "The
Need for Audacity of Thought,"
104; "Nineteen Hundred and
Nineteen," 116, 134, 170, 184,
203; "No Second Troy," 44; "On
a Picture of a Black Centaur by
Edmund Dulac," 139; *On Baile's
Strand*, 32-33; *The Only Jeal-*

ousy of Emer, 89; "The O'Rahilly," 199; "Our Need for Religious Sincerity," 104; *Oxford Book of Modern Verse*, 3, 51, 83, 110, 115, 172; "A Packet for Ezra Pound," 51-52, 53; "Pardon, old fathers," 91, 216, 225; "Parnell's Funeral," 163; "The Peacock," 54; "The People," 44; *Per Amica Silentia Lunae*, 49, 102; "The Phases of the Moon," 185; *The Player Queen*, 32, 176; Poe centenary statement, 15; "The Poet Pleads with the Elemental Powers," 42; "The Poetry of Sir Samuel Ferguson," 23-26; "Politics," 129-30, 171, 172; "A Prayer for My Daughter," 131, 143, 204, 218, 221, 224, 225; "A Prayer for Old Age," 189, 193; "A Prayer on Going into My House," 122; *Purgatory*, 83, 107-10, 117, 176, 177, 210; "Reconciliation," 42; "Red Hanrahan's Song About Ireland," 65, 78; *Responsibilities*, 44, 59, 91, 134, 140, 157, 167-68, 225; *The Resurrection*, 73-74, 157; *Reveries over Childhood and Youth*, 177; "Ribh Considers Christian Love Insufficient," 183; "The Rose of the World" ("Rosa Mundi"), 71, 167; "Sailing to Byzantium," 72, 93, 147, 184, 185, 191, 219, 221; "The Scholars," 44, 189, 221; "The Second Coming," 129, 138-41, 145, 202-03, 214; *The Secret Rose*, 64; *Selected Poems*, 60; "September 1913," 66, 146, 172-73; *The Shadowy Waters*, 33, 42, 71, 122, 210; "Shepherd and Goatherd," 147; "Solomon to Sheba," 150; "The Song of Wandering Aengus," 71, 75, 136; *Sophocles' King Oedipus*, 65,

124, 198; *Sophocles' Oedipus at Colonus*, 65, 124, 198; "The Sorrow of Love," 103; "Swedenborg, Mediums, and the Desolate Places," 49, 52; "Swift's Epitaph," 116, 158; "The Symbolism of Poetry," 32, 214; "The Thinking of the Body," 56; "Three Songs to the Same Tune," 204; "Three Things," 115; "To a Child Dancing upon the Shore" ("To a Child Dancing in the Wind"), 34; "To a Friend Whose Work Has Come to Nothing," 184; "To a Poet, Who Would Have Me Praise Certain Bad Poets, Imitators of His and Mine," 44; "To a Young Beauty," 44, 103, 206; "Tom at Cruachan," 140; "Tom O'Roughley," 191; "To the Rose upon the Rood of Time," 96-97, 167; "The Tower" (poem), 5, 100-101, 123, 134-35, 141, 185, 191, 200, 225; *The Tower* (volume), 8, 85, 134-35, 157; *The Trembling of the Veil*, 26, 27, 228; "Two Songs from a Play," 73-74, 157; "The Two Trees," 37; "The Unappeasable Host," 38; *Uncollected Prose*, Vol. 1, 17, 18, 19, 21, 22, 33; *Uncollected Prose*, Vol. II, 4, 7, 32, 33, 61, 62, 72; "Under Ben Bulben," 185, 221; *The Unicorn from the Stars*, 125; "Upon a House Shaken by the Land Agitation," 163; "Vacillation," 27, 71-72, 100, 117, 141, 176-77, 178, 192, 209; *Variorum Plays*, 106, 107, 126; *Variorum Poems*, 71, 163; *Vision A*, 27-28, 111, 127, 222; *Vision B*, 47, 51-52, 53, 113, 146, 147, 189, 200, *The Wanderings of Oisin*, 42; "What is 'Popular Poetry'?" 23; "When

Yeats, William Butler (*cont.*)
  You Are Old," 61; "The White
  Birds," 36; "Who Goes with Fer-
  gus?" 35, 38, 192; "Why Should
  Not Old Men Be Mad?" 130;
  "The Wild Old Wicked Man,"
  179-80; "The Wild Swans at
  Coole" (poem), 138; *The Wild
  Swans at Coole* (volume), 44;

The Wind Among the Reeds, 37-
  39, 40, 42, 45, 67-68, 120, 192,
  225; *The Winding Stair*, 158;
  "Wisdom," 140; *A Woman
  Young and Old*, 206; *Words for
  Music Perhaps*, 158, 160, 162,
  164, 192, 205, 206; *The Words
  upon the Window-Pane*, 160

LIBRARY OF CONGRESS CATALOGING IN PUBLICATION DATA

Diggory, Terence, 1951-
Yeats & American poetry.

Includes index.
1. American poetry—20th century—History and criticism.   2. Yeats,
William Butler, 1865-1939—Influence.   3. Self in literature.   I. Title.
II. Title: Yeats and American poetry.
PS324.D53   1983   811'.52'09   82-15070
ISBN 0-691-06558-6